DELIGHTFUL CONVICTION

Jonathan Edwards

DELIGHTFUL CONVICTION

Jonathan Edwards
and the Rhetoric of Conversion

Stephen R. Yarbrough
and John C. Adams

Foreword by Bernard K. Duffy

Great American Orators, Number 20
Bernard K. Duffy and Halford R. Ryan,
Series Advisers

Greenwood Press
Westport, Connecticut • London

BT
780
.Y37
1993

Library of Congress Cataloging-in-Publication Data

Yarbrough, Stephen R.
    Delightful conviction : Jonathan Edwards and the rhetoric of
conversion / Stephen R. Yarbrough and John C. Adams ; foreword by
Bernard K. Duffy.
        p.   cm.—(Great American orators, ISSN 0898-8277 ; no. 20)
    Includes bibliographical references and index.
    ISBN 0-313-27582-3 (alk. paper)
        1. Conversion—History of doctrines—18th century. 2. Edwards,
Jonathan, 1703-1758. 3. Preaching—United States—History—18th
century. I. Adams, John C. II. Title. III. Series.
BT780.Y37   1993
230'.58'092—dc20   92-30018

British Library Cataloguing in Publication Data is available.

Library of Congress Catalog Card Number: 92-30018
ISBN: 0-313-27582-3
ISSN: 0898-8277

First published in 1993

Greenwood Press, 88 Post Road West, Westport, CT 06881
An imprint of Greenwood Publishing Group, Inc.

Printed in the United States of America

The paper used in this book complies with the
Permanent Paper Standard issued by the National
Information Standards Organization (Z39.48-1984).

10 9 8 7 6 5 4 3 2 1

Contents

Part I: Jonathan Edwards

Part II: Three Sermons

Series Foreword

The idea for a series of books on great American orators grew out of the recognition that there is a paucity of book-length studies on individual orators and their speeches. Apart from a few notable exceptions, the study of American public address has been pursued in scores of articles published in professional journals. As helpful as these studies have been, none has or can provide a complete analysis of a speaker's rhetoric. Book-length studies, such as those in this series, will help fill the void that has existed in the study of American public address and its related disciplines of politics and history, theology and sociology, communication and law. In books, the critic can explicate a broader range of a speaker's persuasive discourse than reasonably could be treated in articles. The comprehensive research and sustained reflection that books require will undoubtedly yield many original and enduring insights concerning the nation's most important voices.

Public address has been a fertile ground for scholarly investigation. No matter how insightful their intellectual forebears, each generation of scholars must reexamine its expanding universe of discourse, while expanding the compass of its researches and redefining its purpose and methods. To avoid intellectual torpor, new scholars cannot be content simply to see through the eyes of those who have come before them. We hope that this series of books will stimulate important new understandings of the nature of persuasive discourse and provide additional opportunities for scholarship in the history and criticism of American public address.

This series examines the role of rhetoric in the United States. American speakers shaped the destiny of the colonies, the young republic, and the mature nation. During each stage of the intellectual, political, and religious development of the United States, great orators, standing at the rostrum, on the stump, and in the pulpit, used words and gestures to influence their audiences.

Usually striving for the noble, sometimes achieving the base, they urged their fellow citizens toward a more perfect Union. The books in this series chronicle and explain the accomplishments of representative American leaders as orators.

A series of book-length studies of American persuaders honors the role men and women have played in U.S. history. Previously, if one desired to assess the impact of a speaker or speech upon history, the past was, at best, not well marked and, at worst, littered with obstacles. To be sure, one might turn to biographies and general histories to learn about an orator, but for the public address scholar these sources often prove unhelpful. Rhetorical topics, such as speech invention, style, delivery, organizational strategies, and persuasive effect, are often treated in passing, if mentioned at all. Authoritative speech texts are often difficult to locate, and the problem of textual authenticity is frequently encountered. This is especially true for those figures who spoke one or two hundred years ago, or for those whose persuasive role, though significant, was secondary to other leading lights of the age.

Each book in this series is organized to meet the needs of scholars and students of the history and criticism of American public address. Part I is a critical analysis of the orator and his or her speeches. Within the format of a case study, one may expect considerable latitude. For instance, in a given chapter an author might explicate a single speech or a group of related speeches, or examine orations that comprise a genre of rhetoric such as forensic speaking. But the critic's focus remains on the rhetorical considerations of speaker, speech, occasion, and effect. Part II contains the texts of the important addresses that are discussed in the critical analysis that precedes it. To the extent possible, each author has endeavored to collect authoritative speech texts, which have often been found through original research in collections of primary source material. In a few instances, because of the extreme length of a speech, texts have been edited, but the authors have been careful to delete material that is least important to the speech, and these deletions have been held to a minimum.

In each book there is a chronology of major speeches that serves more purposes than may be apparent at first. Pragmatically, it lists all of the orator's known speeches and addresses. Places and dates are also listed, although this is information that is sometimes difficult to determine precisely. But in a wider sense, the chronology attests to the scope of rhetoric in the United States. Certainly in quantity, if not always in quality, Americans are historically talkers and listeners.

Because of the disparate nature of the speakers examined in the series, there is some latitude in the nature of the bibliographical materials that have been included in each book. But in every instance, authors have carefully described original historical materials and collections, and have gathered critical studies, biographies and autobiographies, and a variety of secondary sources that bear on the speaker and the oratory. By combining in each book bibliographical materials, speech texts, and critical chapters, this series notes that text and research sources are interwoven in the act of rhetorical criticism.

May the books in this series serve to memorialize the nation's greatest orators.

Bernard K. Duffy
Halford R. Ryan

Foreword

The conservative rhetorician Richard Weaver suggested that Jonathan Edwards and other clerics helped engender a spirit of rationalism that permeated New England's educational institution and distinguished the Northern religious experience from the Southern. In the South, Weaver argues, religious conviction was not subjected to intellectual analysis, remaining a mystery that required simply a "grammar of assent." It is certainly true that Edwards' life and works demonstrate the reach of human rationality. The gravity and urgency of Edwards' undertaking, to convert his Northampton congregation and save it from damnation, produced a remarkable body of rhetorical artifacts that, as Weaver predicts, are as much a testament to Edwards' intellectual enthusiasms as to his religious commitments. Based upon his exposure to John Locke's empiricism at Yale, Edwards conceived an epistemology that was rooted in sense perception and in the limitations placed upon human knowledge. Fusing the scientific with the religious Edwards made sense perception fundamental to religious experience. Words were Locke's "delegated efficacies," which stood for but could not replace the experiences they represented. That Edwards' rhetoric is rich in sensory imagery, as Yarbrough and Adams indicate, reflects the bond of Edwards' rhetoric with his theological precepts.

One of the key contributions of this book is that it interprets Edwards' oratory not only in the light of rhetorical theory but in light of Edwards' own rhetorical views. For example, the authors explain that it is impossible to understand Edwards' sermons by assuming that he spoke to a homogeneous audience, wholly alike in belief or psychology. In fact, sermons such as "Sinners in the hands of an Angry God" are directed at two audiences, the "saints" who are predestined for salvation and the unsaved, the so-called "natural men." What the saved heard as a forceful and logical exposition of God's divinity, sinners heard as a plea for repentance in the face of God's certain wrath. The sermon therefore was either sublimely assuring or disconcerting in the extreme. Edwards' unexpected relativism suggests a rhetorical perspective that harkens back to the Greek Sophists as, of course, does Locke's empiricism, although Edwards is not, strictly speaking, a Lockean. Adams and Yarbrough emphasize that Edwards departs from Locke in asserting that individual perspectives, not simply sensory data, determine belief. The earthly human experience is, Edwards realized, fettered by perspective, and therefore religious experience required conversion to a more encompassing view. It was equally clear to Edwards that logic alone would not suffice for religious conversion since its premises are bound by perspective.

The authors argue that despite Edwards' belief in the power of grace, he is not a mystic who believes God can be known. He is, rather, one who claims the preferability of accepting grace than living life with the restricted, veiled, and determinate vision that human perspective provides. Yarbrough and Adams believe that in Edwards' theology are the underpinnings of a perspectivism such as is formulated by Friedrich Nietzsche more than a century later. One of the most tantalizing and original suggestions of this book is that if one were to take only the strands of Edwards' perspectivist and relativist views one could even weave them into the fabric of postmodernism.

In light of Edwards' rhetorical relativism it is difficult to make a final judgment on the nature of his sermons. Edwards' unfolded his "fire and brimstone" sermons with commendable clarity and logic. He spoke passionately without betraying an excess of passion in his delivery. Although his sermons created great outpourings of emotion and resulted in hundreds of conversions in Northhampton, his use of pathos reminds us that for Aristotle pathos is the emotional effect words have on the audience not the overt emotionalism of the speaker. Edwards' sermons offer an interesting contrast to his contemporary George Whitefield's voluble exhortations, which reflect the Dionysian temper of the revival conversion experiences Whitefield hoped to elicit.

This learned and original study, a product of Professors Adams' and Yarbrough's fruitful collaboration, is a testament to the importance of an interdisciplinary approach to the study of oratory and orators. The history of oratory is also social and intellectual history, as this book well demonstrates. To explicate Edwards' sermons and to account for their success the authors have provided a fascinating description of what moved Edwards' Northampton audience, of their affections and beliefs. They have also clearly illustrated Edwards' genius, for in meeting the present needs of his congregation he created a perdurable body of discourse.

Bernard K. Duffy

Preface

Although much scholarship has been directed toward understanding Jonathan Edwards' complex theology—its roots in European thought, its relationship to competitive Christian and Enlightenment discourses, and its social and biographical contexts—little has been done to investigate how these and other factors presented themselves as a rhetorical challenge to a man who during most of his lifetime was, for all his talent and intelligence, a pastor of small frontier congregations whose singleminded intent was to convert sinners into saints. From one point of view, a great deal has been done in the way of "rhetorical" analyses. Edwards' use of the traditional Pietist sermon forms, his typological theory, his work's place in the Jeremiad tradition, his use of biblical texts, his borrowings from empirical psychology, his audience's character, his time's political as well as theological debates—these and other issues have been discussed to a greater or lesser extent for many years. Yet, despite all this information, a satisfactory explanation of why Edwards said what he said, the way he said it, has yet to emerge.

The chief reason Edwards' rhetoric remains enigmatic is that we have not yet fully grasped the significance of the ultimate goal of all his discourse: conversion. What, to Edwards, was the difference between the regenerate and unregenerate? So long as scholarship focuses upon the apparent, superficial differences that can be described empirically, such as disputes on dogmatic issues, conflicting social and moral values, and political disagreements, the question will continue to obscure our understanding. For Edwards, the question was absolutely fundamental. Saints did not simply disagree with sinners: they *saw* differently, they *felt* differently, they *thought* differently. In short, they lived in a different world altogether. We will not adequately understand Edwards' sermons until we stress that his rhetorical challenge was not the usual one of persuasion, for in his world the common ground required for persuasive discourse disappears into the abyss between integrity and apostasy.

If Edwards sought to convert rather than to persuade, we should not be surprised that he did not persuade. By all accounts, and by Edwards' own criteria, his oral discourse failed. Not only did the people he believed he had converted during the revivals quickly revert to their old ways, but also his own congregation, almost to a person, finally rejected him. Scholars have suggested numerous reasons for this failure. Some have argued that his flock was intellectually incapable of understanding him, others that democratic sentiment rose against his staunch patriarchism, still others that Arminianism had won the people's hearts. Did something change in Edwards' message between the apparently glorious successes of his revival sermons in 1735 and the minister's inglorious separation from his church after the debates of 1749–50? Did society alter so rapidly during those fifteen years that it outgrew Edwards' antiquated piety? Or, and this is what we answer, did Edwards so clarify traditional Calvinism that its irreconcilability with the values inherent in a growing capital economy was felt too intensely by his congregation for them to tolerate him? The middle-class self-determined individual fit precisely Edwards' definition of the degenerate sinner. Edwards was asking his congregation to give up the identity required to survive in their world.

We may never know how well Edwards understood that the kind of self he attempted to help his listeners become was suitable only to the communal, closed-system, "encyclopedic" economy within which American Puritanism had begun, and that such a self was completely antithetical to the competitive, market economy that nourished a self-reliant, self-determined individualism represented by men like Edwards' contemporary Benjamin Franklin. However, Edwards did understand, more so than any of his Puritan predecessors and increasingly as his career progressed, the full ramifications of the central Puritan doctrines of divine sovereignty and original sin. The deep and unbridgeable gulf Edwards perceived between innocence and apostasy underlies and unifies all the major Calvinist doctrines, and it justifies the uncompromising either/or logic that extends from his attitudes toward dogma into those toward church polity, individual morality, and colonial politics.

Yet, although the uncompromising attitude is certainly visible, almost from the beginning, in Edwards' sermons before, during, and especially after the Great Awakening, the theological rationale for these attitudes does not become clearly visible until after his ouster from his church at Northampton. For this reason, explicating his oratory's rhetorical dynamics requires situating his discourse within his systematic theology, even though he did not fully realize that system until after he had left the pulpit.

Only by first explicating Edwards' system can this book explore its central thesis—that Edwards never intended for his sermons to persuade their audiences, if persuasion means the process, described since antiquity, by which rhetors seek common ground with their audiences and then work from that base toward mutually affirmable goals, ideas, and attitudes. Edwards' primary assumption—that an absolute difference separated the regenerate from the unregenerate—prevented his seeking to persuade in this sense. Instead, he sought to prepare sinners for accepting Christ by undermining or dismantling the belief structures supporting their sense of themselves as independent, self-determined individuals.

Because Edwards' rhetorical intent derives from his theological system, we have chosen to organize the book as follows, first by situating Edwards' work within the context of the concrete sociopolitical, psychological, and economic realities that resisted Edwards' vision of New Israel and thus constituted the rhetorical exigencies that shaped his oral discourse, and then within its complex textual frame.

Accordingly, In Chapter 1, Stephen R. Yarbrough explicates the main tenets of Edwards' conversion theory in terms of the minister's personal conversion experiences; its deviation from the traditional "preparatory model" of conversion experience; its foundations in his perspectivist revision of faculty psychology toward unifying the will, the intellect, and the affections; and its metaphysical foundations in his conceptions of being and time. Along the way, the chapter takes issue with the assumption, commonly held by most previous scholars, that Edwards' metaphysics, and therefore his rhetoric, was derived from John Locke's sensationalism. Despite the Lockean terminology, Edwards departs at key points in favor of a Richardsonian view.

Chapter 2 continues Yarbrough's analysis, showing how Edwards' conversion theory affected his pastoral and rhetorical practices during his first great revival, the "little awakening" at his Northampton church. The chapter's main section analyzes a remarkable sermon, "A Divine and Supernatural Light." The sermon exemplifies Edwards' typical sermon structure; it applies important Edwardsean concepts such as "excellency" and "consent" and his essential distinction between "speculative" and "sensible" knowledge; and it presents his stunningly nihilistic vision of life's meaninglessness in the absence of a sense of divine sovereignty.

Chapter 3 begins with Yarbrough's recounting of the Great Awakening's events and Edwards' part in this historically significant revival, especially his moderating defenses of the revivalists' rhetorical practices against their more conservative detractors while acknowledging the revival's errors and excesses. Then, after Yarbrough's brief exposition of Edwards' conception of personal sin in relation to original sin, John C. Adams rhetorically analyzes what most certainly is Edwards' best-known sermon, "Sinners in the Hands of an Angry God." Adams demonstrates that Edwards' sermons were directed toward dual audiences, the redeemed and the reprobate, and that the sermon's "enthymematic" structure accounts for its original auditors' polarly opposite responses.

In Chapter 4, Adams explains the events leading to Edwards' dismissal from his Northampton pulpit, his subsequent exile to an isolated frontier Indian mission, and his meditative return to the fundamental principles of Puritan encyclopedic order, as demonstrated by his deploying the Pauline "somic" metaphor of the "body of Christ" in sermons such as "True Grace Distinguished from the Experience of Devils." Adams' analysis of "True Grace," perhaps Edwards last great sermon, focuses upon how Edwards invites his clerical audience to identify with Satan himself, a being "educated in the best divinity school in the universe," who most certainly believes, in fact knows, that God is sovereign, and who understands religion better than any human ever will, and yet, because he cannot sense God's beauty and excellency, is damned forever.

In Chapter 5 Adams discusses the complex theological tradition guiding and informing Edwards' own rhetorical theory and practice. Because Puritan theology and rhetoric derived directly from Alexander Richardson's Ramist, encyclopedic philosophy, and because almost no scholarly research has been directed toward articulating Edwards' debt to Richardson, the chapter focuses on those aspects of Richardson's thought most affecting Edwards' own. In a very real sense, Richardsonian encyclopedia forms the dogmatic boundaries beyond which Edwards will not venture. As original as Edwards' metaphysical justification and explanation of orthodox belief may be, he is nevertheless undeviatingly orthodox.

Finally, in Chapter 6, Yarbrough describes Edwards' influence, first upon writers who specifically defended, extended, modified, or attacked his work—including the New Divinity theologians, the New Haven theologians, and the Transcendentalists—and then upon American literary writers. The latter influences are much more subtle and less researched. To indicate the direction future research might take, Yarbrough offers one example of Edwards' literary influence: Harriet Beecher Stowe's Edwardsean conversion techniques in *Uncle Tom's Cabin*.

After writing this book, after risking the accusation of our having only ploughed once more an already deeply furrowed scholarly territory, we are both struck, most of all, by the frightening potential timeliness of Jonathan Edwards' dual vision. From the contented, self-reliant individual's rational, orderly world to the horrific spectacle of abysmal meaningless is but one slippery step, says Edwards; and from that anxiety-filled apprehension to a total surrender, complete abandonment, and absolute obedience to an external, omnipotent authority is but one "turn of the heart." For some reason, Edwards scholars never note just how thorough is his nihilism. As far as he is concerned, unless a completely unified system signifies an omniscient consciousness, the world is nothing, less than nothing. His unrelenting categorical logic led him to nothing, but nothing he would not accept. He grasped the available alternative: it is better, he said, to believe and submit.

In our century, for Martin Heidegger, who himself had once submitted to a totalitarian regime, "The question arises whether the innermost essence of nihilism and the power of its dominion do not consist precisely in considering the nothing merely as a nullity, considering nihilism as an apotheosis of the merely vacuous, as a negation that can be set to rights at once by an energetic affirmation" (*N* 21). A "turn of the heart," an "energetic affirmation"—the suddenness, the surprisingness of the reversals these quiet terms represent should be alarming in an age in which postmodernism's powerful deconstructive instruments are commonly wielded by minds unfortified by history's discipline, in societies unprotected by a centuries-old tradition of mutual responsibility. What happened in New England in the eighteenth century is not disconnected from what happened in Europe in the mid-twentieth. What is happening today is connected to both. However feeble our present attempt may be, it strikes us that studying the conditions allowing conversion to displace persuasion and analyzing the processes of conversion are tasks hardly irrelevant to contemporary life.

Acknowledgments

SERMON TEXTS

The three sermons reprinted in this book follow the text of *The Works of Jonathan Edwards,* rev. and cor. Edward Hickman. 2 vols. (London, 1835. Reprinted. Edinburgh and Carlisle, Pa.: Banner of Truth Trust, 1979).

"A Divine and Supernatural Light Immediately Imparted to the Soul by the Spirit of God, Shown to be both a Scriptural and Rational Doctrine" 2: 12–17.
"Sinners in the Hands of an Angry God" 2: 7–12.
"True Grace Distinguished From the Experience of Devils" 2: 41–50 (edited for length).

SUPPORTED RESEARCH

Part of John Adams' research for this book was conducted in conjunction with an NEH summer seminar for college teachers directed by Lloyd Bitzer. Additional research was conducted in conjunction with a study leave granted by Syracuse University's College of Visual and Performing Arts.

AUTHORSHIP

The order of the authors' names on the title page is arbitrary—it does not reflect a substantive difference in their contributions to this book.

Abbreviations

See Works Cited for complete bibliographic information.

A	Anderson, Wallace E., Introduction. *Scientific and Philosophical Writings.* *See* Miller and Smith
B	Breitenbach, William. "Piety and Moralism: Edwards and the New Divinity."
"CCEB"	Hoopes, James. "Calvinism and Consciousness from Edwards to Beecher."
"CEG"	Edwards, Jonathan. "Concerning Efficacious Grace." *See* Miller and Smith
CNE	Hoopes, James. *Consciousness in New England.*
D	Edwards, Jonathan. "His Diary." *See* Ferm
DO	Owen, John. *Of the Divine Original.*
E	Erdt, Terence. "The Calvinist Psychology of the Heart and the 'Sense' of Jonathan Edwards."
EIW	Miller, Perry. *Errand Into the Wilderness.*
"EN"	Richardson, Alexander. "Ethical Notes." *The Logicians School-Master.*
EW	Edwards, Jonathan. *Ethical Writings. See* Miller and Smith
F	Fiering, Norman. *Jonathan Edwards's Moral Thought and Its British Context.*
"FS"	Edwards, Jonathan. "Farewell Sermon." *See* Hickman (1979)
FT	Mather, Samuel. *Figures and Types of the Old Testament.*
FW	Edwards, Jonathan. *The Freedom of the Will. See* Miller and Smith
G	Goen, C. C. Introduction to *The Great Awakening. See* Miller and Smith

GA	Edwards, Jonathan. *The Great Awakening. See* Miller and Smith
GC	Cohen, Charles Lloyd. *God's Caress.*
GG	Edwards, Jonathan. "God Glorified in Man's Dependence." *See* Ferm
GIC	Bushnell, Horace. *God in Christ.*
"GMP"	Barlow, John. "The Good Mans Priviledge."
"H"	Edwards, Jonathan. "Heaven Is a World of Love." *See* Hickman (1979)
HG	Hollingsworth, Richard. *Holy Ghost on the Bench.*
HP	Pettit, Norman. *The Heart Prepared.*
HU	Locke, John. *An Essay Concerning Human Understanding.*
HWR	Edwards, Jonathan. *A History of the Work of Redemption. See* Miller and Smith
IS	Edwards, Jonathan. *Images or Shadows of Divine Things.*
J	Johnson, Barbara. "The Frame of Reference: Poe, Lacan, Derrida."
JE	Miller, Perry. *Jonathan Edwards.*
"JEAP"	Kuklick, Bruce. "Jonathan Edwards and American Philosophy."
"JEE"	Stuart, Robert Lee. "Jonathan Edwards at Enfield: 'And Oh the Cheerfulness and Pleasantness . . .'"
"JEF"	Laurence, David. "Jonathan Edwards as a Figure in Literary History."
"JENT"	Noll, Mark A. "Jonathan Edwards and Nineteeth-Century Theology."
"JEPI"	Lyttle, David. "Jonathan Edwards on Personal Identity."
"JESH"	Miller, Perry. "Jonathan Edwards on the Sense of the Heart."
"JFA"	Edwards, Jonathan. "Justification by Faith Alone." *See* Ferm
"JG"	Edwards, Jonathan. "The Justice of God in the Damnation of Sinners." *See* Hickman (1979)
JWW	Ward, John William. Afterword. *See* Stowe
K	Kimnach, Wilson H. "The Brazen Trumpet."
LM	Gay, Peter. *A Loss of Mastery.*
LSM	Richardson, Alexander. *The Logicians School-Master.*
"L"	Edwards, Jonathan. "A Divine and Supernatural Light." *See* Part II
"LT"	Kimnach, Wilson H. "The Literary Techniques of Jonathan Edwards."
MCA	Mather, Cotton. *Magnalia Christi Americana.*
MTC	Westra, Helen. *The Minister's Task and Calling in the Sermons of Jonathan Edwards.*
N	Heidegger, Martin. *Nietzsche.*

NRI	Cherry, Conrad. *Nature and Religious Imagination.*
OS	Edwards, Jonathan. *Original Sin. See* Miller and Smith.
PCN	Caldwell, Patricia. *The Puritan Conversion Narrative.*
PF	Morgan, Edmund S. *The Puritan Family.*
PJE	Townsend, Harvey G., ed. *The Philosophy of Jonathan Edwards from His Private Notebooks.*
"PKG"	Edwards, Jonathan. "Pressing Into the Kingdom of God." *See* Ferm
"PMC"	Laurence, David. "Jonathan Edwards, Solomon Stoddard, and the Preparationist Model of Conversion."
PN	Edwards, Jonathan. "Personal Narrative." *See* Faust and Johnson
PRE	Coolidge, John S. *The Pauline Renaissance in England.*
PTJE	Elwood, Douglas J. *The Philosophical Theology of Jonathan Edwards.*
PVM	Haroutunian, Joseph. *Piety versus Moralism: The Passing of the New England Theology.*
R A	Edwards, Jonathan. *A Treatise Concerning Religious Affections. See* Miller and Smith
RHAP	Ahlstrom, Sydney E. *A Religious History of the American People.*
R M	Burke, Kenneth. *A Rhetoric of Motives.*
"RN"	Richardson, Alexander. "Rhetorical Notes." *The Logicians School-Master.*
"ROS"	Miller, Perry. "Edwards, Locke, and the Rhetoric of Sensation."
"S"	Edwards, Jonathan. "Sinners in the Hands of an Angry God." *See* Part II
S A	Armstrong, Hilary. *St. Augustine and Christian Platonism.*
SD	Tompkins, Jane. *Sensational Designs.*
SP	Warch, Richard. *School of the Prophets.*
SPW	Edwards, Jonathan. *Scientific and Philosophical Writings. See* Miller and Smith
SSC-D	Hooker, Thomas. *A Survey of the Summe of Church-Discipline.*
ST	Edwards, Jonathan. *Some Thoughts Concerning the Present Revival of Religion in New England. See* Hickman (1979)
T	Tracy, Patricia J. *Jonathan Edwards, Pastor.*
"TG"	Edwards, Jonathan. "True Grace Distinguished from the Experience of Devils." *See* Part II
TM	Ames, William. *Technometry.*
UTC	Stowe, Harriet Beecher. *Uncle Tom's Cabin.*
V S	Morgan, Edmund S. *Visible Saints.*

W	Winslow, Ola Elizabeth. *Jonathan Edwards: 1703–58.*
WEC	Brown, Arthur W. *William Ellery Channing.*
WKS	Goodwin, Thomas. *Works*, 4.

PART I
JONATHAN EDWARDS

1
Remarkable Seasons

THE EARLY YEARS: 1703–1729

Jonathan Edwards was born October 5, 1703, in East Windsor, Connecticut. He was the fifth child and only son in a family that was to have eleven children. His father, Timothy, with whom he would remain close throughout his life, was the dedicated minister to this small frontier village. His mother, Esther Stoddard, was the daughter of Solomon Stoddard, the most powerful and influential pastor in the Connecticut Valley. Because of this and other family connections, as well as her own strong personality, she, too, was an important personage in the social and political life of the community (W 23).

Always a quiet, studious child, the perhaps pampered only son spent much of his youth either alone or with a few friends playing at religion and observing nature on his father's farm at the edge of the wilderness. In his *Personal Narrative*, Edwards writes of the "secret places" in the woods he went to for his secluded prayer and meditation, as well as the "booth in a swamp" he shared with friends. These are the scenes of the first of "two remarkable seasons of awakening" preceding his true conversion much later (*PN* 57). His letters from the period indicate that he was an unusually serious, self-disciplined, and extraordinarily intelligent boy. It is clear, moreover, that for him only two significant vantage points existed from which one could seriously view life— that of the church and parsonage, and that of the pristine forest, as untouched as if newly made by God. The first was the center and source of social and intellectual life, the other the center and source of beauty and peace.

Then at the age of thirteen, in 1716, Edwards entered Yale College, an institution that had been in turmoil over its permanent location since its founding fifteen years before. Ideological battles raged, as well. The young

Edwards responded primarily by retreating even further into solitary study; but as one biographer has noted, he exhibited the unfortunate traits of criticizing his peers' behavior, displaying his "superior righteousness," and having "a lamentable lack of any sense of humor" (W 69). These circumstances and personal traits tended to isolate him from his fellows. By the time he graduated in 1720, Edwards' personality had set into its intensely grave, introspective aloofness. He was a man capable of discounting the importance of any concerns that were not those of his God.

After graduating, Edwards continued to study at Yale for two years. His life's most important event occurred during this period; his conversion. This event's significance to Edwards' theology cannot be overestimated. Equally important was the turbulent atmosphere at Yale during the months following his conversion while the still very young man was first attempting to comprehend its meaning. In 1722 the Rector and two tutors had openly announced their allegiance to Episcopacy, and when the doctrinal battles had ended Yale emerged even more conservative than it had been before.[1] Edwards' naturally conservative bent undoubtedly was set permanently at this time. Despite his often novel explanations and defenses of orthodox doctrine, never, not even marginally in his private notebooks, would he question orthodoxy's truth.

The young theologian was saved temporarily from the tension at Yale when he accepted the call to his first ministry during August 1722. This newly formed Presbyterian Church in New York City offered him a chance to relax and reflect. That December he began his diary—our primary guide to Edwards' inner life as a young man. Edwards seems to have been happy in New York. His departure was, as he says in his diary, a "melancholy" one (D 125). Nevertheless, the tiny, financially distressed congregation could promise him little future, so in April 1723 he accepted a position in Bolton, Connecticut, and returned to East Windsor to arrange his affairs. However, in the meantime, Yale offered him a tutorship, which he accepted after obtaining his release from Bolton.

The year 1723 was an extraordinary one in Edwards' intellectual development. While in New York he had begun his "Miscellanies," and after returning to Connecticut that summer he worked on his master's thesis and began, among other note series, "The Mind" and "Of Being." That fall, shortly after receiving his M.A. degree, Edwards made the first notes toward developing his central philosophical concept of excellency. About this same time, in October, he wrote his famous letter on migrating spiders, much later than his earliest biographers supposed (A 29–30).[2]

Despite his private achievements, Edwards' nearly two-year stint as a Yale tutor was an unhappy one. The diary reveals him under constant stress. He fell very ill—so ill that he had to return to East Windsor to recuperate during the spring and summer of 1726. Shortly after his return to Yale in September, he received the invitation to assist his grandfather Solomon Stoddard in Northampton, Massachusetts.

When Edwards was ordained in Northampton in February 1727, he must have known that to be the designated successor to the "Congregational Pope of the Connecticut Valley" was a mixed blessing, but he could not have seen it as a curse. Yet, when Stoddard died and in February 1729 Edwards became sole minister to his congregation, the fifty-five years of his grandfather's influence became the weight that twenty years later would pull him down from the pulpit he now controlled with his flock's full consent. Now, however, Edwards saw no conflict between his own beliefs and Stoddard's. As Patricia J. Tracy has noted, Edwards' "initial positions on church sacraments and conversion were thoroughly Stoddardean" (T 73). He practiced open communion in conformity to the Half-Way Covenant, preached the preparatory sequence, and exhorted his audience to reform their behavior, just as his grandfather had done. After his marriage to Sarah Pierrepont shortly after his ordination, Edwards settled into a pattern of ministerial life much like his grandfather's, just as he and everyone else had expected.

However, two sets of forces worked against Edwards' pattern as they had not worked against Stoddard's. One was the powerful force of socioeconomic change in Northampton as it evolved from a frontier village with its social isolation and economic self-subsistence, into a town with its developed economy, more marked class distinctions and intramural social and political life—a society obviously contrary to the ideal encyclopedic order (see Chapter 5). The second, perhaps more powerful, force was Edwards' own mind, one amazingly intolerant of inconsistency. Comparing Edwards' sermons with his private notebook entries during the 1730s reveals that Edwards' public life was heading one way, his intellectual another. A discrepancy existed between Stoddard's conversion theory, with its implications for church polity and sermon rhetoric, and Edwards' personal conversion experience.

CONVERSION

Sometime in his late teens Jonathan Edwards converted. We do not know exactly when the conversion occurred, and he himself "could never give an account, how, or by what means" he became "convinced"; nor, apparently, did he know "at the time, nor a long time after, that there was any extraordinary influence of God's Spirit" involved in his conversion (PN 58). According to biographer Ola Winslow, the conversion "took place in the early part of his second year of graduate study [at Yale], when he was seventeen years old" (W 74). Winslow attributes the date to the Personal Narrative, presumably because in it Edwards states that he went to New York to preach about a year and a half after his conversion began (PN 62). A false conversion preceded his true one, during the second of the "two remarkable seasons of awakening" Edwards describes in the Personal Narrative. It occurred after a long and serious illness—a "pleurisy" contracted "towards the latter part of [his] time at college." After that illness, however, he "fell again into [his] old ways of sin" (*PN* 57–58). Upon his recovery, Edwards did begin consciously to seek salvation, but without "that kind of affection and delight" he had experienced as a boy during his first "awakening." Of the joyless, forced practice of religion that accompanied the second awakening, Edwards doubted "whether such miserable seeking ever succeeded" (*PN* 58).

Of his actual initial conversion, Edwards reports only that before it occurred he had "been full of objections against the doctrine of God's sovereignty," while afterward it no longer seemed "like a horrible doctrine": "But I remember the time well, when I seemed to be convinced, and fully satisfied, as to this sovereignty of God, and his justice in thus eternally disposing of men, according to his sovereign pleasure" (*PN* 58). From this we can surmise only that Edwards' conversion occurred at some particular time and place, and that it took the form of a changed disposition toward a central point of doctrine. Because Edwards does not specify the time and place, we must assume that to Edwards the circumstances did not seem important. His conviction apparently did not occur in response to a sermon, biblical reading, or personal experience. It seems not like an "experience" at all; he describes it as being intellectual, not emotional, in character: "my reason apprehended the justice and reasonableness of God's sovereignty" (*PN* 58). However, from that moment onward, Edwards says, "there has been a wonderful alteration in my mind":

But I have often, since that first conviction, had quite another sense of God's sovereignty than I had then, I have often since had not only a conviction, but a delightful conviction. The doctrine has very often appeared exceeding pleasant, bright, and sweet. Absolute sovereignty is what I love to ascribe to God. But my first conviction was not so. (*PN* 59)

As far as the record shows, the conversion made no other "alteration." If Edwards became a "new man," the new, like the old, still planned to enter the ministry, still wore the same clothes, behaved the same way, espoused the same beliefs, loved the same family.

Nevertheless, the apparently minute changes in Edwards' attitude toward the justice of divine sovereignty, from resistance to consent, then to delight, made all the difference to Edwards' life. Perhaps more important, his accepting that change as his conversion's essential mark eventually made all the difference between Edwards' theology and sermon rhetoric and that of the earlier Puritans.

The young Edwards knew, of course, that his conversion process did not fit the pattern—the "morphology of conversion"—that had become almost prescriptive after two centuries of American development. His diary's first entry, dated December 18, 1722, when Edwards was nineteen and already for six months the minister of a congregation in New York City, demonstrates his concern:

The reason why I, in the least, question my interest in God's love and favour, is, —1. Because I cannot speak so fully to my experience of the preparatory work, of which divines speak: 2. I do not remember that I experienced regeneration, exactly in those steps, in which divines say it is generally wrought. (D 117)

The original model for later conversion morphologies, according to Patricia Caldwell, was Martin Luther's "two-stage theory of repentance": "First, under the work of the law, the sinner saw his sin and was sorry for it; only then, under grace, was he enabled to resolve to amend his life. That resolution was literally a turning point or conversion" (*PCN* 58).

Caldwell has carefully traced these morphologies' evolution. They varied considerably in the number of stages, terminology, and description, but, as C. C. Goen puts it, "By the end of the seventeenth century the steps of the pilgrim's progress had become so fixed in the New England mind as to give the religious experiences narrated by applicants for church membership the appearance of a set form" (G 26). Edwards' diversion from the typical expectation becomes immediately clear when compared to Edmund Morgan's summation of the conversion narratives Michael Wigglesworth recorded in his diary:

First comes a feeble and false awakening to God's commands and a pride in keeping them pretty well, but also much backsliding. Disappointments and disasters lead to other fitful hearkenings to the word. Sooner or later true legal fear or conviction enables the individual to see his hopeless and helpless condition and to know that his own righteousness cannot save him, that Christ is the only hope. Thereafter comes the infusion of saving grace, sometimes but not always so precisely felt that the believer can state exactly when and where it comes to him. A struggle between faith and doubt ensues, with the candidate careful to indicate that his assurance has never been complete and that his sanctification has been much hampered by his own sinful heart. (*VS* 91)

Absent from Edwards' conversion is the experience of "legal fear"—a key element in most morphologies—which in his *Personal Narrative* he expressly denies: "My concern continued and prevailed, with many exercising thoughts and inward struggles; but yet it never seemed to be proper to express that concern by the name of terror" (*PN* 58). Rather than a turning away *from* an old self toward God in fear of God's justice, Edwards experienced a turning *toward* God in appreciation of that justice. Edwards' repentance, according to the *Personal Narrative*, really followed the conversion, and it still was felt not as fear, but as regret: "I often felt a mourning and lamenting in my heart, that I had not turned to God sooner, that I might have had more time to grow in grace" (*PN* 61).

Much later, in his 1746 publication *A Treatise Concerning Religious Affections*, where Edwards laid out his "Twelve Signs of Gracious Affections"— the twelve marks of difference between the reprobate and the saint—he explains at length why terror does not signify grace. He even draws upon William Perkins who, he says, "distinguishes between those sorrows that come through convictions of conscience, and melancholic passions rising only from mere imaginations" (*RA* 157 n. 6), although he denies any certainty to the preparatory steps Perkins and others describe.

However serious Edwards' "least" doubts about his conversion may have been, by May 28, 1725, about a year after his return to Yale from New York to serve as a tutor, he was compelled to enter in his diary "that whether I am now converted or not, I am so settled in the state I am in, that I shall go on in it all my life" (D 142). Unable to question further his own election, Edwards began to question the morphology that put his conversion in doubt. Nevertheless, we go too far if, like David Laurence, we surmise that the difference between the expected preparatory pattern and Edwards' personal experience "eventually led him to reject the step-by-step model of conversion" ("PMC" 266).

An early notebook entry, written probably during either his tutorship at Yale or in the early years at Northampton, while still his grandfather Solomon Stoddard's assistant, shows that Edwards accepted the preparatory model as the "ordinary method" by which sinners come to grace, and that he saw "legal fear" as the typical, although not essential, preparatory step:

> Wherefore 'tis established that, in those that are brought up under the Gospel, God's ordinary way is thus first to convince them; so that there is doubtless ordinarily a preparatory work of conviction. This conviction that causes men to think it worth the while to seek salvation is hardly ever a conviction of the worth of the reward but of the dreadfulness of the punishment. (*PJE* 116)

Laurence correctly notes that Edwards strongly disagreed with Stoddard on the status of "humiliation," which, Laurence claims, Stoddard equated with legal fear.

Edwards understood humiliation not so much as legal fear, or terror before the thought of one's damnation, but as "an utter despair of help from ourselves" in achieving salvation. He accordingly perceived a logical connection between this despair and its opposite: "as they are brought to see that God may damn them if he pleases," so they see that "God may show them mercy if he pleases" (Miscellany 317, quoted in "PMC" 273). Such a connection, obviously, may be perceived immediately or gradually, depending upon the recipient's perspicuity. In another notebook entry Edwards confirms that humiliation, although only "natural [that is, not requiring grace] in religion," is a step that "may be needful to prepare the mind for a sense of spiritual excellency," and he goes further to say that "a sense of the excellency of God's mercy in forgiving sin depends upon a sense of the great guilt of sin" (*PJE* 125).

This would seem to confirm the old morphology, except that in the same entry, Edwards does not argue that the sense of guilt entails terror, but that this "common conviction" of guilt is one of "being made sensible" of the "connection or natural agreeableness there is between" the "great guilt of sin" and the idea of a "dreadful punishment." Sinners, however, are then "brought to see the great need of a satisfaction or something to intervene to make it honorable to that majesty to show 'em favor." For a while sinners are "blind" to the "suitableness" of Christ's sacrifice to this end, but "then afterwards having a sense given them of Christ's divine excellency," they see the "fitness" of the sacrifice and are convinced "that there is indeed acceptance to be had with God in this. And so the soul seemingly believes in Christ" (*PJE* 125–26).

Again, this conforms exactly to Edwards' own conversion experience. On July 4, 1723, he wrote in his diary, "I thought I could go out of the world, as much assured of my salvation, as I was of Christ's faithfulness, knowing that, if Christ did not fail me, he would save me, who had trusted him on his word" (D 129). Also, the rational character of Edwards' "first conviction," as expressed in the *Personal Narrative*, now becomes typified in the notebook entry:

The truth that the soul is most immediately convinced of in this case by a sense of the divine excellency of Christ, with a preparatory sense of the need of satisfaction for sin, is not that the Gospel is the work of [God] . . . but . . . that the way of salvation that the Gospel reveals is a proper, suitable, and sufficient way, perfectly agreeable to the reason and nature of things, and that tends to answer the ends proposed. (*PJE* 126)

Clearly, although grace itself instills a new sense of a doctrine, one the sinner was "often told of before" but had been unable to see or experience, upon receiving this new sense follows a series of rational deductions and inferences that lead ultimately to faith in the Gospel's truth.

Just as clearly, the preparatory step of humiliation, understood as a sense of guilt, receives virtually the same preparatory status as the Gospel: just as hearing the Word necessarily precedes believing it, sensing sin's guilt precedes experiencing God's excellent mercy. Not so clearly, but nevertheless implied, sensing God's sovereignty precedes all of these, for without sensing God's sovereignty, there can be no sensing guilt. These then are indeed links in a rational chain. Legal terror, however, is outside this chain.

As far as Edwards was concerned, the observable steps of a pilgrim's progress argued neither for nor against his or her conversion (see *RA* 161). The Spirit's workings were shrouded in mystery, even if it ordinarily proceeded in the typical manner. By the same token—and this is a point most important to understanding Edwards' sermon rhetoric—knowing those steps was in no way advantageous to the minister in his chief task. Inducing legal fear, the terror of damnation, would not send the sinner further along his journey. Accordingly, Edwards concentrated his efforts less on the steps toward conversion and more on the meaning of conversion itself and on its effects.

Consistent with his own experience, Edwards held throughout his life the Richardsonian view "that the prime alteration that is made in conversion, that which is first and the foundation of all, is the alteration of the temper and disposition and spirit of the mind" (*PJE* 249). Since until the disposition is changed the sinner cannot perceive "spiritual ideas," explaining them to the sinner does no good whatsoever. Edwards says in another early notebook entry:

When we explain spiritual things that consist in mental motions, energies, and operations, though we give the most accurate descriptions possible, we do not fully explain them, no, not so much as to give any manner of notion to them to one that never felt them, any more than we can fully explain the rainbow to one that never saw, though a rainbow is a very easy thing to give a definition of. *(PJE* 245)

The unfortunate corollary to this situation was that the minister's efficacy is severely limited:

From hence it necessarily follows that the best and most able men in the world, with their greatest diligence and laboriousness, most-eloquent speaking, clearest illustrations, and convincing arguments, can do nothing towards causing the knowledge of things of the Gospel. For the disposition, as we have shown, must necessarily be changed first. (*PJE* 246)

In short, conversion is not subject to persuasion.

Rather than attempt to persuade the unconverted, Edwards tried by means of his preaching, in addition to offering the Word, (1) to provide the optimal conditions and circumstances within which conversion might take place, (2) to offer the logical connections between guilt and repentance so that those who have been or are being converted might better understand what is happening to them, and (3) to prevent the misinterpretation of pseudo-religious experience, especially by those who believe they have experienced grace but have not. Understanding that these are the ends Edwards' sermons attempt to achieve—not the conversion itself nor the preparatory steps preceding it—is the prerequisite to understanding his sermon rhetoric.[3]

And here lies the true difference between Edwards and his predecessors regarding the aim of preaching. His predecessors believed that legal fear was the minister's chief instrument. The law was fully rational, and by the law sinners were damned. Norman Pettit summarizes this approach:

The moral law, by the threat of damnation, convinces man of his sins, brings him to despair, and forces him to see that Christ is his only hope for salvation; for God does not allow man to partake of Gospel grace without some foregoing sense of bondage. This convincing work of the law drives the soul to Christ. (*HP* 16)

The conviction of one's just damnation and of one's helplessness to prevent it prepares the heart. Then grace allows the sinner to understand that union with Christ frees him from the law's bondage, for without an understanding of its true meaning, the covenant would not be binding.

Theologically, Edwards saw most of the same elements in the conversion process as his predecessors—the sinner's perception of his violation of God's law, the acceptance of the justice of the law, the sense of helplessness to alter one's condition alone, the joy attendant upon recognizing one's freedom from bondage. Psychologically, however, Edwards saw a different sequence. He asserted that a sinner can be neither "convinced that God may justly damn him" nor "that God may save him if he pleases" (Miscellany 317, quoted in "PMC" 273). Since these perceptions are "like links in a chain," so that one person may consciously experience the former and another the latter, both are manifestly under gracious influence, since each implies the other, and the reprobate can experience neither.

The key element is the justice of the sinner's damnation—the sinner's self-love prevents him or her from truly apprehending it. Both apprehending God's justice in damning and his grace in saving depend upon apprehending God's sovereignty. Unlike his predecessors, Edwards did not believe that rationally comprehending God's sovereignty would necessarily leave "an impression on the heart"; rather, the will had to be moved first, before the intellect would properly comprehend. Addressing the sinner's intellect alone, therefore, would surely be ineffective.

The Will

Edwards believed, as he described it at one point, that "man has, as it were, two wills." One is the "rational will," which does indeed follow upon the dictates of the intellect's last best judgment; the other is an "inclination arising from the liveliness of the idea of, or sensibleness of the good of, the object presented to the mind." In this passage he calls this inclination the "appetite," a term he will abandon in favor of "heart," "inclination," or simply "will" (*PJE* 157–58). This distinction is essential to understanding his theology and rhetoric.

Edwards expresses the key difference between the "rational will" and the "inclination" in a theatrical metaphor. The inclination, he says in *Religious Affections*, "is the faculty by which the soul does not behold things, as an indifferent unaffected spectator, but either as liking or disliking, pleased or displeased, approving or rejecting" (*RA* 96). The metaphor implies that the understanding and the will are really a unitary function appearing as two distinct faculties only because the self may be either disinterested or interested in its results. One thinks, always, from a point of view.

As Perry Miller has noted, Edwards broke completely with the old faculty psychology by that, since Calvin, had led most Puritans to assume a temporal sequence between understanding and willing (*JE* 252–55), an assumption that led them further to explain the will's sinfulness in terms of the faculties' degenerate state. That is, after the Fall, the will chooses evil "because the reason misinforms it or the senses seduce it" (*JE* 252–55). By maintaining compartmental distinctions among the faculties, Puritans left themselves open to the infections of rationalism, especially Arminianism, because, according to the old psychology, if the will is to be moved at all it must be moved through the reason. Moreover, the Arminians charged that if reason cannot persuade the will because of predestination, then religion is useless. As the Arminian Daniel Whitby put it: "To say God seriously invites, exhorts, and requires all Men to work out their salvation, and yet by his Decree of Reprobation hath rendered that Even to the most of them impossible . . . is to make the Gospel of Christ a Mockery" (quoted in *JE* 254).

Edwards, in *The Freedom of the Will*, had argued against the Arminians that "if the dictate of the understanding, and determination of the will be the same, this confounds the understanding and will, and makes them the same." He refused to say whether or not they are the same, but that if they are, and if, as the Arminians say, "liberty consists in a self-determining power in the understanding, free of all necessity," then it follows that moral freedom "must consist in the independence of the understanding on the evidence or appearance of things, or anything whatsoever that stands forth to the view of the mind, prior to the understanding's determination" (*FW* 223). In short, the rationalist argument concludes that to be a free moral agent means to be free from rational persuasion.

Miller and others, such as John E. Smith, have taken Edwards to mean that "a line is drawn between understanding and will, when the distinction means the difference between the 'neutral observer' and one who 'takes sides'; but there is no clear warrant for making this into an opposition" (*RA* 13). That is, they see Edwards as having collapsed the faculties into a unitary "man choosing" (*JE* 254).[4] The "whole man" is always involved, and the whole man is not a free agent. Man understands only as he perceives, he perceives as he desires, he desires as he feels, he feels as he understands. Accordingly, as Edwards uses the distinction, the understanding is the will disengaged from a situation of actual choice—the spectator. This metaphor implies that, just as the spectator judges a play's action differently from any characters in it because their perspectives are different, so too our choices may not follow our understanding. Edwards does not mean, however, as did those rationalists who used the same metaphor, that the disinterested perspective is better because it is more objective.

Quite to the contrary, only those wholly engaged in the Christian drama, only those "thoroughly convinced of the certain truth" of religious things, will persevere in practicing holy actions, while those "never thoroughly convinced that there is any reality in the things of religion, will never be at the labor and trouble" of difficult religious practice (*RA* 395). And for Edwards, the end of grace is "Christian practice," not religious feeling or even spiritual understanding, although these make sustained holy practice possible. The true Christian does not simply perform religious duties, as any natural man might. "When a natural man denies his lust, and lives a strict, religious life, and seems humble, painful and earnest in religion, 'tis not natural, 'tis all a force against nature" (*RA* 296), but a saint sees "the transcendently excellent and aimiable nature of divine things, as they are in themselves, and not in any conceived relation to self, or self-interest" (*RA* 394). Thus where the one does the good because he thinks he should, the other simply wants to do good because "a love to holiness, for holiness sake, inclines persons to practice holiness" (*RA* 394).

By placing the traditional, Richardsonian distinction between the civil and sanctified man on a new psychological footing (see "EN" 128), Edwards revised the Puritan description of grace's operations, clarifying the aims of sermon rhetoric. If Christians are known by their willing Christian practice, grace must change or reposition individuals so that they see their situation in a "new light," so that they see the good as the good and the things of religion as reality. Perceiving the good is desiring the good is doing the good, but the good must be revealed. For Edwards, the problem lies neither with our faculties, nor with the world our faculties perceive. In fact, we misunderstand Edwards entirely if we assume that either must be corrected. The problem lies entirely with the self, with the perceiver's identity, the "for whom" one perceives, thinks, and wills. Instilling fear into sinners' hearts does no good because sinners fear only for their already damned selves. The distinction Edwards makes in *The Religious Affections* is helpful here:

In legal humiliation men are brought to despair of helping themselves; in evangelical, they are brought voluntarily to deny and renounce themselves: in the former they are subdued and forced to the ground; in the latter, they are brought sweetly to yield, and freely and with delight to prostrate themselves at the feet of God. (*RA* 312)

Ultimately, self denial marks the difference between those who understand religious things only rationally and those who sense them with the heart.

Here lies the importance of Edwards' definition of the will to the minister's rhetoric. Since what the disinterested intellect judges to be good may not correspond to what the will senses to be the good,

If a man has only a rational judgement that a thing is beautiful and lovely, without any sensibleness of the beauty, and at the same time don't think it best for himself, he will never choose it. Though if he be sensible of the beauty of it to a strong degree, he may will it though he thinks 'tis not best for himself. (*PJE* 157–58)

Obviously, if the "thing" under consideration is the idea of God's sovereignty, one may either rationally judge it to be beautiful and still resist it, or one may sense its beauty though thinking it bad for one's self. Indeed, since divine sovereignty is antithetical to an independent self, the more one understands its implications the more one will resist its authenticity, fearing oneself's survival. Conversely, the more one senses the authenticity of God's sovereignty, the less one will defend one's self.

Simply put, in Edwards' view, the natural or rational man defines himself as an individual separate from and transcending the world, the world God has made and sustains. As rational, he sees himself as capable of understanding and manipulating the world to his ends, but in fact he is natural, thoroughly determined, a slave to his perceptions and emotions. A sovereign God who really controls the self and the world terrifies such a person, and he resists the notion with all his might. Self-reflection compounds his anxiety, for it reveals that he cannot always do what he knows is best for himself. Eventually, he feels helpless and seeks his salvation. This is "legal humiliation," and it "has in it no spiritual good, nothing of the nature of the true virtue" (*RA* 312). This is simply the sinner as sinner wanting to be saved. But wanting to be saved does not save. In fact, it may simply lead one deeper into sin.

Crucial to understanding how grace changes the will is Edwards' conception of grace's final effects. Negatively a self-denial, positively it effects a complete subordination or "surrender" to God's will, in short, an identification of the self's interests with God's. We find the record of Edwards' conscious expression of faith (which to his grandfather would have been *the* moment of grace) in his diary, dated Saturday, January 12, 1723:

I have this day, solemnly renewed my baptismal covenant and self-dedication, which I renewed, when I was taken into the communion of the church. I have been before God, and have given myself, all that I am, and have, to God, so that I am not, in any respect, my own, I can challenge no sight in this understanding, this will, these affections, which are in me. . . . Now, henceforth, I am not to act, in any respect, as my own. (D 119–20)

Effectively, this represents a typically Richardsonian acknowledgment of a divided self, one an independent, self-determined individual, the other an agent of God, wholly dependent upon an infinitely superior consciousness and antithetical to the personal self.

In the *Religious Affections*, Edwards defines grace's end as the practice of "universal obedience." Doing good and obeying God's will are one and the same. God's will, of course, is expressed in the Bible, but there it is expressed primarily in the Old Testament as a series of "Thou shalt nots," as the law that even the unregenerate can obey, and in the New Testament as the rather vague injunction to "love." What God wants, or needs, or desires, however, is nothing beyond what already is. As Edwards expresses it very early in his notebook, "If God is infinitely happy now, then everything is now as God would have it to be now" (*PJE* 156). The implication is that, although the performance of good works is indeed the chief visible sign of gracious activity, not only are good works ineffective as a means towards salvation, they are unnecessary to furthering Providence's design: everything is already as it should be. What, then, can obedience or Christian practice concretely mean?

Being

For Edwards, true Christian practice is summed up in the term "devotion." But to understand devotion requires a brief detour through Edwards' ontology. Very early in his career Edwards wrote a short treatise entitled "The Mind." In it he defines that which is—being—as "proportion," a term he borrows from Richardson: "For being, if we examine narrowly, is nothing else but proportion. When one being is inconsistent with another being, then being is contradicted. But contradiction to being is intolerable to perceiving being; and the consent to being, most pleasing" (*SPW* 336). Although Edwards means this quite literally, for us today it is probably better to substitute the term "meaning" for "being" here: what something means, its significance, is determined by its perceived relation to other meanings.

Edwards' concept is essentially structural to the extent that he sees all being or meaning as relational. However, unlike post-Saussurian structuralism, which conceives meaning within differential systems, so that the meaning of any one element is determined by its differentiation from other elements, Edwards' "structuralism" is based upon sameness or likeness. His key term is "excellency," defined as "the consent of being to being, or beings' consent to entity [nonperceiving being]. The more the consent is, and the more extensive, the greater the excellency" (*SPW* 336). Consent is, roughly speaking, an element's assent or contribution toward the whole's "direction" or inclination or end. No element can exist (be significant) in itself, not because alone it cannot differ, as in modern structuralism, but because alone it cannot consent:

One alone without any reference to any more cannot be excellent; for, in such a case, there can be no manner of relation, no way, and therefore no such thing as consent. Indeed what we call "one" may be excellent because of a consent of parts, or some consent of those in that being that are distinguished into a plurality some way or other. But in a being that is absolutely without any plurality there cannot be excellency, for there can be no such thing as consent or agreement. (*SPW* 337)

Edwards distinguishes between two kinds of beings, the perceiving and non-perceiving. Finite, non-perceiving "sensible" things' consent to one another Edwards normally terms "beauty." Excellency he reserves for spiritual, or conscious, beings' consent to one another.

Sensible things may consent "by equality or by likeness or by proportion." Proportion's complex beauty is more satisfying than the simple beauty of equality or likeness, and he inevitably draws upon human art to exemplify proportionate beauty:

By proportion one part may sweetly consent to ten thousand different parts. All the parts may consent with all the rest and, not only so, but the parts taken singly may consent with the whole taken together. Thus, in the figures or flourishes drawn by an acute penman, every stroke may have such a proportion, both by the place and distance, direction, degree or curvity, etc., that there may be a consent in the parts of each stroke, one with another, and a harmonious agreement with all the strokes and with the various parts composed of many strokes and an agreeableness to the whole figure taken together. (*SPW* 380–81)

However, a sensible thing's real being or meaning, its beauty, is ultimately determined by its reference to the totality of things, so that a thing appearing agreeable or disagreeable from a lesser perspective may appear (and therefore be) quite the opposite from a greater.

Edwards considered sensible aesthetics analogous to spiritual, except, of course, that the latter is much more complex. Whereas consent to sensible things entails assuming the spectator's disinterested attitude, consent to other spiritual beings as spiritual being requires accepting its sameness or likeness with oneself. As Edwards puts it, the consent of "minds towards minds . . . is love" (*SPW* 362). Similar to his distinction between perceiving and nonperceiving beings is his distinction between finite, created minds and infinite mind or "being in general"—God (*SPW* 363). As sensible beings or meanings depend fully upon perceiving beings, finite mind depends fully upon infinite mind: "As to bodies, . . . they have no proper being of their own. And as to spirits, they are communications of the great original Spirit, and doubtless, in metaphysical strictness and propriety, He is and there is none else" (*SPW* 363–64). Accordingly, as a sensible thing's beauty or being is gauged by its consent or contribution to its context—and ultimately to the total sensible universe—so too a spiritual being is gauged by its consent to or dissent from other spiritual beings and ultimately to God.

These relationships can get rather complex. "Deformity" or "disagreeableness" may range from "only merely a dissent from being" to a "dissent from, or not to consent with, a being who consents with his being," while "consent to being" includes "dissent from that which dissents from being" (*SPW* 363). In short, spiritual beings are spiritual to the extent that they consent to other spiritual beings' existence, and since one spiritual being is infinite, all other spiritual beings are part of, or are "communications," of the infinite spirit.

To Edwards, communication with God—which amounts to a reflection upon the self as a reflection of God's reflection upon Himself—or devotion, is the highest end to human activity. In his notebooks Edwards argues against the rationalist and Arminian contention that there "may be a degree of devotion that may hinder one from their being so useful to the rest of the creatures as they might otherwise." Edwards says this contention stems from believing the world was made, like a clock, "to have all the parts of it nicely hanging together and sweetly harmonious and corresponding," so that, in such a world, "the highest end of a particular creature was to be useful to the common good of creatures in general." However, says Edwards, "if the highest end of every part of a clock is only mutually to assist the other parts in their motions, the clock is good for nothing at all" (*PJE* 126–27). For Edwards, our works are good or useful to others only insofar as we know what being useful means, that is, insofar as we know our place in the great scheme.

Time

Edwards' belief that human activity's highest end is devotion implies that judgments made from anything less than an infinite, total vision are inadequate and doomed to error. Thus, to guide their actions human beings depend entirely upon the Word of the God who has that total vision. Belief in that total vision further assumes that time does not limit God's perception, as it does human beings', but that God observes reality immediately and completely, not sequentially and partially. Like being itself, time, its medium, is perceptual. Grace, in altering the person by altering the perspective, ultimately changes temporal perception. The shift from self-love to love of God, from a limited, finite perspective toward a total, infinite one, is also a shift from considering perpetually unfolding future possibilities toward urgent immediate judgment. God's time is now, not later. There can be no deferral. Grace disposes the heart toward present devotion.

Modern scholarship's failure to acknowledge adequately the temporal dimension in Edwards' theology often has led to misunderstanding his work's relationship to prior writers. Most important is the assumption that Edwards used the phrase "a new simple idea" as Locke would have in describing grace instead of as the metaphor it was, an assumption that has been often repeated since Perry Miller first advanced it.

For example, James Hoopes recently has noted that at least one seventeenth-century New Englander, Charles Norton, in *The Spirit of Man* (1693), had, drawing upon both traditional Augustinian sources as well as the new "perceptual model of the inward life," emphasized the "disposition" or "heart" and had "described religious conversion as a renovation, not of the traditional faculties, but of personal disposition" (*CNE* 58). Despite this self-provided clue to Edwards' true position, Hoopes clings to Miller's interpretation, saying "redemption, for Edwards, was not a matter of achieving ideal apprehension generally but rather particularly with respect to a single new idea—holiness—which was perceivable thanks to a divine influx" (*CNE* 82).

A new idea of this sort requires, by the Lockean model, a new sense organ, a spiritual one beyond the five external ones, and so Hoopes, like Miller and others, speculates that Edwards meant that grace gives a saint "a new, exclusive sense" (*CNE* 85). The argument is based upon a passage from Miscellany 782 (and Hoopes quotes Miller's quotation here):

An awakened sinner looks anew at the world and, achieving an "ideal view of God's natural perfections," realizes that nature's creator must be a very great being. But this powerful feeling of the heart is not redemptive since it contains no new intellectual or speculative knowledge; the sinner has been told since childhood that God is great. The sinner's experience in awakening is an "ordinary influence of God's Spirit," that is, the communication of "a sensible knowledge of those things that the mind had a speculative knowledge of before." In redemption, on the other hand, "the extraordinary influence of the Spirit of God. . .imparts speculative knowledge to the soul." (*CNE* 82; see also "JESH" 136, 141, 139–40)

Unfortunately, within the ellipsis lie the words "in inspiration"—and these two words destroy the entire argument. For inspiration, as Edwards says in "A Divine and Supernatural Light"—the sermon that draws heavily upon the materials first worked up in Miscellany 782—is the basis of revelation, and the ordinary convert should not pretend to it:

This spiritual light is not the suggestion of any new truths or propositions not contained in the word of God. This suggesting of new truths or doctrines to the mind, independent of any antecedent revelation of those propositions, either in word or writing, is inspiration; such as the prophets and apostles had, and such as some enthusiasts pretend to. (Miscellany 782)

It may be, as Hoopes insists, that "utterly new knowledge requires a new sense. (*CNE* 83), but by the same token, seeing the same old knowledge in a new light does not require a new sense. Not a sense organ, anyway—it requires a "new light," a new perspective.

The new perspective, or new disposition, enables the individual to have new ideas about religion; a new idea does not alter his disposition. In one of the few places where Edwards uses the phrase, this emphasis is clear:

The godly man's idea of God consists very much of these spiritual ideas, that are complicated of those simple ones [of] which the natural man is destitute. But as soon as ever he comes to have the disposition of his mind changed, and to feel some of the operations of mind by which he gets those simple ideas, [so] that he sees the beauty of them, so he gets the sight of the excellency of holiness and of God. (*PJE* 246)

Rejecting Locke in favor of Richardson, Edwards concludes that the perspective, or disposition, makes the person, not his or her ideas.

On the question of what makes a person, of personal identity, Edwards broke with Locke very early.[5] In entry 11 of "The Mind" Edwards had sided with Locke ("Well might Mr. Locke say that identity of person consisted in identity of consciousness, for he might have said that identity of spirit, too, consisted in the same consciousness"); by entry 72, however, Edwards was claiming quite the opposite:

It was a mistake that it [identity] consists in sameness or identity of consciousness—
if by sameness of consciousness he meant having the same ideas hereafter that I have
now, with a notion or apprehension that I had them before, just in the same manner as
I now have the same ideas that I had in time past by memory. (*SPW* 342, 385–86)

For Edwards, one's present disposition toward ideas, not the ideas' continuity,
constitutes one's identity.

It is not enough to examine, as many scholars have, Edwards' subjective
metaphysics of being; his subjective metaphysics of time founds his notion of
personal identity, and upon this notion Edwards secured such traditional Puritan
dogmas as original sin, providence, and free grace. Very early on Edwards began
to conceive personal identity as a product of the individual spirit's being "in
place":

No doubt that all finite spirits, united to bodies or not [as the angels], are thus "in
place"—that is, that they perceive, or passively receive, ideas only of created things
that are in some particular place at a given time. At least a finite spirit cannot thus be
in all places at a time, equally. (*SPW* 339)

A spirit separated from God is defined by its spatial and temporal finitude, a
finitude rendering it dependent upon "sensation or some way of passively
receiving ideas equivalent to sensation" (*SPW* 390).

Unlike animals, however, human beings have the capacity of "voluntary
actions about their own thoughts" (*SPW* 374). This reflective capacity underlies
our ability to partially transcend finite limits by psychologically reordering
events. The succession of events determines their "number"—according to the
OED, "That aspect of things which is involved in considering them as separate
units of which one or more may be taken or distinguished"—their identity and
significance (how they count):

Number is a train of differences of ideas, put together in the mind's consideration, in
orderly succession and considered with respect to their relations one to another, as in
that orderly mental succession. This mental succession is the succession of time.
One may make which they will first, if it be but the first in consideration. The mind
begins where it will and sums through them successively one after another. It is a
collection of differences; for it is being another in some respect that is the very thing
that makes it capable of pertaining to multiplicity. . . . To be of such a particular
number is for an idea to have such a particular relation (and so considered by the mind)
to other differences put together with it, in orderly succession. (*SPW* 372)

The process of differentiation and ordering is temporality itself. It is subject to
the will. What the spirit wants to be first in order is what is first for that
spirit—it determines the very world in which it is situated.

The fact that "duration . . . is nothing but a mode of ideas" (*SPW* 372) is the
root of the Puritan dilemma—that awful position of knowing that doing good is

the mark of salvation and yet in no wise its cause—for it implies that individuals will the moral circumstances within which they judge their own actions. Interpretation produces the perceived circumstances. Thus Puritanism was a religion of piety, not morality. Morality is purely circumstantial—"there is no action [that] is either moral or immoral but considers things with their circumstances" (*PJE* 208)—and circumstances change: "Thus the action of killing a man is in no wise a moral evil abstracted from its circumstances." Similarly, "circumcision is nonetheless a duty of eternal reason because it is a duty at one time and not another, any more than brothers and sisters marrying together is not an immorality of eternal reason because it is a sin at one time and not another" (*PJE* 208). The point is not to do the right thing; the point is to do one's duty, to obey. Not what one does, but for whom one does it determines the state of the soul. "Moral virtue does not primarily and summarily consist on truth," says Edwards, but in "love" (*PJE* 209).

Accordingly, we consider what we ought to do in the future based upon how we perceive the present in relation to our past. Duration is but a "mode of ideas" founded ultimately upon a finite being's limited perceptions ordered "in place" from a historically situated standpoint.

Reason, furthermore, does not transcend this historicity: "Reasoning does not absolutely differ from perception any further than there is the act of the will about it" (*SPW* 373). Itself temporally linear, reasoning presupposes that every effect has its cause. This proposition is an "innate principle, in that sense that every soul is born with it—a necessary, fatal propensity so to conclude, on every occasion" (*SPW* 370).

Neither perceiving nor reasoning from a finite perspective can situate properly the individual toward spiritual reality. Just as beings' references to the totality of things ground their reality, so too spirit's reference to total circumstance, that is, to eternity, grounds its reality. Perception and reason, products of finite time and space, falter before those questions that must be referred to infinity, and, ultimately, all questions must be so referred. Even something as simple in our experience as the perception that "something now is" confounds reason:

> For if something now is, then either something was from all eternity or something began to be without any cause or reason of its existence. The last seems wholly inconsistent with natural sense and the other, viz., that something has been from eternity, implies that there has been a duration which is without any beginning, which is an infinite duration, which is perfectly inconceivable and is attended with difficulties that seem contrary to reason. (*PJE* 224)

These temporal paradoxes help explain how grace operates. Here his argument is that reason is insufficient and revelation necessary, but the paradoxes also suggest why those who have received revelation might not heed it: they are not in a position to. From the position of rational finitude, "past eternity is . . . an endless duration of successive parts, as successive hours, minutes, etc."; the other alternative, "an eternal duration without succession," is simply inconceivable, "incompatible with any faculty of understanding that we have" (*PJE* 224). The latter is God's.

To Edwards, humans' existence in a temporal modality different from God's goes far toward explaining many paradoxical theological doctrines, including foreordination:

Degrees of our everlasting state were not before our prayers and strivings, for these are as much present with God from all eternity as they are the moment they are present with us; they are present now as He decrees, or rather the same, and they did as really exist in eternity with respect to God as much at one time or another. (*PJE* 157)

Another paradox is that although "conversion is a work that is done at once, and not gradually" ("CEG" 562), regeneration is a lifelong process. Another, that although the converted "cannot sin" they continue to err and to backslide and beg forgiveness for the rest of their lives ("CEG" 563). All these paradoxes assume a conversion from the ordinary experience that "something now is" to the conviction that *only* "now" is.

Subordination to the divine will therefore entails a shift from the individual's personal moral perspective to the total, divine perspective, not only spatially but also temporally. Being finite, the individual does not see "as God," of course, yet clearly for Edwards the saint senses such a perspective's actuality and its rightness. But to sense or feel eternal presence, the "now," as he puts it, can produce opposing effects. To sense that one has no time can, on the one hand, produce extreme anxiety; on the other hand, to need no time can produce ecstasy. The effect depends upon the perspective. To an individual with needs and desires, sensing that the time in which such desires could be fulfilled is ending is horrifying. To one subordinated to duty, sensing that things are already as the One to whom one serves would have it is liberating—everything is as it should be. Again, the difference lies in one's attitude or disposition toward divine sovereignty.

2
The Little Awakening

Edwards' metaphysical investigations reinforced, rather than challenged, his traditional Calvinist beliefs: ultimately, things are as they should be, by God's providence; striving for worldly gain is sinful and striving for personal salvation is futile; the aim of human existence is devotion and the mark of salvation is obedience. In short, human beings depend absolutely upon God. For this New England minister, these and other points of dogma derived logically from the premise that there is one all-powerful, sovereign God. His sovereignty—the sense of it, the conviction of it—is everything. This is the theme uniting Edwards' life, his preaching, and his writing.

On the surface, Edwards' thought seems hardly different from any other conservative minister's. To his contemporaries, his orthodoxy, his focus upon orthodoxy's central doctrine, distinguished him from the beginning. When the Boston clergy invited him to give the Public Lecture on July 8, 1731, his sermon, "God Glorified in Man's Dependence," won him immediate recognition and his first publication. Its encyclopedic doctrine, "That there is an absolute and universal dependence of the redeemed on God for all their good," Edwards laid out clearly, plainly: man can do nothing to save himself, good works avail a man nothing but are a glory to God alone, faith is a gift and not to be achieved (GG 145). If a difference existed between Edwards and his contemporary orthodox brethren, it was that his mind simply could not tolerate inconsistency. He tested every idea and action by the doctrine of sovereignty. Every word he spoke from the pulpit was ultimately connected to it. Every pastoral initiative he took was motivated by it. So if we want to know why the great revivals in the Connecticut Valley spread, initially at least, from a spark ignited in

Northampton, we must explore why Edwards' parishioners would respond so emotionally to a doctrine that was, for him who preached it, as logical as it was affecting.

One reason they responded so strongly to Edwards' persistent theme of man's spiritual dependency upon God was that it symbolically legitimized the economic and social dependency already endured and anticipated by those converted during the revivals. Scholars have often noted that most were young, unmarried men and women, averaging ten years younger than those responding to the call during ordinary years. Unlike their parents and grandparents, these adolescents could not expect to live independently until well into their adulthood.

Because the population was exceeding the available tillable land, by 1705 Northampton had ceased offering land grants, so that within Edwards' congregation, as Patricia Tracy has noted, "although 94% of the eligible grandfathers had received land grants, and 48% of the eligible fathers did so, only 1.3% (3 men of 236) of the native-born Edwards converts were given land by the town" (T 100). This meant that most eldest sons could look forward only to living with and working for parents until death released the family land to them. Many other young men were forced to consider relocating further into the frontier or entering lines of work for which their parents could not have trained them. Daughters, of course, were always dependent, but these could look forward only to marrying dependent young men. Whatever their personal situation, Edwards' converts during the "little awakening" of 1734–35 were mostly young, disappointed with what future their parents could offer them, and already viewing each other as competitors.

The last could be said for the town as a whole. A few years before, the greatest challenges to the Northampton citizens' survival and prosperity were nature and the Indians. Now they competed with other Northampton citizens. Fear and distrust were turning inward. Edwards himself noted in 1751 that "there has for forty or fifty years been a sort of settled division of the people into two parties, somewhat like the Court and Country party in England" (letter to Gillespie, *GA* 562). Thus, in addition to family tensions and competitive tensions, there were class tensions as well. However, for Jonathan Edwards, a man who for all practical purposes had endured no period of adolescence and had always known who he was or at least what he was going to do, the "surprizing" conversions described in *A Faithful Narrative* were exactly what they seemed—a "work of God."

It must have seemed so, for Edwards offered his people nothing new—no new ideology, no new economic system, no new regime—nothing that great exhorters, from Luther to Cromwell to Lenin, usually offer their hearers. He apparently offered only what had always been available to them, and certainly no great new social, political, or theological ideal. But from a rhetorical perspective, he did offer something new: he dignified and, indeed, sanctified those feelings of helplessness, aimlessness, and uselessness already being experienced, though now loathingly, by the young. By repeatedly, week after week, hammering on the theme of dependency, by telling them, again and again, that they were *supposed* to feel helpless, Edwards provided a means to reenchant the disenchanted, to sublimate their rage, to raise the lower to the higher, to let them seem superior to their merely half-way elders. All this without, really, changing a thing, without their having to do anything or sacrifice anything. God the Father was substituted for their real fathers who had, in their eyes, failed them. Moreover, to a lesser degree, Edwards substituted himself for God.

To some extent, this was expected of him. Like most Puritan divines, Edwards shared Alexander Richardson's encyclopedic vision of social order, a circular order of mutual dependency. As Edwards describes it in *The Nature of True Virtue,* "There is a beauty of order in society. . . . As, when the different members of society have all their appointed office, place and station, according to their several capacities and talents, and everyone keeps his place and continues in his proper business" (*EW* 568). Within this order, there were three governing institutions—family, church, and state—each with its prerogatives and peculiar responsibilities.[1]

The power of these institutions' heads—father, minister, and magistrate—was, within their proper spheres, nearly absolute. The minister, in particular, commanded extreme deference with respect to spiritual affairs because he received his commission directly from Christ. As Edwards put it, "For this commission that he gives to his apostles [in Matthew 28] in the most essential part of it belongs to all ministers" (*HWR* 364). All congregationalists accepted, in theory at least, the minister's spiritual authority, but that authority's bounds had been questioned for some time. The Stoddardean practice of open communion, in particular, had been eroding pastoral control. The Great Awakening would erode it further. With so many ministers on the road, and with so much open, hostile controversy, and so much confusion about right doctrine, congregations would soon learn that they could choose what to believe. But in the early 1730s, no one, as yet, was doubting the minister's authority, least of all Jonathan Edwards.

Edwards, in fact, seems to have had an unusually inflated view of the minister's power. In an early notebook entry he wrote out his notion of ministerial power, asserting that "ministers are to teach men what Christ would have them to do, and to teach them who do those things and who doth not." Then he shifts to first-person discourse, claiming further that "if I in a right manner am chosen the teacher of a people, so far as they ought to hear what I teach them." Edwards' main point is that to the extent that the people believe that he speaks for Christ, he has legitimate power over them, even to the extreme that "if it were plain to all the world of Christians that I was under the infallible guidance of Christ . . . then I should have power in all the world" (*PJE* 200).

This passage, probably written shortly after Edwards' return from his first pastorate in New York City, has been read as being no more than a youthful fantasy (T 65), as a hint of a lust for power ("LT" 26), and as an index of Edwards' "apostolic tendencies" (*MTC* 33). It more likely argues against the Roman Catholic system than reveals his dreams of being the next "Congregational Pope." One thing is clear, however. The passage suggests that early in his career Edwards was prepared to accept whatever degree of spiritual authority might be offered to him. And as the record prior to and during the "remarkable" awakening of 1734–35 shows, that power began to be offered.

During 1733, Edwards had been preaching largely upon a Christian life's practical benefits. Apparently, the young people were listening, for, as Edwards recounts in *A Faithful Narrative*, when one autumn Sunday he chastened them for "mirth and company-keeping" on Sabbath evenings, they ceased. Actually, the sermon urged the fathers to exercise their control, "to govern their families and keep their children at home at these times," but apparently the young people, without waiting for parental instruction, obeyed Edwards directly (*GA* 147). Through no fault of his own, Edwards essentially bypassed parental governance and, for the first time, directly exercised spiritual authority over the young people who implicitly offered it to him.

Edwards did not let that authority go, but before openly exercising it, the Arminian controversy came to Northampton. Arminianism was the term loosely applied to the belief that one could, through good works, proper living, righteous attention to religious ritual, and so forth, earn one's way into heaven. This, of course, struck orthodoxy's very core, and Edwards—despite some influential men who felt that such controversial matters should not be addressed from the pulpit (see W 160)—struck back. During 1733–34, most notable sermons, including "A Divine and Supernatural Light" (August 1733), attack some aspect of Arminianism, and thus emphasize man's dependency. Most effective was a sermon series on "Justification by Faith Alone." All in the series took for their theme "that we are justified only by faith in Christ, and not by any manner of virtue or goodness of our own" ("JFA" 221).

In one of these sermons, "The Justice of God in the Damnation of Sinners," Edwards takes his explication of God's sovereignty to its extreme, proclaiming, "From what has been already said, it appears, that if men were guilty of sin but in one particular, that is sufficient ground of their eternal rejection and condemnation" ("JG" 670). He then in the application lists several particular sins, aimed no doubt specifically at young people, for the list begins with lust and goes on to describe vividly dishonor to parents, worldliness, pride, sensuality, childhood lying, and unearnest participation in communion. "Seeing you thus disregard so great a God," he asks, "is it a heinous thing for God to slight you, a little, wretched, despicable creature; a worm, a mere nothing, and less than nothing, a vile insect, that has risen up in contempt against the Majesty of heaven and earth?" ("JG" 673).

The time apparently was right for Edwards to add humiliation to the theme of dependency. It was also time to add urgency. In April 1734, a young man had died suddenly from pleurisy, a death that "much affected many young people" (*GA* 147). While the "Justification" series was being preached, a young woman, recently married, also fell ill, but she apparently converted before she "died very full of comfort, in a most moving manner warning and counseling others" (*GA* 148), on February 13, 1735.

The next week Edwards preached "Pressing into the Kingdom of God," a sermon stressing urgency, the shortness of time:

You that have a mind to obtain converting grace, and to go to heaven when you die, now is your season! Now, if you have any sort of prudence for your own salvation, and have not a mind to go to hell, improve this season! Now is the accepted time! Now is the day of salvation! ("PKG" 280)

Now must also have seemed to Edwards the time to exert his spiritual authority. In the same sermon he says:

God is now calling you in an extraordinary manner: and it is agreeable to the will and word of Christ, that I should now, in his name, call you, as one set over you, and sent to you to that end; so it is his will that you should hearken to what I say, as his voice. ("PKG" 281)

Yet Edwards had already begun to assert that authority, to substitute his own for parental control, as well as to offer his voice as the voice of God.

A few months before, he had "undermined the deference of his special constituents to their parents by gathering them into age-graded groups for prayer and study under his own supervision" (T 111). As Patricia Tracy has said, "Essentially, the evening frolics became legitimized as 'social religion'" (T 111). More important, Edwards allowed himself to become the agency through which the young could transfer their sense of dependency from their parents to God. When the conversions began in December 1734, and included a young woman "who had been one of the greatest company-keepers in the whole town," Edwards was harvesting a ground he had carefully prepared (*GA* 149).

Throughout the spring of 1735, the entire town was in a religious frenzy. Over three hundred people were converted as Edwards continued to mix humiliation with consolation, God's sovereignty with human dependency. Word spread beyond Northampton, and revivals took place in several surrounding villages. Yet as the enthusiasm reached its peak, as some could not find in themselves what everyone else seemed to be finding, nerves began to snap. In late March, Thomas Stebbins attempted suicide; in June, Edwards' own uncle, Joseph Hawley, slashed his throat and died. Other attempts followed. According to Edwards, the Devil was taking his revenge. Even some ordinarily normal people "had it urged upon 'em, 'Cut your own throat, now is good opportunity: *now, NOW!*'" (*GA* 206–7). Although the conversions continued through the summer and into fall, enthusiasm fell. By 1736, Northampton had begun to experience a "very lamentable decay of religious affections" (*GA* 544).

"A DIVINE AND SUPERNATURAL LIGHT"

Edwards delivered "A Divine and Supernatural Light" in August 1734, just prior to the revival's beginning. As Perry Miller reports, "according to legend" the sermon "so delighted [Edwards'] people that they persuaded him to publish it" (*JE* 44). It has continued to delight its scholarly audiences. Douglas J. Elwood says it is "Edwards' most significant sermon, by modern standards" (*PTJE* 131). Ola Winslow believes it is "one of the most notable sermons of [Edwards'] life and also one of the most individual" (W 159). Miller thinks "it is no exaggeration to say that the whole of Edwards' system is contained in miniature within some ten or twelve of the pages in this work" (*JE* 44).

As that last statement by Miller might suggest, the sermon may be rendered very complex once philosophical analysis is brought to bear upon it. One might, as Miller has, wonder how a congregation could have understood and appreciated it enough to encourage its publication. Yet its initial audience by this time had been hearing Edwards from the pulpit and receiving his personal instruction for several years. Moreover, Northampton people were extremely sophisticated in theological matters compared to today's churchgoers. In fact, after his ousting, Edwards would blame their pride in that knowledge—high even by eighteenth-century Puritan standards—as the source of their temerity to challenge his authority (see *GA* 563). Furthermore—and Edwards says this in the sermon itself—its main message is so extremely simple, that "babes are as capable of knowing these things as the wise and prudent."

That message is contained in the title: "A Divine and Supernatural Light, Immediately Imparted to the Soul by the Spirit of God, Shown to be Both a Scriptural and Rational Doctrine." Light, the conventional image for knowledge, is of two kinds. The supernatural kind—saving grace—is a knowledge that cannot be achieved through natural, that is, rational, means; and because it is supernatural, it is rational to believe that such knowledge should not be rational. At first, this appears to be a merely tautological, specious argument, as it would be if Edwards were referring to the same knowledge emanating from two different sources. As it turns out, however, supernatural knowledge is really about the significance of natural knowledge. Affective rather than cognitive, it is knowing in the biblical sense.

In this sermon, a counterargument to Arminianism and rationalism of all sorts, Edwards concedes to the rationalists that one may learn the difference between right and wrong naturally. That is, one may deduce from natural and historical facts the moral order of things—including the existence of God, of justice and retribution, of good and evil. Nevertheless, such knowledge does not save us, because to *know* good and evil does not ensure that we *want* good and not evil. To know the law, even to follow the law, does not make us love the law. To natural men, the good is a burden, and to be good is to fight always against one's natural inclinations. This is not salvation.

To be saved, one must desire the good for its own sake, but the good is established from the divine, not the finite human perspective. What is good for the individual within his or her limited world may be, in the largest sense of things, evil. To truly want the good, then, the individual must cease to see things from his or her limited position. For a finite being, this is impossible. Yet one may believe that one is a part of that Being who has that perspective once one has seen how a human might participate in the divine. Christ in the Gospels provides this example, but again, to know of this example is not to believe in it. To believe in it, one must sense what Edwards calls the excellency of it, the beauty of it. This sense comes from grace, and to have it is to be saved.

Sermon Structure

Edwards laid out this message within a format conventional in New England and hardly altered by him. Such sermons always were divided into three sections: the Text, the Doctrine, and the Application. These three sections, as Wilson H. Kimnach as said, "if well contrived, fit one another like rings in a pool of water" (K 279). The Text is usually a brief biblical passage, followed by a literal paraphrasing, sometimes with historical background, and always a careful teasing out of the apparently obvious thematic elements that will become the subject of analysis in the Doctrine. The Doctrine is the sermon's "formal heart" (K 278). It is divided, quite mechanically, into major propositions. These are usually numbered, and as each is taken up, it too is further subdivided into its "reasons." Finally, the Application or Improvement, as formally structured as the Doctrine, views more concretely the same material, "indicating," as Kimnach says, "the point of the Gospel's impingement upon life, and focusing the metaphysical doctrine upon a social, or even personal situation" (K 278). In short, "the center of attention in the sermon moves from *statement* in the Text to *concept* in the Doctrine, and finally to *experience* in the Application" (K 279).

It is worthwhile to reflect briefly upon this simple structure's implications. Note first of all that the Text is not merely epigrammatic or illustrative. It is the *sine qua non* of the sermon. As "A Divine and Supernatural Light" itself declares, the Word is the subject of the light of grace, and receiving it is the necessary precondition for salvation. The Word was not to be played with. Edwards, who was as capable of symbolical and allegorical interpretation as anyone, kept very strictly to literal readings. Today, to think of these sermons as interpretations of the texts is tempting. But neither Edwards nor any other Puritan minister ever made the slightest suggestion that these biblical passages might be ambiguous or subject to varying readings.

Similarly, to suppose that the Doctrine explicates or explains the Text is anachronistic. The Doctrine may lay out the Text's implications, but this is in passing. Primarily, the Doctrine argues for the Text's rightness, its reasonableness, its coherence with remaining scripture and other doctrine. Its effect may be explication or interpretation; still, the speaker's assumption never seems to be that the audience does not understand the text's meaning. No matter how complex the doctrinal analysis may be, Edwards' tenor is really that of a reminder to the believing and a rejoinder to the rest: You know this is what the Bible says, you know this is what it means, you know it cannot mean anything else. Overall, the Doctrine proclaims that the Text, as the minister assumes the congregation understands it, makes sense.

The Application, however, generally does undertake explicative work. But rather than explicate the text by the measure of experience, it explicates the hearer's experience by the measure of the text. Edwards has often been faulted for his lack of poetry, for his literalness and conventional figuration. Winslow, for example, says,

His sermon style was seldom heightened. At its best it was as unadorned as Bunyan's, although lacking Bunyan's distinction. His figures of speech were always strictly scriptural. When he needed briars and brambles, pastures and water brooks, a cloud the size of a man's hand, the high places of the forest, he took them from David and the Prophets and the Evangelists, as though he had never had a farm boyhood of his own, and had not every year of his life spent weeks in lonely horseback journeys through woods, breathtaking in their spring and autumn beauty. (W 246)

To expect Edwards to convert biblical theology into the images of everyday experience is to expect him to have meant for his message to make everyday experience meaningful. That expectation is romantic. Edwards, quite to the contrary, sees the Gospel's message as rendering meaningless our everyday, natural experience.

The sermon Applications, almost always aimed at two audiences, measure the listener's life against the standard of the Gospel. The unredeemed are shown to fall short. Their fears, their confusions, their inadequacies, are explained by their departures from biblical expectations. In contrast, the redeemed are usually reminded of their present difference from their past life and from their fellows who remain unsaved. The key principle in the Applications is differentiation, not the identification governing the use of such rhetorical figurations as metaphor and simile. Edwards does use such figures, albeit with little originality, in order to vivify the meaning of damnation. In sermons such as "The Justice of God in the Damnation of Sinners" and "Sinners in the Hands of an Angry God," the images of everyday life may intensify the horrible end he envisions for the unregenerate, but that is because apocalyptic horror is the natural extension of the everyday. Apocalyptic glory, however, is a different thing entirely from life as it is ordinarily known, and so the language of everyday experience cannot adequately express it.

The Text

The text for "A Divine and Supernatural Light," a sermon that does celebrate divine glory, comes from Matthew 16:17—"And Jesus answered and said unto him, Blessed art thou, Simon Barjona: for flesh and blood hath not revealed it unto thee, but my Father which is in heaven." After briefly placing the passage in its context, Edwards immediately focuses upon two key points. The first is the term "blessed." Because of what Peter knows, he is saved. The second is the clause "for flesh and blood hath not revealed it unto thee." Peter is saved because of the way he learned what he knows. The text Edwards then quickly translates into a philosophical statement he can analyze: "He [God] imparts this knowledge immediately, not making any use of any intermediate natural causes, as he does in other knowledge" ("L" 110). In turn this statement is transformed into the doctrine: "That there is such a thing as a Spiritual and Divine Light, immediately imparted to the soul by God, of a different nature from that obtained by natural means" ("L" 111)

Immediately evident to today's reader is just how much interpretive activity has already taken place, apparently without Edwards' being conscious of it. Most obvious is his reading of "blessed," a term often applied in the Gospels to objects other than human beings, and therefore one that cannot be assumed to designate a state of salvation. Similarly, Edwards reads "flesh and blood" very broadly, to include not only the other people from whom Peter might have learned, but also his own body and brain, his senses and rational faculties, so that Edwards can claim that Peter did not infer his answer from the evidence at hand. As a final example, consider the term "revealed," which Edwards translates into an indication of a special kind of knowledge, a kind that could not have been gotten any other way, as if the only knowledge the biblical God revealed could not be gotten naturally.

It is safe to say that if Edwards had been confronted with such objections it would not have bothered him one bit. Yes, he could say, "blessed" does not necessarily mean "saved," the sense of "flesh and blood" could be more restricted, and, yes, God does in the Bible reveal things that could have been learned by other means. But he would say that arguing about the passage's possible meanings is pointless. The real question is whether the doctrine gleaned from it is true or false. What his sermon argues is not his reading's probable correctness, but the doctrine's truth.

What Edwards means by "truth" in this instance is best understood by examining Miscellany 782, the long notebook entry from which Edwards drew most of this sermon's philosophical material. In the entry's final paragraph, Edwards says, "But this is the truth the mind firstly and more directly falls under the conviction of, viz., that the way of salvation that the Gospel reveals is a proper, suitable, and sufficient way, perfectly agreeable to reason and the nature of things, and that which tends to answer the ends proposed" (*PJE* 126).

An extreme form of skepticism undergirds this statement. Life is ultimately, utterly meaningless without absolute truth, justice, and beauty. Individuals may, within their finite limited experience, find temporary approximations to these, which may, for a time, satisfy them, but time and change will alter the conditions that made these illusions possible. Eventually each person is forced to stare into the abyss, to confront the fragility of the meanings and values for which he or she has lived, to recognize the insignificance of personal yearnings and hopes in the face of the eternal and death.

The Christian message, according to Edwards, is that the self who falls prey to this existential horror is not the true self, but an illusion. By accepting the Gospel's claim that the true self is a part of the infinite God with whom, through Christ, one may identify, thus escaping the finitude defining the natural self, the person may find not only satisfaction with the limited role he or she is destined to play, but also may look forward to participation in ultimate power.

The Gospel message, of course, is thoroughly irrational; that is, it is beyond "the power of human reason of itself to discover" (*PJE* 126). It is not, however, unrational: neither reason nor experience can disprove its possibility. Therefore, to accept the Gospel message is better, more rational, than to content oneself with the message of nature and man, which offers only meaninglessness and death.

Edwards does not set out to prove the existence of God and grace. It is unprovable. His more limited task is to demonstrate that the Gospel reveals "a proper, suitable, and sufficient" way to escape the horror of a meaningless existence. It is, really, a practical rather than a metaphysical argument.

The Doctrine

The Doctrine of "A Divine and Supernatural Light," then, sets out three tasks: first, to "show what this divine light is"; second, to explain "how it is given immediately by God, and not obtained by natural means"; and third, to "show the truth of the doctrine" ("L" 111). Of the three tasks, defining grace is the most crucial. Edwards offers a functional definition describing grace's effects upon the recipient. This form of definition affords the listener a standard by which to measure his or her own spiritual state. It is also true to its object, for grace turns out to be a divine action changing the individual's perception of his or her spiritual condition. Thus, while grace itself—the change in condition—is immediate, its effects upon the individual are gradual, as the perceiver gradually attunes to the new conditions.

Edwards defines grace first negatively, then positively. In the first part of the negative definition, he distinguishes saving (or "special" grace) from "common" grace (or "conscience") and "inspiration." Edwards' insistence that common grace is not saving grace must have tasted bitter to some in his audience. "Some sinners," admits Edwards, "may have a greater conviction of their guilt and misery than others," and some may have "more apprehension of truth than others" ("L" 111). They may apprehend right and wrong, justice and retribution. He further admits, explaining why some unbelievers might be good, civil men, that the Spirit is at work upon them, assisting "the faculties of the soul to do that more fully which they do by nature" ("L" 111). Nevertheless, although such persons may be good, moral agents, behaving rightly and legally, they remain unsaved. The reason, says Edwards, is that with such persons the Spirit is only "assisting natural principles, and not infusing any new principles" ("L" 111).

What Edwards means by "natural principles"—and here it is helpful to read between the lines, or at least the notebook entries behind the sermon—is, ultimately, the principle of self-interest. Such sinners may recognize that it is in their self-interest to curry "the favor of so great a being, His mercy, as it relates to our natural good or deliverance from natural evil, the glory of Heaven with respect to the natural good that is to be enjoyed there." They also may naturally fear "the dreadfulness of God's wrath and . . . the punishment of Hell" (*PJE* 123–24). Such responses, however, are motivated entirely by love of oneself. They result from perceiving God as a tyrant, as a power over and against the individual, as an agency exterior to, differing from, and conflicting with the individual. And, in fact, toward such unregenerate persons, God acts exactly as they expect: "He acts upon the mind of an unregenerate person as an extrinsic, occasional agent" ("L" 112). In short, God is to natural men as Nature, as an impersonal, material force, "for notwithstanding all his influences that they may be the subjects of, they are still sensual, having not the Spirit" ("L" 112).

God is nothing more than material force to the self produced by impersonal, material forces—the socioeconomic historical self, finite, the result of environment and temporal contingency. And who history produces, history will destroy. To the saint, God is entirely otherwise. It is not that the saint's body ceases to be conditioned materially, quite the contrary. But to the saint's mind God acts as "an indwelling vital principle" and not as an "extrinsic, occasional agent" ("L" 112). God's actions become "holy influences" and "peculiar communications of himself."[2] The change lies in the perceiver's different dispositions toward the same influences that had confronted him or her before. In Edwards' words, the saint acts upon principles now "restored that were utterly destroyed by the fall" ("L" 112). Rather than acting upon the principle of love to self—a self defined by its difference from other spiritual selves—the saint now acts upon the principle of love to God—consent to spiritual "being in general."

Emphasizing his main point that conversion entails a change in disposition toward what is already apprehended rather than a change in what one apprehends, Edwards confirms in the second, third, and fourth parts of his negative definition that grace does not directly affect the faculties. Confuting Antinomians and enthusiasts, he denies that grace necessarily induces visionary experiences, inspires new doctrines, or produces strong emotional responses. Grace does, as he will say in the positive definition, assist the faculties, so that conversion may enliven the imagination, strengthen the intellect, and affect the emotions, but these are secondary effects, and do not necessarily result from special grace.

Positively, saving grace is "a true sense of the divine excellency of the things revealed in the word of God" ("L" 113). This sense "in his heart" convinces the person of their truth. Of all the concepts Edwards employs in his theology, the "sense of the heart" has received the most scholarly attention, although arguably "excellency" is the more important of the two key concepts he employs here. Most scholars have agreed that to Edwards "conversion is a perception, a form of apprehension" (*JE* 139) and that "what constitutes perception . . . is not the import of the object, for the object is without significance, but the object as seen, the manner of the view, and the state of the mind that views" (*JE* 255). Some scholars have even described conversion as "a qualitatively different perspective and valuation of a Reality already accessible to the mind" (*PTJE* 132).

Most of these scholars, unfortunately, have followed Perry Miller's lead in attributing the concept of the "sense of the heart" to Edwards' reading of John Locke. However, as Terrence Erdt has shown convincingly, Edwards draws not only the concept and term, but also many of the metaphors and examples he uses (such as the taste of honey's sweetness as opposed to the knowledge of its sweetness) directly from traditional sources, such as John Calvin, William Ames, and John Wollebius. Ames, for example, in *The Marrow of Theology*, a standard textbook used at Yale, says that "Faith is the resting of the heart on God. . . . It is an act of choice, an act of the whole man—which is by no means a mere act of the intellect" (quoted in E 176).

Even the term "excellency" Edwards probably derived from traditional sources. As Erdt points out, Alexander Ross' translation of Wollebius' *The Abridgement of Christian Divinity*, a standard textbook at Harvard, employs the term "to describe the quality perceived through redemption" (E 176). Thus, it is difficult to accept Miller's suggestion that Edwards' audiences were not "judicious enough to understand what they admired," that his notion of conversion would have seemed "enigmatic," that his words were to them as "a foreign language" (*JE* 30–34).

In "A Divine and Supernatural Light," Edwards defines the "sense of the heart" as a form of "sensible" knowledge, and he differentiates it from "speculative" or "notional" knowledge ("L" 114). By a speculative knowledge of the good Edwards means a rational inference, based upon experiential evidence, that an action toward or by an entity will have positive or beneficial results upon the perceiver. From the responses of those tasting honey that honey is sweet, the speculative knower may conclude that honey would be sweet to anyone, assuming that the faculty of taste is the same in all. But it may not be. Honey, to some, may be sour. Only tasting honey oneself will yield the sensible knowledge that can sufficiently engage the will toward desiring honey.

Differing responses to the Gospel are similar. One may hear about spiritual things from the Gospel, even believe them to be true, but that is not the same as personally experiencing their excellency. Just as you may lead a barbarian to a beautiful work of art but cannot make him appreciate it (though you may convince him to buy it), you can lead a sinner to Christ, but you cannot make him love Christ.

The analogies Edwards offers might suggest that differing appreciations of the same perceived objects indicate differences in the perceivers' faculties. Edwards does not mean this. He means only that in order to know something sensibly, the taster or beholder must perceive presence in a relation to him or herself. The defining characteristic of speculative knowledge is the distance between perceiver and object. Sensible knowledge closes that distance. The sense of the heart is an intimate personal union between perceiver and perceived. Heart knowledge is therefore concerned knowledge. It is concerned with

those properties . . . that immediately relate to [the] end of all our knowledge, and [to] that in the objects of our knowledge on the account of which alone they are worthy to be known, viz. their relation to our wills and affections and interest—as good or evil, important or otherwise—and the respect they have to our happiness or misery. (*PJE* 120–21)

To sense God's excellent gloriousness in one's heart, then, is to recognize that "the object beloved is of supreme excellency, of a loveliness immensely above all, worthy to be chosen and pursued and cleaved to and delighted [in] far above all" (*PJE* 205). Such a shift—from the finite individual's sensing only limited goods and beauties, to the saint's sensing God's infinite excellencies—devalues both limited goods and the limited self which formerly valued them.

The distinction between speculative and sensible knowledge may be, as Edwards has said, "the most important of all" the distinctions he makes in his theology. Unfortunately, many scholars have concluded that because the sensible is the key form of knowledge involved in conversion, Edwards developed what Miller calls a "sensational rhetoric" in order to assail directly the emotions. Miller, however, never really says that Edwards attempted to utilize emotive language. Commenting on one of Edwards' sermons, Miller says, for example: "The achievement of this passage is the nakedness of the idea. There is no figure of speech . . . , nothing perjorative; it is as bare as experience itself, as it would be to the sense that suffers" (*JE* 161). Miller tries to explain Edwards' use of language through Lockean sensational psychology, but as Miller well knows, the Lockean view of language as pure convention makes any attempt to describe the unconventional, the other-worldly, impossible. Miller resorts to claiming that Edwards achieved his effects by "a stupendous assertion of will: he must *make* the words convey the idea of heaven, he must *force* them to give the idea of hell" (*JE* 160).

Edwards' conception of language, which for the most part is indeed Lockean, recognizes that the "great part of our thought and the discourse of our minds concerning [things] is without the actual ideas of those things of which we discourse and reason" (*PJE* 113). Thus, if one has not experienced the things the signs designate, one may read and understand speculatively without understanding sensibly, that is, without really sensing their import or relevance. To the extent that our understanding rests upon signs, and not ideas themselves, the world and its language are meaningless, signifying nothing.

Edwards' contribution to this theory lies in his recognition that the things of which we have ideas derive their ideality from a framework, structure, or context of ideas and signs. We do not simply sensibly know "chair" but chairs within a context of sitting, in conjunction with tables, in relation to meals and conversations, and so forth. Moreover, he recognizes that things may have value in one framework but not in another, and that frameworks may change, contract or expand, so that what may seem valuable and significant in one instance may seem trivial in the next.

To sense God's excellency, for Edwards, is, really, to sense totality, the infinite and final structure, or to sense that there is such a final structure. At the same time, it is to sense any incomplete structure's inadequacy. A minister's preaching may not be able to convey the sense of totality or excellency, except in the lamest way, to those who as yet have not experienced it. But he may convey, and intensify, his audience's prior sense of their present existential inadequacy. "I am not afraid to tell sinners," says Edwards, "that are most sensible of their misery, that their case is indeed miserable as they think it to be, and a thousand times moreso; for this is the truth" (quoted in *JE* 159).

Eventually, Edwards concluded that most sinners will not seek salvation unless they first sense what they are being saved from. He believed that a sinner's life was already miserable, that his or her ends and purposes were limited, that ultimately their values were meaningless. But sinners themselves must sense this. Thus, even before writing "A Divine and Supernatural Light" he would consider that "it may be needful to prepare the mind for a sense of spiritual excellency" by first bringing the sinner to a sense of sin (*PJE* 125).

For Edwards, misery or damnation was the perfectly logical outcome of leading a limited, narrow life. But he would not teach it only logically; nor would he resort to emotional outpourings or rhetorical pyrotechnics. During the revivals to come, Edwards' depictions would be so horrifying because they would remind his audiences of what they already faintly sensed—that their lives were meaningless and insignificant, and that they were helpless to change them alone. Edwards would merely intensify that sense. He would lead his flock to look into the abyss above which they were already dangling so that they might appreciate and desire the ground of total vision once it was offered them. For now, however, he taught only the vision's desirability.

Once the total vision is received, once the sinner has sensed divine excellency, the foundation is laid for faith, for "a conviction of the truth and reality" of the things in the Gospel. In this sermon, Edwards says that the sense of divine excellency leads to conviction in two ways: first, indirectly, by removing the heart's prejudice against the Gospel and by increasing our interest in and therefore our capacity for attending to spiritual things; second, directly, by "a kind of intuitive and immediate evidence," because the Gospel message appears so sublime that it could not possibly have been a merely human creation ("L" 115).

The Doctrine's second major proposition is that saving grace "is immediately given by God, and not obtained by natural means" ("L" 115). The thrust of this section is to show that, on the one hand, speculatively knowing divine things is in itself insufficient for salvation while, on the other hand, speculatively knowing of divine things is salvation's necessary precondition. Human reason is the "subject and not the cause" of divine light, and the Gospel is "the subject matter of this saving instruction" ("L" 116)

A few implications of this proposition are worth noting. One is that, because the Gospel is a necessary precondition, religion is to a certain extent social. Inspiration, rare as it may be, can come to heathens with no access to scripture, but the grace Edwards speaks of can come only to those who have been instructed. Moreover, because the Gospel is sufficient "to the ends proposed," inspiration is unnecessary to a religious society and therefore highly unlikely. Accordingly, preaching the Biblical Word is the minister's essential duty. But because the Word "is no proper cause" of grace, in a religious society the real danger to the soul is spiritual pride—believing that one is saved when one is not.

His doctrine laid down and explained, Edwards proceeds to the third major proposition, showing the "truth" that "this doctrine is both *scriptural* and *rational*" ("L" 116). Scriptural evidence may carry no philosophical and very little rhetorical freight for most audiences today. For Puritans, however, scripture superseded all other evidence. As always, Edwards draws conclusions from scriptural passages directly, with no interpretive mediation, from both the Old and New Testaments, with no hint that the words' meanings might be tied to a specific historical, rhetorical situation, as he recognized was the case with ordinary human language. He uses scripture to support the points he has already made, to show that "this knowledge . . . cannot be a mere speculative knowledge," that "it is as immediately from God," that it is "an arbitrary operation, and gift of God," and that from it arises "a true and saving belief of the truth of religion" ("L" 117). Edwards says that scripture "abounds" in passages supporting what he has taught, and he piles passage upon passage after saying he "shall mention but a few texts out of many" ("L" 116). Such abundant evidence must have been convincing to a people whose entire social, moral, and legal framework rested upon the Bible's sacredness.

The second part of the proposition, the claim that the doctrine is rational, was intended to be secondary. It does not offer positive proof of supernatural grace, only a demonstration that if there were supernatural grace, then it is "not unreasonable to suppose" that the points of doctrine Edwards expounded would be correct. In short, Edwards claims only that reason does not stand in belief's way. Reason can proceed only from the evidence handed over to it. Those who cannot believe lack evidence; those who believe do not lack reason. Accordingly, it is rational, that is to say, not unrational, to accept the proposition that divine things "are vastly different from things that are human" ("L" 119). "Upon what account should it seem unreasonable," he asks, "that there should be any immediate communication between God and the creature . . . if we own the being of a God?" ("L" 120).

Rhetorically, Edwards relies here upon the unthinkability of God's nonexistence. For him, thinking there is no God was impossible, since for him if God was anything he was everything. To think there is no God would be the same as having an idea of nothing, since if there is a truly sovereign God, all depends upon him. As he demonstrated satisfactorily to himself in his early essay "Of Being," "There is no such thing as absolute nothing." Even to inquire of its possibility is to "speak nonsense." There is nothing only in respect to something, so to think of absolute nothing "we must think of the same that the sleeping rocks dream of" (*SPW* 9).

We must remember that to Edwards the sovereignty of God was *the* overwhelming fact. For there to be God, he must be sovereign, absolutely. Without that sovereignty, there is only relativity, meaninglessness, nothingness—unthinkable. If there is a sovereign God, upon whom the very existence of everything immediately depends, then it is rational to suppose that he would act and speak in ways that reason, relying upon evidence gathered from a finite perspective, could not predict. Finite human beings could not possibly know what to do, what to value, what to want, unless this sovereign being who does know were to tell them. God has told them, in scripture. Believe this, says Edwards, or surrender your life to oblivion.

Application

Edwards concludes his sermon with "a very brief improvement." The first of his Application's three major points may seem quite paradoxical to the student of Edwards' theology: "a saving evidence of the truth of the gospel is such, as is attainable by persons of mean capacities and advantages, as well as those that are of the greatest parts and learning" ("L" 121). The complexity of Edwards' arguments about grace may divert us from what he argues, namely, that grace lets us see that God is worth relying upon. To accept grace is, in many respects, to revert to childlike dependency, to believe that you need not know and master the world because the world already has a master and he can tell you what you really need to know. That "babes are . . . capable of knowing these things" may be an understatement. They may be more capable of relinquishing their as yet undeveloped independent selves. As we have already seen, Edwards prior to and during the little awakening was directing his sermons toward the youth. Here he proclaims that inexperience and dependency are not obstacles to be overcome, but in fact ease the way to salvation.

His second major point is that the doctrine provides a guide by which individuals may examine themselves for signs of saving grace. Edwards' use of an if/then argument allows him to address two audiences, the redeemed and unredeemed, simultaneously: "If there be such a thing indeed, then doubtless it is a thing of great importance, whether we have thus been taught by the Spirit of God" ("L" 122).

He then, less timidly, moves to the third point: "All may hence be exhorted earnestly to seek this spiritual light," and proceeds to explain why it is worth seeking ("L" 122). One may wonder why Edwards exhorts "all" to seek the light when presumably he thought that at least some in the audience were saved. The answer is that although different in kind from natural light, or reason, there are varying degrees of supernatural light. Conversion is instantaneous, but sanctification is a slow process.

The reasons Edwards offers for seeking salvation are all positive ones: "it is the most excellent and divine wisdom that any creature is capable of"; it is "knowledge . . . that . . . is above all others sweet and joyful"; it "assimilates the nature to the divine nature"; it "has its fruit in a universal holiness of life" ("L" 122–23). At the same time, he speaks of the price to be paid—the personal self: "it effectually disposes the soul to give up itself entirely to Christ"; "it will effectually dispose to a universal obedience"; "it shows God's worthiness to be obeyed and served" ("L" 123)

In this pre-revival sermon, Edwards was still, perhaps from personal predilection, emphasizing God's positive side. As his notebooks testify, however, he was already considering that the negative might be more effective. Clearly, as he delivered this sermon, Edwards felt that he was describing an experience that he shared in common with most of his audience. Perhaps, even as late as August 1734, he was still building his ethos, showing that he indeed knew whereof he spoke, and that through him spoke "the voice of God." This would not be the last time that Edwards would preach on God's glory, on the positive side of religion, but it would be one of his last times to do so exclusively. The revival to come would convince him of the effectiveness of preaching the misery that results from not knowing God, and conflicts with his congregation would convince him that not so many of his listeners as he thought shared his vision. After the revival began, he would preach more to convert and less to share the joys of conversion. He would take on more spiritual authority, even to "teach them who are Christians and who are not."

3
The Great Awakening

NORTHAMPTON: 1737–1742

In *A Faithful Narrative*, Edwards laments that after the 1735–36 revival "there was a gradual decline of that general, engaged, lively spirit in religion, which had been before" (*GA* 207). He also notes a number of occurrences and issues that diverted the people's attention from religion to other affairs. One was the building of the new meetinghouse (*GA* 208).

In the fall of 1735, the old meetinghouse swollen with the recently converted, Northampton passed a formal vote to build a new church. It was not completed and the old house torn down until spring 1738. In the meantime, the gallery of the old house fell during a Sunday morning service in March 1737—an event that was, of course, taken by Edwards and his flock as a sign to repent their sins (W 169–70). Although the accident was the most dramatic event to take place during this process, the most important was the seating arrangement for the new pews.

As Patricia Tracy has analyzed this affair, there were several significant departures from custom. One was the minister's exclusion from the seating committee. Another was the revision of the criteria for ranking—from the former policy of considering age first, followed by wealth and usefulness, "to a new order considering wealth first, then age, then usefulness. The last departure from custom was the privilege accorded to the rich of sitting with their families, even to the extent that wealthier young sons would outrank elder saints" (T 125–28). The elevation of wealth and family above age and usefulness implied a secularization of values contrary to the traditional Puritan convictions that estate and family are merely temporal and that usefulness is the central criterion of the encyclopedic order (see Chapter 5).

Edwards could not have been pleased with the abrupt shift in his congregation's concerns from those spiritual ones exhibited during the revival, only a year before, to the secular ones displayed in arranging the pews. On the first Sunday of the new arrangement, December 25, 1737, Edwards used as his text John 14:2, "In my father's house are many mansions," and he admonished the elite:

You that are pleased with your seats in this house because you are seated high in a place that is looked upon hungrily by those that sit round about . . . consider that it is but a very little while before it will [be] all one to you whether you have sat high or low here" (quoted in T 129)

More evidence of secularization came in the March 1738 decision to erect a townhouse. Whereas civic business had before been conducted in the pulpit's shadow, now church and town activities were physically separate (T 130). The message to the minister that the encyclopedic ideal was eroding could not have been more clear.

During this period before the Great Awakening, however, Edwards seems to have been dwelling more on the glories of the recent past than on the clear signs of dissolution in the present. In May 1735 he wrote a letter to Benjamin Colman, pastor of the Brattle Street Church in Boston, describing the events of the awakening of 1735–36. After being published later as *A Faithful Narrative*, it became "a strong competitor for designation as 'Edwards' most widely read book'" (G 90).

The importance of *A Faithful Narrative*'s popularity to the coming awakening is that it would serve as a kind of handbook of revivalist response. In the narrative Edwards stresses above all else, as he always stressed, the new convert's sense of God's sovereignty. He describes "the joy that many of them speak of . . . which they find when they are lowest in the dust, emptied most of themselves, and as it were annihilating themselves before God," when they feel "they are nothing and God is all" (*GA* 183–84).

A second theme Edwards stresses is the preparatory model's inability to describe the revival's conversions. Here he describes the "endless variety in the particular manner and circumstances in which persons are wrought on," and he claims it shows "that God is further from confining himself to certain steps, and a particular method, in his work on souls, than it may be some do imagine" (*GA* 185). And the third theme, that it "was very wonderful to see after what manner persons' affections were sometimes moved and wrought upon" (*GA* 174), runs throughout the narrative, with Edwards reporting laughter, tears, "loud weeping," shouting, and "raptures" of "joy and delight."

Notwithstanding Edwards' insistence that calmness followed upon such experiences, and despite his assurances that "great care has been taken both in public and in private to teach persons the difference between what is spiritual and what is imaginary" (*GA* 189), even for someone fully aware of Edwards' theological stand on these matters it is difficult to read this document without sensing that he was condoning, indeed promoting, an enthusiastic frenzy, one that no rules could contain and no reason could explain. Given this, it is particularly unfortunate that Edwards chose two exceedingly sentimental cases as his primary examples—a pathetic, dying young woman, Abigail Hutchinson, and a four-year-old upstart girl, Phoebe Bartlett. The overall effect upon the readers of *A Faithful Narrative*—at least for those who did not carefully attend to the unemphasized caveats among all the sensation—must have been to conclude that even the ultra-orthodox Mr. Edwards taught that common sense is to religion as oil is to water.

Thus to no small degree Jonathan Edwards prepared the way and set the tone for the intense revival that spread throughout the Middle Colonies and New England during 1740–42, although this time he and his Northampton congregation were on the fringes, rather than at the epicenter, of the spiritual earthquake. As a preacher, Edwards certainly contributed to this general awakening, and it fell to him, as the revivalists' greatest intellect, to provide the movement's defense. By providing it, in the long run he would influence American religion more than any of his peers.

But the immediate instigator and central figure of the Great Awakening was George Whitefield, an English itinerant preacher, who in style, temperament, and intellect was as different from Edwards as he could have been and still fight in the same cause. Whereas Edwards delivered his sermons in a steady voice and with distinct enunciation, his hands on the lectern and his eyes straight ahead, the flamboyant Whitefield gestured vigorously, modulated his voice, shouted, wept—he was the envy of England's best actors. Whereas Edwards' sermons were structured, logically impeccable, and traditional, Whitefield's assaulted the emotions directly. He preached without notes, working his audience for effect. Whereas Edwards' messages were complex, difficult, learned arguments, Whitefield's were simplistic, sometimes incoherent, if not inane, and repetitive. Both men, however, could send listeners into hysterics.

Whitefield landed in New Jersey in September 1740. For over a month Whitefield stormed through New England and the Connecticut Valley, never stopping for more than a day or two. Upon his heels that winter followed Gilbert Tennant, the "leader of the Presbyterian revival in the Middle Colonies" (G 50), and then that summer came James Davenport, an extremely emotional enthusiast who exhibited almost no control. Nearly all America was by this time in religious turmoil.

Edwards, of course, did not sit to the side through all these events. He had written Whitefield that February, urging him to visit Northampton during his visit to the colonies. Whitefield reached Northampton on Friday, October 17, 1740, where he preached from Edwards' pulpit several times over the weekend, apparently quite successfully sparking a revival there. Edwards kept the revival going at home, but like so many ministers, he frequently went on the road himself, for by now it had become obvious to everyone that a strange voice was far more likely to stir an audience's fervor than one grown too familiar. On one of these trips, on July 8, 1741, at Enfield, Connecticut, he preached what has become his most famous sermon, "Sinners in the Hands of an Angry God."

Before leaving on another preaching journey during the spring of 1742, Edwards invited a young preacher, Samuel Buell, to replace him in his absence. Buell so whipped Edwards' people into excitation that even Edwards' wife went into ecstasies excessive enough that some parishioners feared for her life (W 204; T 137). That Edwards asked Buell to stay on for a few weeks after his return says a great deal about the elder minister's selfless character, though it may lead one to wonder about his practical judgment.

However, Edwards would judge religious experiences by theological principles he had already made perfectly clear. On September 10, 1741, shortly after the enthusiast James Davenport had left New Haven in turmoil, Edwards arrived to deliver the commencement address at Yale. The sermon, expanded and published shortly afterward as *The Distinguishing Marks of a Work of the Spirit of God*, distinguishes between nine "no signs"—observable behaviors that argue neither for nor against the validity of a spiritual experience—and five positive signs— observable alterations in attitude and action that confirm that a spiritual change has occurred. As Ola Winslow has observed, in the *Distinguishing Marks* Edwards "consistently maintained a middle position" (W 201), admitting to the revival's excesses yet insisting that the excess does not detract from the value of the whole.

In the sermon's Application, he strongly warns against "the unpardonable sin against the Holy Ghost" (*GA* 275) by the revival's detractors, not only those who condemn spiritual acts when convinced the acts are genuine, but also those ministers who refuse to assist in the work of the Spirit although they believe it to be genuine (*GA* 276). He goes on to warn that Christians are not to judge the inward spiritual states of others, only their visible actions—a distinction that later became of great importance in Edwards' struggle to retain his ministry.

Of importance to understanding Edwards' rhetoric in this period's sermons is the ninth negative sign: "'Tis no argument that a work is not from the Spirit of God, that it seems to be promoted by ministers insisting very much on the terrors of God's holy law, and that with a great deal of pathos and earnestness" (*GA* 246). Edwards argues that the dreadful reality of hell demands urgent, lively pleading. As an analogy, he asks if any man in his audience, seeing his child in a burning house, "would speak to it only in a cold and indifferent manner" (*GA* 247). Ministers, he goes on, who warn sinners of hell in a cold manner "contradict themselves; for actions . . . have a language to convey our minds, as well as words" (*GA* 248). Thus Edwards, in this extension of his contextual semiotic theory, insists that there be an agreeableness, consent, or correspondence between verbal and behavioral signs, much as in his discussions of beauty and excellency he insists that parts relate coherently to a whole:

And certainly such earnestness and affection in speaking is beautiful, as it becomes the nature of the subject. Not but there may be an indecent boisterousness in a preacher, that is something besides what naturally arises from the nature of his subject, and in which the matter and manner don't well agree together. (*GA* 248)

Propriety demands, in preaching, a symmetry between actions and words.

Piety demands a similar symmetry in the lives of confessed saints. As Edwards reports in a letter to Thomas Prince, dated December 12, 1743, Edwards composed a covenant that was owned by his congregation March 16, 1741. Generally, the covenant is a promise to act fairly and honestly as Christians to one another in all matters, public and private. Mention of this covenant comes in the letter immediately after Edwards' description of Buell's February visit and the trances, rantings, and other extravagant behavior it induced: "But when the people were raised to this height, Satan took the advantage, and his interposition in many instances soon became very apparent: and a great deal of caution and pains were found necessary to keep the people, many of them, from running wild" (*GA* 550). Although he does not say so in the letter, it was probably this chaos within his own village that started Edwards on the path toward exerting more ministerial control and insisting, after 1744, that converts should make a public verbal profession of faith.

He did not, however, here or elsewhere, condemn the enthusiasm he witnessed. In fact, shortly afterward, he used his wife's raptures under Buell's influence (without using her name) as his example of authentic religious experience in *Some Thoughts Concerning the Revival*, published in 1743. In this second major defense of the Awakening, he repeats and expands the arguments of the *Distinguishing Marks*. Particularly interesting are his remarks on preaching in the third part of this four-part treatise.

In this part of *Some Thoughts*, Edwards answers ten charges against revivalist ministers, including contentions that they address the affections rather than the understanding; preach terror to those already terrified, instead of comforting them; preach too frequently; induce bodily effects; allow too much singing; and encourage religious meetings for children. Of these, Edwards' rejoinder to the first is the most rhetorically significant. He admits that reasoned argument and structured discourse "have been of late, too much neglected by ministers" (*GA* 386), but he denies that the understanding should be addressed instead of the affections, because it is a mistake to assume that these faculties are distinct. "All affections do certainly arise from some apprehension in the understanding"; therefore, the question is whether the apprehension to which the affections respond is "agreeable to truth, or else be some mistake or delusion" (*GA* 386). Whether the apprehension is arrived at by means of "learned handling of the doctrinal points of religion, as depends on human discipline, or the strength of natural reason," or by means of a direct presentation of "divine and eternal things in a right view" is beside the point. The point is that "the real nature of things" be apprehended, and "not only the words that are spoken, but the manner of speaking, is one thing that has a great tendency to this" (*GA* 386).

Despite his acknowledging the shortcomings of revivalism, with the publication of the *Distinguishing Marks* and especially of *Some Thoughts,* Edwards found himself aligned with the "New Light" revivalists against the "Old Lights" in a theological conflict that only intensified as the Awakening itself diminished.   When the revival had first gathered momentum, ministers suspicious of the numerous sudden conversions had at first remained silent, but after witnessing the excesses preachers like James Davenport displayed, they began to publicize their doubts.   Some revivalists hotheadedly charged that ministers who questioned the conversions were themselves unconverted, that they were Arminians substituting works for grace, or Deists replacing spirit with reason. The ministers charged back that the revivalists were Antinomians who believed they had received immediate revelations from God.

The clerical community soon split into New Light and Old Light groups. The Old Lights, led by Charles Chauncey, held to the traditional preparatory model of conversion, asserting that grace first illumines the intellect to judge the good before the will moves the heart to accept it. New Light extremists tended to assert that "saving faith was the faith of assurance—a person's certain belief that Christ's righteousness is applied to him for his pardon" (B 182).

Clearly, Edwards differed significantly from both extremes, but in the tumult of the hour he became identified with the New Lights. He could not, of course, have predicted the eventual political consequences of this unsought affiliation. Even if he had, he probably would not have altered his stance. To him, the excessive effects of the revival were understandable and predictable, and he could not have denied the actions of the Spirit that he believed had caused them.

During the Great Awakening, Edwards was moved to justify the rhetorical methods of ministers whose styles differed significantly from his own. He could not deny their success, although he might lament their excess. Nevertheless, his arguments defending these exhorters were logical extensions of the philosophical conclusions he had arrived at long before, and they really apply more directly to his own preaching than to the bombast of the Whitefields, Tennants, and Davenports. There was a theological precision to the "apprehensions" raised by Edwards' sermons that simply cannot be found in the others. Audiences, of course, may not have been able to distinguish between the doctrinal exactitude of an Edwards and the sloppy thinking of a Whitefield, and Edwards himself may have "read in" the logic that would justify the emotional pyrotechnics of others, so long as they did not divert too far from the orthodox path. However this may be, the fact that both Edwards' quiet, eyes-straight-ahead style and Whitefield's flaming oratory produced identical, "affecting" responses must have been proof, to Edwards at least, not only that it was the power of God, rather than the oratorical power of men, that produced the revival, but also that his philosophical conception of the unity of the faculties was correct.

Concept Of Sin

During this period in his ministry, Edwards witnessed several episodes of what to him appeared as genuine mass spiritual awakenings, followed by obvious displays of the community's increasingly secular values. Some parishioners who apparently experienced intense religious conversions reverted quickly to their old habits; others who displayed more, or less, intense visible effects became solid, pious Christians. He noticed that sermons, both fiery and restrained, produced similar audience responses, and that individuals' responses to the call were completely unpredictable. Sometimes those previously callous and indifferent responded readily, while those most obviously desirous of light sometimes remained untouched.

Such uncertainties only confirmed Edwards' belief in human dependency, in the ineffectualness of human effort, in the unreliability of human knowledge, and in the absolute sovereignty of the Almighty. Evil is insidious, deceptive; human life and human knowledge are uncertain. In fact, sin, as Edwards understands it, can be defined as acting, thinking, or speaking as if one were certain when in fact one cannot be certain. Only one thing is certain—the truth is God's only, and it is revealed only in His Word.

Edwards adhered to the orthodox doctrine that all sin resulted from the original sin of Adam, the first man. Everyone is born into sin, and subsequent sins are repetitions, further instantiations, of this first one. Conversion leads the Christian away from sin; therefore, to understand conversion and the rhetorical practices intended to assist conversion, one must understand what sin is, and to understand sin, one must understand original sin.

Edwards did not fully articulate his view of sin until very late in his life, in *The Great Christian Doctrine of Original Sin Defended* (1758).[1] However, there is no reason to suspect that this treatise represents any alteration to his earlier conceptions. In a fairly early notebook entry, he writes:

The best philosophy that I have met with of original sin and all sinful inclinations, habits, and principles is that of Mr. Stoddard of this town of Northampton; this is that it is self-love, in conjunction with with absence of the image and love of God— that natural and necessary inclination that man has to his own benefit, together with the absence of original righteousness. (*PJE* 242–43)

This early conception of original sin, influenced by his grandfather, is the same one the later treatise expounds at length: sin is simply acting from self-love when one conceives of oneself as an individual distinct from and undetermined by God.

To Edwards, human beings are not distinct, self-determined beings. As in Richardson's encyclopedia, in Edwards' theology all beings are interdependent, part of a vast system of Being, the totality of which is God. Thoughts, affections, and actions are not intrinsically good or evil; rather, whether these are good or evil depends upon whether they are appropriate to the being's place within the system:

If any creature be of such a nature that it proves evil in its proper place, as in the situation which God has assigned it in the universe, it is of an evil nature. That part of the system is not good, which is not good in its place in the system; and those inherent qualities of that part of the system, which are not good, but corrupt, in the place are justly looked upon as evil inherent qualities. (*OS* 125)

Somehow or other, all human beings have gotten out of place. "We are," he wrote in a very early notebook entry, "the highest species with the lowest excellencies. We have the easiest and greatest delight in things that in themselves are least delightful" (*PJE* 241). How did this terrible state of affairs come about?

To answer this question, first, Edwards stresses, one must concede that God neither caused Adam's fall nor actively changed Adam's nature once he fell. Adam was responsible for both. God had implanted in Adam both "self-love" and certain "superior" principles "summarily comprehended in divine love; wherein consisted the spiritual image of God," but when Adam sinned "these superior principles left his heart" (*OS* 381, 382).

In the Edenic state, Adam was one with God. God, as the source of unity and identity, is the absolute unity of being and consciousness—of things being as they are thought—and God as infinite consciousness comprehends all possibility in the "moment," outside all time. Consequently, to be one with God is to be completely without want, content, without desire, and obedient. Adam, however, had finite comprehension. So when presented with a choice, simply by wanting to choose he set in motion what must be described as a chain of events, but which occurred simultaneously. Wanting to choose creates a difference between a conception of how things are and how things might be—a present and a future—that is, time. Being in time separated Adam from God, who is outside time. Separation from God, the loss of His image, creates a self defined by its difference from God, and that self, being finite, becomes subject to death and to sin. Human beings will choose because, being finite, they are ignorant of the consequences and can know of no reason not to choose, and they are inclined to choose because, by contrast with their prior condition, they are discontent.

Thus, by virtue of their being the same kind of creature as Adam, subsequent persons, having been born into Adam's identical metaphysical condition, will, like Adam, choose. They will choose evil over good because, like Adam, having lost the image of God, that is, their identity with God, they are left only with self-love, and whereas self-love impels toward the good when the self is one with and subordinate to God, after the Fall there is consciousness only of the personal, finite self. Any desire to save the personal self is merely further sin, a further differentiation of time, and an increased separation from God.

For Edwards, then, a finite soul, or consciousness, is nothing more than an image, a reproduction of God, that has lost sight of the original and sees itself as being original. Yet its originality, its self-sustaining power, is an illusion, just as one's own image in a mirror is an illusion. A mirror image, he notes, "that exists at this moment, is not at all derived from the image that existed the last preceding moment." Interpose something "between the object and the glass, the image immediately ceases" (*OS* 403). Similarly, if God removes himself from us, to us we are lost, but to him, nothing is lost. As individuals, it is only to the extent that we are in God's consciousness that we exist at all. As individuals, we are "depraved": we are not who we believe we are. Being depraved, we are inclined to think and act for, and from the perspective of, whom we believe we are.

Accordingly, when we act, it is not what we do, but for whom we do it that determines whether the act is virtuous or depraved. Wanting to be saved, we may do good in an attempt to earn salvation. But the self, the finite individual self, cannot be saved. It will die. The soul, however, if it returns to the infinite God and sees itself as part of Him, subordinate to Him, can be saved. Self-love is sin only if one loves a false self.

The rhetorical coherence of Edwards' so-called "sermons of terror," such as "Sinners in the Hands of an Angry God," relies upon this principle. What is the point, many have asked, of terrifying sinners with warnings of hell, if they can do nothing to save themselves? What is the point of convincing people that they deserve to be damned, when they can do nothing to prevent their damnation? The answer is simple: one always loves oneself, one always perceives from one's own point of view, so if one really does perceive the justice of one's damnation, it is not oneself one damns, but one's old, unregenerate self, for conversion has already occurred.

"SINNERS IN THE HANDS OF AN ANGRY GOD"

Edwards' opening biblical verse, "Their foot shall slide in due time" (Deut. 32:35), sets the tone of utter helplessness that works its way through "Sinners." It is a sermon filled with striking images of dangling, slipping, falling, sliding—of unanticipated accidents or unforeseeable catastrophes where one completely loses self-control: "he that walks in slippery places is every moment liable to fall, he cannot foresee one moment whether he will stand or fall the next; and when he does fall, he falls without warning" ("S" 125). In images such as these one's fate is determined by outside forces, beyond the reach of one's finite will. No matter how carefully one measures one's steps, slipping and tripping and falling are possible—anywhere, any time, no matter how clear and straight one's path through life may seem. This is the human condition.

In keeping with the belief that sin is confusion of the finite self with the true self through the illusion of self-determining independence, "Sinners" functions primarily to heighten awareness of how salvation completely depends on God's arbitrary will. If sinners are to be saved they must realize that their finite human values and finite human identities are thoroughly groundless—that as sinners they are damned and think that they are not. No matter what material comforts sinners may have in the present, no matter what temporal successes they have achieved, no matter what their visible civil status may be, salvation is not signified by their "natural" condition.

Sensationalism

Edwardsean studies commonly claim that John Locke's sensationalism at least partially guides Edwards' rhetorical practice. For example, Perry Miller in "The Rhetoric of Sensation" argues that Edwards crafted his sermons so that his imagery would encompass both rational and emotional senses, and he implies that Edwards' emotive appeals aim primarily to sensually impress, move the passions, and thereby convert his auditors. Miller sees this as an extension of certain aspects of Locke's orientation toward language (see "ROS" 167–83).

Indebted to seventeenth century Puritan authors whose repeated denouncements of the "Papist" doctrine of implicit faith suggest a developing empiricism, Edwards sought to fit the emerging "New Science" to his Protestant religious interests. Lockean empiricism legitimized experiential faith, as Locke himself would seem to attest in his *Essay Concerning Human Understanding*:

Men most commonly . . . pin their Faith [on] *the Opinion of others*; though there cannot be a more dangerous thing to rely on, nor more likely to mislead one; since there is much more Falshood and Errour amongst Men, than Truth and Knowledge. And if the Opinions and Perswasions of others, whom we know and think well of, be a ground of Assent, Men have Reason to be Heathens in Japan, Mahumetans in Turkey, Papists in Spain, Protestants in England, and Lutherans in Sueden. (*HU* 657)

Along with their willingness to "pin their Faith [on] . . . the Opinions and Perswasions of others," such persons are likely to demand that others obey their dictates, for they have no reasons to support them, other than some alleged authority. The result is an unappealing political situation; in Locke's words, "the assuming an Authority of Dictating to others, and a forwardness to prescribe their Opinions, is a constant concomitant of this bias and corruption of our

Judgments" (*HU* 698). Like Edwards, Locke recognizes that one's "bias" or sensibility will affect one's judgment.

From what Locke says in the *Essay* about "enthusiasm," he seems opposed to Edwards' elevating the affections over the understanding in matters of faith. However, this is not necessarily the case. When Locke condemns "revelation" in connection with enthusiasm, he means direct, scripturally unmediated revelation—he is opposing the Antinomian heresy (*HU* 698). Edwards agrees with Locke that "Reason and the Scripture" may provide "unerring Rules to know whether it [revelation] be from GOD or no" (*HU* 705), although Edwards further requires in religious matters that assent, an operation of the will, be directed by holy affections.

Both Locke and Edwards accept religious experience that can be linked to biblical proof texts, and both reject direct revelation, unwarranted by Scripture. Accordingly, Locke's linkage of faith to revelation, as a "communication" from God (*HU* 689), could well serve Edwards' tenets of experiential faith. In short, Edwards fit Locke's empirical philosophy to a stream of Protestant thought that had been developing progressively since the Reformation.[2]

While fairly accurate, the view of Edwards' rhetoric as Lockean is incomplete. It assumes Edwards addressed his sermons solely to sinners and that conversion and persuasion are the same, but Edwards knew his sermons would affect sinners and saints differently. In Edwards' view, sensually impressive words alone will not arouse holy affections, yet the capacity for experiencing holy affections distinguishes the saved from the damned. Since pathetic appeals may arouse sinners' natural emotions through intense natural imagery, they have their place in sermons. However, a saint would experience the same imagery quite differently. No longer finding their identity in the natural order, saintly auditors would hear Edwards' so-called brimstone sermons as tokens of God's divine justice and love.

Edwards' rhetorical practice assumes that experience grounds faith. In "Sinners," rhetorical devices of suspense and vivid concrete imagery aptly convey the fate of unassured "natural men":

Natural men are held in the hand of God over the pit of hell; they have deserved the fiery pit, and are already sentenced to it . . . hell is waiting for them, hell is gaping for them, the flames gather and flash about them, and would fain lay hold on them, and swallow them up; . . . all that preserves them every moment is the arbitrary will, and uncovenanted, unobliged forbearance, of an incensed God. ("S" 129–30)

Despite Edwards' reputation for brimstone preaching of this sort, God's angry justice does not find its way into all of his sermons. For example, in his sermon "Heaven Is a World of Love," Edwards poses images of tranquil loveliness:

Heaven is a part of creation which God has built for this end, to be the place of his glorious presence. And it is his abode forever. Here he will dwell and gloriously manifest himself to eternity. And this renders heaven a world of love; for god is the fountain of love, as the sun is the fountain of light. . . . And therefore seeing he is an infinite Being, it follows that he is an infinite fountain of love. . . . It follows that he is a full and overflowing and inexhaustible fountain of love. ("H" 369–73)

There is a sharp contrast between heaven and hell, a place for saints and a place for sinners. Their difference illuminates the unbridgeable gulf between salvation and damnation.

Although "Sinners" pursues the theme of divine ire and retribution, and "World of Love" follows the theme of divine love and reward, they share a common characteristic: their vivid striking imagery. However, it is Edwards' images of fear and suffering that compel attention and arouse the strongest emotions. His images of heaven are thin in comparison. The "infinite fountain of love" does not have the rhetorical power of hell's gathering flashing flames. This is so for one important reason: "natural men" easily identify with images of bodily sensation, and these images are truly hellish as far as damnation entails an eternity of bodily torture.

The finite body is the site of pain, and pleasure too—but sources of earthly pleasure, when overstimulated, may turn to sources of pain. That is, a pleasurable sensation maintains its positive charge for a short period of time. It is hard to imagine a natural analogue for infinite joy. Not so with pain—in this lifetime it can be chronic, just as it is in hell. Since hell is a world of retribution and corporal punishment, hell is rhetorically and sensually "speakable." It is the analogue of the natural world—its only difference is the total absence of pleasure. While one's natural life may be lived in dialectical tension between pleasure and pain, in death the tension ends.

For Edwards, the tension is eternally resolved in either of two extremes: torment or pleasure. However, the pleasures of heaven are vastly different from the pleasures of earth, hence they may not be portrayed as effectively in sensual imagery. But clearly, the torments of hell are well within a framework of earthly description, because one may have a natural "taste" of hell right here on earth. Natural people (who are believers) know what hell is and certainly want to avoid it. No sane person willfully seeks torture. However, as "Sinners" so effectively shows, the earthly desire to avoid eternal torture is no ground for actually doing so—it is all in God's hands. If this is the case, how does the occasion of hearing a sermon such as "Sinners" possibly result in a positive "saving" experience? One must assume that Edwards was trying to do *some* good as he spoke at Enfield.

Even though "Sinners" ends on a seemingly positive note, apparently holding out hope, the motive to turn to Christ flows directly from the preceding horrific images. The last lines of "Sinners" read:

Therefore, let every one that is out of Christ, now awake and fly from the wrath to come. The wrath of Almighty God is now hanging over a great part of this congregation: Let every one fly out of Sodom: "Haste and escape for your lives, look not behind you, escape to the mountain, lest you be consumed." ("S" 137)

As Robert Lee Stuart has pointed out, the "exhortation to flee to the *mountain* is in direct and intentional contrast to the previous images of sinful man's falling *down* to damnation" ("JEE" 58). The congregation is called to a sure-footed return to Christ, up the mountain trail. However, there is no vivid portrait offered of the view from the mountaintop. The inducement to climb the mountain is wholly negative. There is a drastic difference between fleeing up the mountain and climbing up it out of regard for the vista from the summit. The motive to "fly out of Sodom" is not hope, as Stuart's reading of "Sinners" wants to make it.

If it is true, as eyewitnesses state, that there were both "moaning and great distress" and "cheerfulness and pleasantness of . . . countenances" (quoted in "JEE" 46) among the listeners at Enfield, what accounts for the difference, given all persons in attendance heard the same sermon and were plied with the same fearsome imagery? There must have been something outside of Edwards' sensual imagery that determined auditors' responses that day. Somewhere between the auditor and the sermon is an affective locus that is compelling to the will, outside the will's control, but conducive to totally opposed experiences of the same discourse—joy and terror. The "determining" compulsion is not a matter of choice, and sensing this, one may come to appreciate more deeply God's sovereign will.

Auditor's Response

Edwards explains why liveliness tends to move the will in *Freedom of the Will*:

The agreeableness of the proposed object of choice will be in a degree some way compounded of the degree of good supposed by the judgment, the degree of apparent probability or certainty of that good, and the degree of the view of sense, or liveliness of the idea the mind has, of that good; because all together concur to constitute the degree in which the object appears at present agreeable; and accordingly volition will be determined. (*FW* 146)

However, Edwards goes on to write, a person's "state of mind" will influence how he or she perceives an object's "agreeableness" or disagreeableness (*FW* 146). He attributes the various mental states and the conflicting judgments they may yield to "the particular temper which the mind has by nature, or that has been implanted and established by education, example, custom, or some other means; or the frame or state that the mind is in" (*FW* 146–47). Accordingly, upon hearing a sermon that vividly presents an object of choice, the auditor's mental state will determine his or her experience of its imagery.

Further, Edwards' distinction between "natural goods" and "spiritual goods" continually stresses the affections' importance. In *A Treatise Concerning Religious Affections*, as he distinguishes between "natural goods" and "spiritual goods," Edwards contrasts "worldly joys" (and carnal delights) with "holy affections." "True religion" consists of the holy affections. Unlike natural affections, holy affections are "of a vastly more pure, sublime, and heavenly nature, being something supernatural, and truly divine, and so ineffably excellent; the sublimity and exquisite sweetness of which there are no words to set forth" (*RA* 95).

While Lockean sensationalism may have affected the way Edwards crafted his sermon imagery, his sermons can more accurately be read as enthymematic descriptions or depictions of actual holy experiences—personal encounters with God. Auditors must have prior experiences that give divine words their holy beauty and complete their meanings. The sermons celebrate God's glory, for His glory, but their images wait upon sanctified auditors to complete the celebration—to be affected with "cheerfulness and pleasantness."

Saintly auditors fill Edwards' words with their own spiritual experiences; speaker and auditor join in imagining what is "ineffable" or "beyond words." That is, Edwards' words do not do something *to* his saintly auditors in a vehement onrush of pathos; rather, the saints do something *with* them.

Edwards' sermons have a twofold appeal, depending on his auditors' "frame of mind." Saints may hear his sermons as psalmlike celebrations of God's glory— the rolling thunder and leaping fire may, in Edwards' words, "rejoice" one. In contrast, so-called natural persons may hear only pathos-charged sensationalism as they await an effect directly from the speech. For example, the damned will identify with the sinner held over hell's flame by God's hand. They may shriek with terror. On the other hand, saintly auditors will identify with the hand of God. They may shriek with joy. Grounded in assurance, saints are able to discern the awesome beauty of God's justice—they have been to the mountaintop. Thus, the sermon affects two kinds of listeners very differently. Similarly, Edwards' images of tranquil loveliness may make unregenerate auditors feel alienated, rejected by their own inability to appreciate the infinite depth and beauty of God's "unspeakable" benevolent love.

In *Religious Affections* Edwards makes explicit the twofold impact of his sermons:

God hath appointed a particular and lively application of his word, in the preaching of it, as a means fit to affect sinners, with the importance of the things of religion, and their own misery, and necessity of . . . a remedy provided; and to stir up the pure minds of the saints, quicken their remembrance, and setting them before them in their proper colors, though they know them, and have been fully instructed in them already. . . . And particularly to promote those two affections in them, which are spoken of in the text [2 Pet. 1:12, 13], love and joy. (*RA* 116)

This passage distinguishes between the two qualities and levels of experience that may be had upon hearing a sermon.

Evidence that Edwards intentionally aimed his sermons at twofold audiences may be found in his practice. For example, in the conclusion of "The Justice of God in the Damnation of Sinners," Edwards first addresses the "natural men" (four paragraphs from the end of the sermon), and finally, "the godly" in his audience (from the penultimate to the final paragraph):

I will finish what I have to say to natural men in the application of this doctrine, with a caution not to improve the doctrine to discouragement. For though it would be righteous in God for ever to cast you off, and destroy you, yet it would also be just in God to save you . . . I would conclude this discourse by putting the Godly in mind of the freeness and wonderfulness of the grace of God towards them . . . O! what a cause here for praise! . . . You have reason, the more abundantly, to open your mouth in God's praises . . . he alone hath made you to differ from others. ("JG" 679)

In short, the meaning of Edwards' sermons varies among auditors, depending on their varying spiritual conditions—on their taste for the holy spirit. Thus, the auditors' interpretive frameworks will affect their experiences of listening to sermons.[3]

"Sinners" should be read with sensitivity to Edwards' judgment of its multifold intention. In his sermonizing the distinction between natural and holy affections is set by the distinction between rhetorical techniques of arousing pathos and enthymematic processes of recollecting holy beauty.[4] An auditor's state of heart or inclination determines his or her particular sense of a given sermon's aim. For the so-called natural man, "Sinners" is a pathos-charged exhortation; for the so-called sanctified man, it is a celebration.

Auditor's Character

When reading "Sinners" one should be mindful of the variety of experiences that may attend it. To be sure, the sermon pointedly portrays mortals' helplessness to do anything on their own about their spiritual state. But in the context of Edwards' theology and understanding of religious affections, the sermon in itself is not terrifying. It may, in fact, joyfully celebrate God's sovereign glory. It all depends on one's self-concept and inclination to identify with either God's hand or the "poor sinner" it holds over hell's pit. Even if one feels held over hell, in the light of saving grace, dangling over the pit is not terrifying, the hand not angry. Rather, in faith viewing the abyss may be a wonderful, joyful experience. God's hand will never let go of His elect.

Nevertheless, somewhere beyond screaming terror and joyful tranquility is apathy. If "Sinners" fails to give one an emotional charge, if reading it bores, such disinterest marks the truly damned. For in the apathetic auditor's case, God has already let go his hand. So, the twinge of fear may not be hope, but it may be reason for hope, and perhaps during the Great Awakening this was Edwards' central message. If one cannot feel joy, fear may be the next best thing. It may signify conversion. The idea that one "may already be saved" can be thought only from a perspective acknowledging just damnation, for God's justice acknowledges only sinners and saints. One cannot be neither.

Thus "Sinners" appeals to a variety of perspectives. Its hermeneutic strategy resonates with Puritan linguistic values. Above all, Edwards emphasizes the role that the auditor's character plays in his or her response to a sermon message. This central insight helps explain the role of preaching in his rhetorical thought. Like many contemporaries he divided persuasion from conviction, but further, he divided conversion from both, although he still believed it was occasioned most often by hearing the Word. His imagery, like that of his Puritan forebears, is rational and sensually impressive. While its converting potential is enthymematic, the "missing premise" is in the unwilled inclination of a saint to experience the Word in a saving way—with an uncommon affection.

4
An Apostle in Exile

DISMISSAL FROM NORTHAMPTON

With the Great Awakening's end people wanted a return to normalcy. Although the Awakening had reaped a harvest of souls for the church, the people of Northampton and the surrounding communities were beginning to express reservations about the spiritual value of revivals—many who had been "saved" during the Great Awakening had returned to their former vices. To many prominent citizens, it seemed that revivals were not the best way to do God's work. There was a growing consensus that Whitefield's and Tennant's itinerant preaching, and especially Davenport's outrageous behavior, may have caused more problems than they solved.

The Great Awakening had left the Protestant churches sharply divided over issues centering on the conversion experience and the experiential grounds of saving faith. In this climate of conflict and discontent, during the mid 1740s Edwards' Northampton congregation began turning on him. A number of theories exist as to why this happened, but disputes centered on the parishioner's typical reluctance to pay the preacher's salary, and more important, on community and church discipline. It was bad enough that for the past fifty years the church had not required its members to profess their faith in Christ before admitting them to the Lord's Supper, but now the congregation's youths seemed unable to act civilly in public. Their collective moral failure became a community issue in the "bad book" episode, initiating the series of events that culminated in Edwards' dismissal from his church in 1750.

A book on midwifery was circulated among the young people of Northampton—boys and girls (see W 215-67). Given the subject, of course, vulgar talk accompanied its reading, and the young people seemed conspiring with Satan to play out their sexual impulses inappropriately. Following the usual policy of bringing alleged immoral behavior to the congregation's attention, Edwards publicly named the young persons he wanted to question concerning the episode.

Unfortunately, he named both the innocent witnesses he wished to question and the persons he intended to accuse and possibly punish for circulating the book. This infuriated some members of the congregation because the list mixed persons from the best and worst of families—it showed that when it came to adolescents' preoccupation with sex, lineage or community standing did not matter. Moreover, the list made it seem as if all parties were potentially guilty of the same immoral behavior.

The subsequent hearing developed into a challenge of Edwards' authority. He was accused (among other things) of overstepping his bounds and interfering in the members' private lives—as if this prerogative was something new for New England preachers. In New England, generations had understood that the pastor had not only a right, but an obligation to monitor his parishioners' lives. Now, Edwards won the battle, but he lost the war. Although the young people openly confessed to their "crimes" and sought forgiveness, their backsliding and admission of guilt did not lead to the usual round of revivals; communal guilt did not motivate collective promises to reform.

In Edwards' view, things were surely getting out of control. At this time he probably began to question more deeply than ever the liberal membership practices his grandfather Solomon Stoddard had instituted when he opened participation in the Lord's Supper to persons who had not professed their sanctity—in Stoddard's church the Lord's Supper became a mere "converting ordinance." Clearly, his Northampton church no longer very closely approximated the invisible church. It was failing to meet his Puritan forebears' hopes to have their Calvinist churches made up of visible saints—professing Christians.

While general circumstances probably affected Edwards' emergent sense that reform was needed, everything came to a head in 1748. Edwards decided to require new applicants to profess that they were converted. This was an old practice, and as Edwards proposed it, it was not a radical expectation. But in the context of the boiling controversies over ministerial power, prominent community members seized the opportunity to challenge Edwards' right to make such demands. They called for his dismissal. Battle lines were drawn, and to make a long story short, his church dismissed him in June 1750. Eventually, he ended up in the wilderness community of Stockbridge ministering to the Indians and a small population of white settlers.[1]

In his "Farewell Sermon" Edwards gives one a sense of what he believed led up to his dismissal. Clearly, he is referring to the "bad book" episode:

It has been exceedingly grievous to me, when I have heard of vice, vanity and disorder, among our youth. And so far as I know my heart, it was from hence that I formerly led this church to some measures, for the suppressing of vice among our young people, which gave so great offence, and by which I became so obnoxious. I have sought the good and not the hurt of your young people. I have desired their truest honour and happiness. ("FS" ccvi)

In this passage (and others) Edwards shifts responsibility for his downfall to his congregation, who no longer know what is good for them.

When a flock is mostly made up of goats, congregational church polity breaks down. Where there is no interest in establishing a church of visible saints, after two or three generations, a congregational pastor's authority is bound to erode. The encyclopedic relation between minister and people disintegrates, and attempts to reinstate the founding ethic of relative relations between pastor and flock may be misread as despotism. Or, put another way, Edwards' patriarchal gestures were obnoxious to a community of people who were not able to see the positive value of being related as a family to a forbearing father. Paul's somic metaphor of the "body of Christ" had lost its power to unify, and the Richardsonian doctrine of usefulness had given way to hierarchies of wealth and lineage—of outward spiritual pride, which may even manifest itself "under the disguise of extraordinary humility" ("TG" 155).

In Edwards' view, most of his congregation, and most of his peers, were damned, and they did not know it, or even suspect it—they had succumbed to the Arminian heresy of good works, forgetting the Richardsonian distinction between restraint and sanctification, common grace and special grace. They had become comfortable with their "natural" civil inclinations and misread them as tokens of salvation.

After his forced departure from Northampton, as Edwards sat in exile at the lonely crossroad settlement of Stockbridge, he maintained his sense of purpose and commitment to Calvinist ideals. With unremitting zeal he wrote out his thoughts in the idle hours his missionary duties afforded. So, when Edwards was called out of the wilderness to address the Synod of New York in September 1752, the opportunity must have compelled him to distill his thoughts in preparation for public speech before such an important body.

SYNOD OF NEW YORK: 1752

When Edwards stood before the Synod of New York and presented his sermon "True Grace Distinguished from the Experience of Devils," he carried forward a long tradition of claims concerning religious experience, especially those of his Puritan forebears, who privileged "experience" or "experimental faith" over abstract or "speculative" understanding. Although Locke's critique of language influenced how Edwards expressed himself, more significantly, what he expressed derived from long-standing controversies over the grounds of saving faith: the quality of experience entailed in reading or hearing holy themes.

In fact, Locke's commentary on pineapples, on the difference between biting into one and hearing reports from others who had tasted them, resonates with a traditional Puritan attitude toward language, or human testimony, and its incapacity to substitute for direct experience in questions of assurance or spiritual knowledge. In his *Essay Concerning Human Understanding* Locke had written:

Simple Ideas, as have been shewn, *are only* to be *got by* those *impressions* Objects themselves make on our Minds, by the proper Inlets appointed to each sort. If they are not received this way, all the *Words* in the World, *made use of to explain, or define any of their Names, will never be able to produce in us the Idea it stands for*. . . . He that thinks otherwise, let him try if any Words can give him the taste of a Pine-Apple, and make him have the true *Idea* of the Relish of that celebrated delicious Fruit. (*HU* 424)

For Puritans, the difference between historical faith and experiential faith is like the difference between tasting the pineapple and hearing a report from someone who had. Testimony alone cannot produce or arouse the quality of feeling attached to direct experience. Together, speculative, or abstract knowledge, *and* experience constitute the grounds of saving faith. Or, put another way, speculative knowledge may provide an intelligible linguistic medium for objectively or formally explicating spiritual doctrine, while spiritual experience legitimates or "proves" the truth of doctrine by its sudden arousal of affection, not simply for the Gospel, but for the person of Christ himself.

In order to appreciate what Edwards was getting at in "True Grace," aside from the intradenominational power struggles he stood to address, one must hear in it the deeply encultured relationship between taste and understanding as Edwards perceived it.

Taste

While the Puritans' concept of affection certainly echoes the belief-love complex extant in Plato's *Phaedrus*, its emphasis on "taste" gave substance to the image of word-as-manna, partially deflecting both Plato's privileging of sight as the primary affective channel and his debasing of taste in the *Gorgias*. The *Gorgias* compared rhetoric to cookery and characterized it as a knack of dressing or seasoning speech in such a way as to make whatever it dishes up appealing. The connection of cookery to rhetorical seasoning carried over into the Puritan tradition via the Ramist influence.

Omer Talon's *Rhetorica*, a key text in Puritan pedagogy, limited rhetoric to the canons of style and delivery, and Puritan exegetes (such as Richardson in "RN") explained the suasory function of rhetoric through clothing and gustatory imagery. Their conception of rhetoric as seasoning emphasized the way the canons of style and delivery appeal to the will, tending it toward embracing goodness, whether apparent or real. However, unlike Plato, and significantly for understanding Edwards, Ramist-Puritan poetics described rhetoric not so much as a technique for adding sweetness *to* truth, but as a technique for presenting the sweetness *of* truth.

In this vein, drawing on biblical proof texts, seventeenth century Puritans compared their experiences of saving grace to tasting or smelling sweetness. For example, Thomas Goodwin wrote: "God hath put into every creature a taste, and discerning of what shall nourish it . . . the understanding made spiritual is the palate of the soul" (*WKS* 4:305). In his *Of the Divine Original* (1659), John Owen wrote: "He [God] gives *aisthesin pneumatiken*, a spiritual sense, a Tast of the things themselves upon the mind" (*DO* 94). Drawing on Paul's epistle to the Romans (8:38), in his *Holy Ghost on the Bench* (1656), Richard Hollingsworth wrote: "He that sees the Sun knows it is bright and light; he that tastes honey, knows it is sweet" (*HG* 76). Finally, in his *Figures and Types*, Samuel Mather wrote: "And the Gospell of Christ hath not only a sweet sound, but a savory smell, and cordial refreshing virtue to refresh the heart. 2 *Cor.* 2. 15, 18. The Gospel produceth such fruites, as are sweet and savory: therefore the Church is compared to an *Orchard of Pomegranates*, Cant. 4. 13" (*FT* 633). Such gustatory and olfactory images tended to be directed toward explaining the indubitability and particular quality of personal, subjective religious experience, most usually conversion.

The references to taste in seventeenth-century Puritan literature echoed the protracted controversy over the articulation of spiritual experience then taking place within the Congregational churches of New England. Similarly, Edwards' emphasis upon grace as an alteration of taste conditioned his desire to reinstitute membership practices of the early colonial churches. Aside from the "bad book" episode, his dismissal from Northampton resulted finally from his attempt to revive pre-Stoddardean tenets that limited full church membership to the visibly elect—especially to those who would sincerely profess their conversion (see "FS" cxcix).

Rule of Rational Charity

In Congregational church polity, the members decide who is to be admitted, excluded, or excommunicated. The Puritans hoped the so-called "visible" church (the temporally gathered church of professing Christians) would come as close as possible to the "invisible" church (the actual body of the elect known only to God). In short, they wanted their churches to be constituted of saints—persons who had experienced an infusion of saving grace and were predestined for salvation. Although there were many controversies over requiring a conversion narrative, the seventeenth century winners of the controversies (whose victory was short-lived) articulated criteria for judging the sincerity of candidates' avowals of saving faith. These criteria shifted the judgment's locus from the narratives themselves to the church members' predispositions. Divines such as Thomas Hooker in his *Survey of the Summe of Church-Discipline* urged the members to apply what was termed "the rule of rational charity," which is "love directed by the rules of reason and religion" (*SSC-D* 24).[2]

The rule of rational charity requires that the congregation affect a loving attitude toward candidates when judging their professions of faith. Thus, the judges construct the narrative's credibility in reference to their own preferred character attribute. In this view the judge's character influences the judgment's outcome, not his perception of the candidate's character. To be sure, in judgments of sincerity the artifact itself must cover certain substantive territory in a coherent and meaningful way, but at the same time, the listener must be able unhesitatingly to impute a motive of sincerity to the speaker, although knowing fully that the candidate may be deluded, or worse, a lying hypocrite.

Given the emphasis on taste and affection, its biblical proof, and its doctrine of experiential faith, naturally the ability to judge conversion narratives charitably became associated with having a sensibility, affection, or "taste" for the kinds of experience avowed in the professions. In this association, having a "taste of" leads to having a "taste for" the kinds of things candidates avow. As Jonathan Mitchell wrote in his "Proposition" (1664): "None can be such *self-examining* and *discerning* Christians without some *experience* of the work of grace, (or without *grace in exercise*) so as to have an experimental savoury acquaintance, with the *essentials of effectual calling*" (quoted in *MCA* 1:84). Since the "experimental savoury acquaintance" or sensibility results from the listener's prior conversion experience, competent or proper judgment implies a spiritual quality of character. Since it is spiritual and rooted in saving faith, the conversion experience must infuse it. That is, saints have a quality of taste that the unsaved do not possess; taste and character are inextricably linked.

These complex interrelations of grace, taste, and the judgment of texts influenced Edwards' battles with his congregation over restoring the requirement of making a profession. Since his congregation was composed of persons who had been admitted without a required avowal of their conversion, he had no way of knowing whether the members were able to judge competently candidates' professions. In fact, Edwards may well have taken his congregation's uncharitable disregard of him as a token of their sinful condition, as his "Farewell Sermon" seems to suggest. That is, they had no "taste" for his conservative reforming tendencies, and hence, sent him on his way.

In his *Treatise Concerning Religious Affections* Edwards extends the concept of taste to cover instances of spiritual discernment, and to characterize the interpretive experience of the saintly exegete, whose grace-filled taste enables him or her to correctly interpret and fully appreciate scripture (and virtually everything else) differently from the unsaved (see *RA* 287). Just as there is natural taste, "so there is likewise a *divine taste*, given and maintained by the Spirit of God, in the hearts of the saints, whereby they are in like manner led and guided in discerning and distinguishing the true spiritual and holy beauty of actions" (*RA* 286). Taste is the sensibility which most informs spiritual experience. It gives the saint confidence and a heightened capacity for understanding spiritual matters (see *RA* 286).

By anchoring grace in taste, Edwards lifts spiritual judgment from the discursive sphere, making taste the will's primary arbiter. Or, put another way, one's taste is what one wills, and what one wills is determined by a character attribute that is itself unwilled. "Divine taste" results from grace, not ethical training or other apparently "edifying" educational pursuits (see *RA* 286).

To be sure, in order to read scripture one must be literate, but not much more secular education is required of the saint for proper practical action. A saint, in short, is a bearer of *phronesis*—a person of practical wisdom who is able to act appropriately in any circumstance. However, Edwards understands this construction of practical wisdom in the context of his Puritan religion. He translates the Grecian cultural ideal of *phronesis* into the Puritan ideal of grace— literally a propriety or poise circumscribed and informed by the decalogue. It motivates the saint to act dutifully for God's glory as an expression of love, rather than self-interest. The difference between the saint and the sinner is one of motive. This difference creates an unbridgeable gulf between the damned and the saved. They may like the same things, and believe the same things, but for entirely different reasons.

"TRUE GRACE DISTINGUISHED FROM THE EXPERIENCE OF DEVILS"

Edwards' subjective indicator of saving grace is "divine taste"; it finally distinguishes the saints' experience from the damned. Edwards articulated this standpoint most strikingly in "True Grace Distinguished from the Experience of Devils." He traveled down from exile in Stockbridge and preached the sermon before the Synod of New York at Newark, New Jersey, on September 28, 1752.

His text is drawn from James 2:19: "*'Thou believest that there is one God; thou dost well: the devils also believe, and tremble.'*" This sermon is especially noteworthy since it comes at a time in Edwards' career when (as an exile) it meant everything to him to show that his position on saving grace was not only doctrinally sound, but also, when put in sermon form, potentially converting.

As he explains the "experience" of devils and contrasts it to true grace, it becomes quite clear that his dismissal from Northampton still affects him. His traditional emphasis on taste operates to deflate the spiritual pride of persons who believe they are saved because they believe in God and Christ, and who may have had some deeply emotional spiritual experience. It shows quite strikingly that there is finally only one determining difference between Satan and saints—one that makes the difference between being damned and being saved.

Resting his main point on the concept of "experiential difference" keeps Edwards in the Puritan tradition of experimental faith. However, while "Sinners" exploits natural imagery to amplify and engage the terrifying experience of realizing one's utter helplessness, "True Grace" addresses an even more insidious side of the experience of being damned—one's assurance of being saved, when in fact the experiential grounds of one's faith may be identical to Satan's. As Edwards catalogued devilish attributes and "no signs" of salvation, he probably had his Northampton congregation in mind, who truly thought they were serving the Lord when they dismissed him from his pulpit. In fact, as "True Grace" unfolds, one becomes aware of how well founded Satan's experiential faith seems.

In "True Grace," in an unremitting either/or logic that leaves no room for doubt, Edwards rests everything concerning personal assurance on the "divine taste," distinguishing it sharply from cognitive (speculative) knowledge. As his proof text declares, "*devils also believe, and tremble*"—devils may experience deep terror, not unlike those apparently converted during the Great Awakening. Furthermore, the sermon shows that devils and saints may be equal in their knowledge and veneration of God and Christ. Saints and devils both believe in God; in fact, Lucifer, the head of all devils, has better reasons than all living persons to believe in God and Christ.

As Edwards points out, Satan is an immortal witness to all that is holy:

Thus the devil has undoubtedly a great degree of speculative knowledge in divinity; having been as it were, educated in the best divinity school in the universe, *viz.* the heaven of heavens. He must needs have such an extensive and accurate knowledge concerning the nature and attributes of God, as we, worms of the dust, in our present state, are not capable of. And he must have a far more extensive knowledge of the works of God, as of the creation in particular; for he was a spectator of the creation of this visible world. ("TG" 144)

According to Edwards the primary difference between devils and saints rests on their capacities of taste. Devils: "will see what [Christ] is, and what he does; but his infinite beauty and amiableness, . . . they will not see. Therefore in a sight or sense of this fundamentally consists the difference between the saving grace of God's Spirit, and the experiences of devils and damned souls" ("TG" 154). As the title of the sermon suggests, everything rests on inner experience when it comes to discerning spiritual difference. Edwards' privileging of taste places the final emphasis of religious experience on subjective awareness.

As we have seen, the rule of rational charity for judging conversion narratives shifts the burden of proof to the visible saints, whose frames of mind were supposedly shaped by Christian interests. A similar interplay of taste and conversion informs Edwards' rhetorical thought. He uses taste as a vehicle to describe how sermons, biblical texts, and other divinely authored phenomena affect saints. "Divine taste" provides an interpretive framework enabling saints to experience the Word (and world) differently from the unsaved; and this difference means everything to the Puritan. Edwards' concept of divine taste sets an unbridgeable gulf between two kinds of persons—the saved and the damned. In Edwards' theology there is no in-between; one is either saved or damned.

This is the awful, absolute distinction Edwards' concept of divine taste offered his contemporaries, and increasingly, many of them damned him for it. Addressing such a message to his contemporaries at the Synod of New York, Edwards surely knew he would alienate some of his auditors. His reference to Satan's attendance at the "best divinity school in the universe" surely must have struck a hostile chord in the minds of some of his listeners, especially given Edwards' status as an exile and the continuous theological controversies during the period.

In Edwards' view it was far better that auditors be alienated and know it, than to live their lives under the delusion that they were saved. To be sure, this sermon, perhaps more than any of his works, operates by a principle of contrast. Auditors unable to identify with Edwards' characterization of the saint *must* identify themselves as damned. "True Grace" pointedly invites unsaved auditors (who may be believers) to identify themselves with Satan. If anything, then, one's disgust at being so much like Satan may be the first sign of a budding spiritual taste. Self-disgust is only possible from the perspective of being saved. It implies self-criticism from a point of view other than doctrinal knowledge or fear of damnation—a questioning of one's identity that may evidence a new inclination, projecting a psychic break from the past. In short, identifying with Satan may inspire a qualitative judgment about one's self from a new sense of being, evidencing a new inclination that is enabling, but itself is unwilled.

For Edwards, as well as for his Puritan forebears, it is the whole person who is saved. People are rational yet passionate beings, and grace is a "delightful conviction." Thus, "True Grace" may be taken as a vivid character sketch of Satan, providing Edwards' preacher-auditors with an easily identifiable image of their own experiences and the ways they may have mistakenly taken them as signs of salvation.

Final Word Is Love

Like "Sinners," "True Grace" may induce identification, but the incentive for identification comes from outside the text. It comes from the auditor's character, whether damned or saved. In "Sinners," Edwards provides an opportunity for the damned to identify with the person suspended over hell, angrily held aloft by God's arbitrary forbearance. In "True Grace," Edwards provides an opportunity for the damned to identify with Satan. In both cases, one's own "self"—one's inclination—compels identification.

Nowhere does the sermon give a reason to be disgusted with Satan's experience and knowledge; on the face of it, Satan is spiritual. Like the rest of Edwards' sermons, "True Grace" constructs a grand enthymeme, a bridge that only one's inclination to love Christ can cross over. The missing premise is not speakable. There may be words for it, such as grace, divine love, or spiritual taste, but the words are neither the sense itself, nor do they make or implant the sense in a listener or reader. That is, the word cannot implant the inclination to love, because the inclination supplies the word's sense. Self-love would prevent sinners from seeing themselves in Satan's image; only grace could cause the soul's separation from one's prideful self-image, allowing it to revolt and turn disgusted from its former self. Grace is just a word until the heart registers sickening self-disgust. Thus, Edwards' sermonic message provides a medium for salvation but not a motive to experience its meaning in a saving way.

That motive, conversion, must come from God. It is a gift of the spirit. Edwards is sensitive in "True Grace" to the way conversion functions as a mimetic return to oneness with God, a recognition of one's true self-image as God's spirit lifts the veil of pride and self-interest. Edwards says in "True Grace," as well as in other sermons, that the "*sense of divine beauty* is the first thing in actual change made in the soul in true conversion, and is the foundation of every thing else belonging to that change" ("TG" 155). In contrast to this vision of true conversion, further on Edwards offers what amounts to a critique of the Great Awakening:

When false religion, consisting in the counterfeits of the operations of the Spirit of God, and on high pretences and great appearances of inward experimental religion, prevails among a people—though for the present it may surprise many, and may be the occasion of alarming and awakening some sinners—[it] tends greatly to wound and weaken the cause of vital religion, and to strengthen the interest of Satan, desperately to harden the hearts of sinners . . . more than open vice and profaneness, or professed atheism, or public persecution, and perhaps more than anything else whatsoever. ("TG" 156)

These lines read as a repudiation of the Great Awakening. More pointedly, however, they may refer to the "hard hearted" people at Northampton who sent Edwards off to the wilderness of Stockbridge.

As Edwards' "Farewell Sermon" attests, they were mistaken in their judgment of him because of their uncharitable inclinations. On Judgment Day

then it will appear, whether my people have done their duty to their pastor, with respect to this matter; whether they have shown a right temper and spirit on this occasion; whether they have done me justice in hearing, attending to, and considering, what I had to say . . . and whether . . . righteousness and charity and christian decorum have been maintained; or, if otherwise, to how great a degree these things have been violated. ("FS" cciv)

Thinking that their judgment was impeccable, his congregation dismissed him. As much as anything, then, "True Grace" offers a pointed warning to persons who judge uncharitably—who may think they are doing the work of God, but through their failure to affect christian decorum are actually doing Satan's work. Everything comes down to a question of self-identity and a recognition of one's true commitment to loving relationships with people and God, through one's love of Christ.

If Edwards had lived until the decade's end, perhaps he could have heralded a post-awakening fervor founded in a principle of love. It seems he discovered toward his short life's end that the Great Awakening was an awakening from simplistic concepts of experiential faith to an astonishing realization of the complexities and pitfalls of Protestant religion, especially in its Puritan and Calvinist guises.

After his grievous dismissal from Northampton, and once settled into the tumult and intrigues of the wilderness community of Stockbridge, Edwards seems to have doubled his strenuous intellectual efforts, focusing them more sharply on the Pauline tradition of Puritan thought. An apostle in exile, he maintained that edification—building up the Christian community (the "body" of Christ)—is Gospel's aim. Perhaps his sojourn in Stockbridge, where as a missionary he worked the margins and the center—the so-called Indians and Whites—recalled his youthful commitment to the Richardsonian ideal of encyclopedic social order. In his last years, Edwards sought to mobilize Paul's somic image and reinfuse the Colonial *sensus communis* with the spirit of Christian love. He never backed down from his Calvinist commitment. He never altered the pattern of thought learned from his father Timothy. In the neoteric spirit of Richardsonian philosophy, he used whatever he could to keep the Puritan ideal alive, not simply in the heads, but in the hearts of his Colonial contemporaries.

Approximately six years after he delivered "True Grace" to the Synod of New York, he accepted a call to the College of New Jersey at Princeton. Before he could have any significant impact in the office of president, Jonathan Edwards died in 1758 of a smallpox vaccination.

5
The Richardsonian Heritage

Jonathan Edwards' most fundamental intellectual commitments flowed from the Ramist Alexander Richardson's encyclopedic philosophy of art—*the* Anglo-Puritan philosophy—contained in the preface to Richardson's *Logicians School-Master* (1629; 1657).[1] It is Puritan and Ramist, and it echoes in Edwards' private writings such as *The Mind* and *Miscellanies*, and in *Images or Shadows of Divine Things*. Initially, Edwards received the Richardsonian tradition from his father, Timothy. It exerted an influence when Edwards was a student at Yale through the *technologia* that Richardson's student William Ames developed.[2] Recurring continually in Edwards' writings, Richardson's basic themes and assumptions constitute a deeply embedded body of received opinion substantially guiding his thought.

UNDERPINNINGS IN CHRISTIAN PLATONISM

The Greek term *techne* is of primary importance in understanding the Platonic substructure of Richardsonian thought. The ancient Greeks defined *techne* as "craft" or "skill"—a systematic means of doing something. Plato, in the *Phaedrus* and *Statesman*, developed the meaning of *techne* that, in Lee W. Gibbs' words, would most affect "the classical philosophical understanding of art" (*TM* 18, 68). According to Gibbs, this conception of art includes the following components:

(a) a distinction between an end and a means to that end; (b) a distinction between a preconceived idea or thought and the activity of imposing that form or idea on some kind of matter; (c) an order where an end is conceived before the means in thought but

where the means are first in execution, so that the end is attained through them; and
(d) the hierarchical relation among the various arts or crafts, where one art uses what
another provides so that the matter or means of one art is the finished product of
another. (*TM* 18–19)

In contrast to the Aristotelian view of his contemporaries that *techne* is derived
from observing human action, Richardson characterized *techne* as the "frame" or
structure of reality or "being" (*ens a primo*). Richardson developed this neo-
Platonic conception of *techne* in an attempt to articulate the grounds of the
reformed Ramist curriculum.

Although Peter Ramus had rejected the schools' metaphysics when reforming
the arts curriculum, he had not formulated his own first philosophy, one that
would delineate the general nature of being and thus reorganize knowledge.
Richardson's major task was to fill this void in Ramus' plan of reform, first by
developing a philosophy of art from a consideration of being and then by
"grounding [his] rules of art upon it" (*LSM* 1).

Richardson begins his search for the grounds of art, as Samuel Thomson
claims in the foreword to the *School-Master*, by "div[ing] deep, even unto the
bottom of Entity," considering God as the first cause of being, and considering
being as artistically framed and, therefore, expressive of the Divine Artist's
techne. The relationship between God and creation is analogous to that between
artists and their artifacts. Similarly, God's calculated praxis (action) creates and
sustains particular beings. The world is a concrete body existing in accord with
God's idea and will. Since the supremely good agent's willful praxis deliberately
makes being, it has a quality of God's goodness about it.

The whole and completed end of being is twofold: (1) to glorify God by its
own proper performance, or eupraxie (existing in accord with God's will and
idea), and (2) to symbolize God's idea and will to people, as a way to God and a
guide to a person's own proper performance, for the glory of God.

The two-tiered concept of creator and artifact originated in Plato's *Timaeus*,
probably followed from Philo into the Augustinian tradition, and was clearly
explained by Origen:

It is the Platonic representation of a universe on two levels, of which the higher, that
of the divine, is the model of the lower, its symbol, where the world of the senses is
to be found. This, because it is a symbol, is not self-sufficient and has no existence
which is not a means to an end and derived: its end is to lead the soul to the divine,
and sin consists in stopping the movement of the intelligence to it, putting it in
place of the divine. Into this point of view, borrowed from Platonism, the
sacramental structure of the time of the Church fits harmoniously. (quoted in *SA* 13)

However, where for Origen the intelligence moves toward God's idea and will
through contemplating an artifact God's praxis has created, for Richardson
contemplation seeks to symbolize the soul's atunement to God's idea and will

through proper praxis—through applying contemplative knowledge to practical, productive, and stewardly human activities.

Since the principles (or arts) of derived being are God's ideas, through observing "things" one may know, communicate, and learn to act by attending to them:

So that we may see, that art is the Wisdom of God, but yet as it is *energetick* in the thing, so it is called *Ars*, So that mark this, that Art is the Law of God, whereunto he created things, whereby he governeth them, and whereunto they yield obedience. Mark this well, for the Schooles run into many absurdities, whilest they have thought Art is in a mans head, and not in the thing. (*LSM* 19)

Art is "*energetick* in the thing." It is the active quality of God's *techne* that affects human consciousness.

Puritan typology, a principle of reading usually reserved for a scriptural interpretation, presupposed *techne's* active quality. Puritans normally used typology to establish the Old and New Testaments' common divine authorship, thus legitimating the New Testament. The Old Testament (the "type") was read as a prophetic prefiguration of Christ's coming in the New Testament (the "antitype"). This hermeneutic strategy created an order of continuity between Old Testament and New so that the New Testament would appear to be "shadowed" in the Old, making them one complete text. For example, the story of Jonah's three days in the whale's belly was read as a type of Christ's burial (antitype).

Richardson adapts this hermeneutic strategy Platonically, viewing the ideas of art in God's mind as archetypes of the created world. Art in the created world he views as "entypes" of the archetypal ideas that "frame" art's existential acts. When persons experience and understand art, their "ideas of art" are called "ectypes." However, Richardson interchanges type-antitype terminology (from biblical hermeneutics) and archetype-entype-ectype terminology (from Platonic Idealism). For example, "Art is the wisdom of God, in *ente a primo*, and the frame of the creature is in the antitype of this wisdom, and is a subject of Art" (*LSM* 20). Thus, "reading" the created world as both the embodiment of God's idea of art and as an antitype of scriptural types is possible. John Flavel's *Husbandry Spiritualized or the Heavenly Use of Earthly Things* (London, 1669) is an example of a typological reading of natural order, as is Edwards' *Images or Shadows of Divine Things*.

According to Samuel Mather in *Figures and Types of the Old Testament*, "type" comes from the Greek *typos*, which means an "exemplar" (*FT* 76). However, his proof text suggests another possible Greek derivative. He refers to John 20: 25, where "doubting" Thomas, who missed Christ's first appearance to the other disciples, claimed he needed more than their testimony to convince him of Christ's resurrection: "The other disciples therefore said unto him, We have seen the Lord. But he said unto them, Except I shall see in his hands the print of the nails [*typon to on*], and put my finger into the print of the nails, and thrust my hand into his side, I will not believe."

In order to believe, Thomas had to see and touch Christ's wounds, the "print of the nails" remaining after the nails have been removed. "Print" here extends the concept of *typos* to encompass the Greek *typton*, which may mean (among other things) "to strike." The nail prints are "exemplars," but at the same time, as wounds, they are signs resulting from an impact. This extended etymology of "type" is consistent with Richardsonian epistemology, where one knows only God's ideas through their imprint. Analogies in common experience are the impress upon minted coins or the lingering reddish trace left on the flesh that suggests a slap (*typton*). Richardson characterizes the process of creation as that of being struck: "so that every creature must take a blow of God" (*LSM* 10).[3]

Thus, the world is a medium. Through it, God actively communicates divine artistic principles to human beings. Since knowledge results from a mediated "blow," it is not willfully constructed. It is *nomos*, but God, not human culture or tradition, inspires it. Accordingly, "we know that Logick [or *logismos*] carries from the thing to man, and speech from man to man, that which he sees with his Logick" (*LSM* 10). Metaphysically, the art of logic is the act of God's *logismos*. Through it humans may observe all the other arts in being. Logic is the "key" to all the arts and to derived being, and because it is the expression of *logismos*, it is reason's proper subject.

Although derived from Puritan typology, Richardson's concept of *logismos* closely parallels the Stoic belief that yielding to, or living in harmony with, the natural *logos* is the highest good. However, while the Stoics allowed that the *logos* is God's soul permeating being, therefore admitting a sort of pantheism, Richardson separates God from derived being by making it an expression of God's idea and will. Here the *logos* doctrine more consistently understands *logos* as "word"—as willfully created, rational, and intelligible, but mediated—existing apart from the being that expresses it. *Logos* in this version avoids pantheism, and it gives being a rational intelligible principle (*logismos*), a way to God's idea, not to God, but to the sum total of His commandment "let there be." Accordingly, since the *logos* is not God's soul permeating being, but God's expression of being, *logismos* can be applied to humanity's stewardly role—human alterations of being do not violate the divine presence.

Similarly, Richardson's *logos* doctrine diverges somewhat from the Platonists'. In Richardsonian thought, the *logismos* leads a person's soul to the divine, but only so far as God exhibits His wisdom to inform humanity's practical stewardly role. Richardson's way to God intends to reveal God's purpose for people, whose artistic actions constitute their humanity insofar as they are inclined to harmonize with God's will and idea. All knowledge is finally useful to humanity's stewardly role because knowing the principles of things ends in practically applying them, for the glory of God, and for the good of people.

Richardson's Christian Platonism provided a theological bridge from the seventeenth to the eighteenth century that eclectic Puritan thinkers such as Edwards smoothly traversed. Edwards was able to accommodate Newtonian physics and Lockean epistemology to the Richardsonian doctrines of emanation and the divine communication of *techne* by conceiving natural "forces" (resistance and gravity) as the media of God's creative actions. In Edwards' writings, Newtonian streams of "atoms" become continuous pulses of God's Idea; Lockean impressions communicate ideas because they are configured pressures. However, unlike the "scientific" thinkers he revised, Edwards thought such "pressures" or "resistances" were not objective configurations. Since they convey God's ideas, their reception relates people to God. Thus, an idea emanating from being is not purely speculative or contemplative because its felt quality implies the character of its divine source (see *LSM* 13).

Yet, while the world may constitute a text revealing God's idea, one's sense of its end is not in the text. Perceiving solely through natural order cannot grasp God's will; rather, His will must be read beyond the text of nature, by imputation, through faith and scripture. Put another way, the world's spiritual meaning is not in the world, but in the motive for its creation. Faith is a disposition toward imputing a divine motive to being. This imputation simultaneously makes the world the intelligible entype of art and the affective antitype of God's will. As Edwards writes in *Images or Shadows of Divine Things*: "It is very fit and becoming of God, who is infinitely wise, so to order things that there should be a voice of His in His works, instructing those that behold them and painting forth and shewing divine mysteries and things appertaining to Himself and his spiritual kingdom" (*IS* 61).

The "mysteries" apprehended through the divine *logos* or typological "voice" result from a pious awareness of one's special relationship to God. People experience the same world differently because they perceive its relational dimensions differently. Saints experience the world's content aware of its mediated relationship to God, so that the natural order has a divine voice. The unsaved experience only nature's nonmotivated causes or forces, so that for them the world is not the trace of some divine other's idea and will.

In Richardsonian philosophy, nature expresses holy literary significance because God authored it for a reason. Similarly, Edwards' references to one's sense, temper, inclination, or disposition in reading the world results partially from his viewing it as a divinely authored text. A long-standing tradition in Puritan thought regarded words' effects to be the consequence of listeners' prior inclinations. Words do not arouse affections in persons not predisposed to respond to them.

As we have seen in earlier chapters, for Edwards one's inclination or disposition is a function of one's identity—of one's perception of oneself as either an independent being or as an integral and subordinate part of a larger whole. The notion that one's stance derives from one's position within a system derives from Richardson's concept of encyclopedia.

Encyclopedia, as part of Richardson's abstract plan of art in general, supplements Ramus' conception of arts and their ordering (see *LSM* 343). Richardson derived his idea of encyclopedia partly from his etymology of the Greek *paiedia en kuklo,* which means to Richardson *"Circulus Artium* [the circle of art]" (*LSM* 14). For Richardson, encyclopedia is *"qua omnes artes comprehenduntur pro subordinatione finium* [that by which all arts are comprehended according to the subordination of their ends]" (*LSM* 14). In encyclopedic order, all artistic activity becomes a corporate enterprise because all artistic actors use what others produce, and produce what others use. Richardson's philosophy might be summarized as follows: *Art is God's idea of things' proper performance. When people methodically observe the encyclopedic order of art's true scientific precepts, these precepts' harmoniously mixed and subordinate uses guide and conjoin humans' activities in their mutual stewardly roles.* As Richardson says, "God is the beginning and end of things, and the Alpha and Omega of the Arts" (*LSM* 15).

Richardson's encyclopedic plan unifies all members of society who work purposefully as stewards, glorifying God by using His creation and acting like Him as artisans. As actors playing out their chosen callings in an encyclopedic circle of useful subordination, the individuals' harmony in artistic action symbolizes a proper performance of God's command for humanity. Thus, while derived beings passively obey, properly perform, and thus symbolize, God's true, just, and wise idea, the social order actively represents to God His peoples' understanding of His idea and their obedience to His will. People glorify God through their artful conduct, expressing their love and collective "turn" toward God, constituting a relationship not only among people, but between people and God.

Glorifying God must be a communal effort, because people are finite, and alone they cannot experience, observe, or know and do all things. A person may competently practice a specific calling and thereby master a part of God's idea, but playing one's role depends upon one's fellow stewards. The community produces a social order out of practical reciprocal activities. Usefulness is moral because it furthers the communal purpose of glorifying God. That which a relative artist cannot use properly because of defective workmanship or *malpraxis* breaks the harmonious circle of art and subverts the community's symbolic progress toward unity with God.

Each person is responsible to God as a steward and to the community as a useful part of the whole. Artists depend upon each other at the point of use. For example, the miller's ground wheat will be only as good as the wheat the farmers supply. Since relative arts pass around and use others' products, and since a rule of reason guides their praxis, the communal circle may rationally critique their products' usefulness respecting the accuracy of, or adherence to, logically derived principles and precepts.

While individuals choose a calling, they must contract together in groups or singly with those whose products they use, and they must fulfill their obligations to those who use their products. No steward can rightfully fulfill his or her stewardly role outside the circle of art. A baker, for example, must contract with a miller in order to fulfill his obligation to the user of his baked goods. While selecting a calling is voluntary, the type of artist one contracts with is not. That is, the baker needs the miller, and vice versa—no milled grain, no bread. Reciprocal necessity, then, makes or breaks the social contract at the point of use. No steward can properly perform his or her role and meet his or her obligation to God in isolation, outside the circle of art. To be properly performed, all human roles must exist through conjoinment with counterparts in some sort of relationship, ultimately rooted in, and guided by, God's idea and will. For example, one could not be a lender without a borrower, a husband without a wife, or a minister without a congregation.

Such an order's primary social ethic is that no community member is above rebuke because each is responsible to the persons who use his or her product. Artists choose their callings, but their choices are judged by their products' usefulness to those who need them to practice their own callings. Utility, then, becomes a focus of political power and moral restraint, providing relative users a voice in judging who has a legitimate right to practice and produce what in each area. The greater the product's useful scope, the greater the number of people who may call its producer to task. All callings are divinely mandated, but the right to claim a calling depends temporally upon the products' utility. Even a king's subjects may judge his right to rule by his utility toward producing a commonwealth according to laws and principles, for the use and good of its citizens.

Because it emphasizes glorifying God, the Richardsonian philosophy of art is theocentric. It preserves the schools' temper while metaphysically rejecting the principle of hierarchical social order implicit in their distinctions between *scientia*, *praxis*, and *poesis*. Richardson's philosophy allows any legitimate social role that glorifies God and shows concern for one's neighbor to be a source of human happiness.

This philosophy is consistent with Christ's gospel of piety and charity and with Paul's epistles. In 1 Corinthians (12: 4, 6–7), Paul's somic metaphors unprecedentedly characterize the general spiritual unity among diverse special callings within the "body" of the Christian community (*PRE* 36–38). Quoting Corinthians, John S. Coolidge points out that Paul's special use of the somic metaphor, adopted by the Puritans, emphasizes not just the "order" the bodily metaphor implies, but the order's *quality* as it intersects its members' spiritual and social lives: "Now there are diversities of gifts, but the same Spirit. . . . And there are diversities of operations, but it is the same God which worketh in all. But the manifestation of the Spirit is given to every man to profit withal" (*PRE* 17). The somic image extends covenant theology to include virtually all human activity, making the community a single consenting relationship constrained by relative relationships to the complete performance of God's will.

Of course, people, as stewards, exist not only in relationship to one another but also in a relative relationship to God. To consent to God in stewardly tasks is to accord with God's ideal image of humanity, reflecting God's own image of Himself—a Holy Artisan. Harmony between Lord and steward is the ultimate source of human happiness because it constitutes a return to the proper relationship with God, the relationship that Richardson's Platonic philosophy describes through its constructions of art and artful conduct.

Thus, on a wider scale, the encyclopedic community is the antitype of a prelapsarian ideal of *communitas*. Social interaction attuned to God's idea and will constitutes a mimetic return to God. As the community itself becomes the image of God's idea and will, it virtually realizes His artful end as eternal love in creative action. This mimetic return to an Edenic state is clearly captured in Paul's epistles: "Now the Lord is that Spirit: and where the Spirit of the Lord is, there is liberty. . . . But we all, with open face beholding as in a glass the glory of the Lord, are changed into the same image from glory to glory, even as by the Spirit of the Lord" (2 Corinthians 3:17–18).

In this passage Paul employs the metaphoric gaze into a looking glass to characterize conversion as the soul's ectypal mimesis (or *imitatio*) of holiness mediated through a reflected image or entype of God's glory. The "open [or unveiled] face beholding" enables an unwilled seeing, one that thrusts the lapsed soul back into the divine image, transforming it as it is "struck" by the reflected type of God's holy spirit. God's grace lifts the veil of self-interest, harmonizing the soul with the love (*caritas*) that the sovereign image of God's all-commanding glory orders. One's sanctified love is inclined toward the infinite— one "sees" one's true self-image (see "L" 122).

To the saint the world expresses God's desire for complete consent with His idea, which finally constitutes His will. The Richardsonian philosophy frames God's idea and will within actual empirical experience—a saint sees, hears, smells, tastes, and may mimetically become God's glory. Richardson's student, John Barlow, in his sermon entitled "The Good Mans Priviledge" (1618), succinctly contrasts speculative ("notionall") and experiential ("experimentall") knowledge: "Knowledge is either Notionall, or experimentall. Notionall is the bare apprehension of the truth of an Art, or rule in any science: but experimentall knowledge is, when we have seen and felt the truth of a thing, verified either in our selves, or others" ("GMP" 3–4).

For Edwards and his Richardsonian forebears, saving grace is a "felt" experience of spiritual truth. Feeling the holy truth is as indubitable as tasting the sweetness of honey, but it is reserved for the elect. Upon hearing a saving sermon, the rational understanding and loving affection consenting together toward the holy word betokens a sanctified character. Love's inclination to embrace the divine idea may be experienced, in Edwards' words, as a "delightful conviction."

The Richardsonian philosophy outlined above permeates Edwards' thought. In nearly everything he writes, his piety toward his sovereign God is evident. Edwards' notions of experiential faith, Christian virtue, social order, and church polity derive from Richardsonian philosophy. His account of the conversion experience in terms of "speculative" and "affective" knowledge echoes traditional Puritan distinctions between the "notionall" and the "experimentall." Finally, Edwards' typological reading of natural order exhibits a marked continuity between his thought and that of his Puritan ancestors.

In his career as a pastor he maintained this Puritan stance. However, no matter what Edwards' intentions were, like any thinker who leaves a literary trace, his works were bound to be appropriated, interpreted, and employed to a variety of ends. There is no guarantee how one's legacy will be used by one's heirs.

6
The Edwardsean Legacy

Describing Jonathan Edwards' influence is a difficult task, speculative, if not necessarily revisionist, at best. In the first place, influence is itself an extraordinarily problematic critical concept. Its mechanisms, although clarified considerably by Harold Bloom, remain subject to a strenuous debate.[1] Second, Edwards as a minister and theologian was so very self-consciously orthodox that distinguishing his influence from that of other Congregationalists is, in many instances, impossible.

Publication history complicates the problem, for although when he died many of Edwards' sermons and treatises were in print, the notebooks containing his metaphysical speculations were not; and if we, nearly two and a half centuries later, can easily discern the relationship between his metaphysics and his theology, we can also doubt that those coming immediately after Edwards could detect the ramifications of his peculiar formulations. As we have seen, even after some of the more important documents were collected, edited, and published in 1829, Sereno Dwight's misdating of these materials led scholars to misjudge their importance to his mature work.

Finally, we have the problem of historicity: an audience's situation will always condition any judgments of Edwards' significance. Critics have labeled Edwards as a thinker "representative" of his culture, as "the last Medieval American" (*LM* 116), and as a pre-modernist revolutionary misunderstood by his benighted contemporaries. These judgments and others like them say as much or more about the critics' own times and predilections as they do about Edwards. The present study, as well, is no different.

Written in the postmodern era, this study cannot but describe Edwards' work through discursive strategies in many ways completely foreign to him—indeed, foreign to Edwards scholars until very recently. For example, Edwards' theory of language, described by Miller and others as being influenced by Locke, as no doubt it is, seems more structural, if not poststructural, than empirical when we note that Edwards' differentiation between the speculative and sensible relationships to signs—which he believed to be his most important philosophical distinction—rests upon his claim that the ideas to which signs refer derive their ideality from a framework or context of ideas and signs.

As we have seen, for Edwards these frames may be more or less "excellent"; that is, they may in varying degrees approximate the total, infinite frame of God's consciousness. Since reference to this total frame is unattainable except through divine influence, without that influence the truth, even when written plainly in the Bible, is, in postmodern parlance, "undecidable," illusory. Thus Edwards' contention—that "the universe is one vast general frame consisting of an innumerable multitude of lesser frames," and that if it were not for God one random "wandering particle" would be sufficient to "destroy the harmony" of the whole system (*PJE* 101)—sounds remarkably like a tenet of Derridean deconstruction.

A postmodernist such as Barbara Johnson can ask, "If 'comprehension' is the framing of something whose limits are undeterminable, how can we know what we are comprehending?" (J 336). Her final answer seems uncannily familiar: "If we could be sure of the difference between the determinable and the undeterminable, the undeterminable would be comprehended within the determinable. What is undecidable is whether a thing is decidable or not" (J 349). As Edwards would have put it in his time, if we could be sure of the difference between faith and apostasy, then faith would not be faith, but apostasy. Precisely *what* we must believe is *that* we must believe.

Similarly, Edwards' reconfiguration, or abandonment, of faculty psychology may seem to modern eyes "as far from the psychology of our time as from that of the middle ages" ("CCEB" 207), but to the postmodernist, his characterizing the self as a mirror image may seem to foreshadow Jacques Lacan's revision of Freud's substantive ego into a positioned subject. Edwards explicitly rejects Locke's definition of personal identity as the continuity of consciousness, that is, as an explicitly maintained referral to personal memories.

From a post-Lacanian perspective, this rejection is more than a philosophical tour de force designed to avert Arminian attacks upon original sin. More than explaining how the soul may be responsible for an act it did not perform and cannot remember, Edwards' description of "dependent identity" (*OS* 400)—the notion that personal identity is not self-perpetuating but is generated through repeated references to an original pattern—serves to explain not only why "men may be and often are ignorant of their own hearts" (*PJE* 73), that is, why they may be unconscious of their true motivations, but also why they may be incapable of acting upon their conscious, rational judgments. Essentially, Edwards describes the fallen self as a floating signifier that no longer has its "place" within a semiotic system. At least his descriptions of degeneracy can be read that way.

If, historically distant as we are from Edwards' writing, we discover embryonic formulations of present-day concerns, how much more so may Edwards' language have provided rhetorical patterns guiding subsequent writers' arguments, some perhaps subverting Edwards' original. Whether specific ideas, concerns, terminology, or rhetorical strategies, what is passed down may transform in meaning considerably as it assumes a new function in a new situation. Similarly, a later writer employing an entirely different style, diction, and genre may be furthering a purpose a prior writer originally conceived. Thus, a later writer's relation to an earlier may be essentially conservative, one fully intending to pass on the legacy, however it may be (mis)conceived, to the next generation; it may be antagonistic, fully intending to discredit and disempower; or it may be agonistic and revisionary, diverting earlier rhetorical energies into new channels and new purposes.

INFLUENCE VISIBLE

Since the present book is concerned with rhetorical influence, and specifically with the influence of Edwards' conversion rhetoric, we will discuss only briefly Edwards' undeniable, visible influences—on writers after Edwards who specifically defended, extended, modified, or attacked his work. These influences could include his impact not only upon subsequent theological and philosophical developments, what we might call the conceptual legacy, but also upon American religious and social history, or what we might call the ministerial legacy. The latter, however, is confined primarily to the effects of Edwards' revivalist activities, and these, as we have seen, were not unique to Edwards, except for his immediately influential published defenses of the revival.

The conceptual legacy was passed, first and foremost, to a group of disciples who taught and wrote during the decades immediately following Edwards' death. These leaders of the New Divinity movement, as its detractors labeled it, included Joseph Bellamy (1719–90), Samuel Hopkins (b. 1721), Jonathan Edwards, Jr. (1754–1801), and Nathaniel Emmons (1745–1840). Clearly, each of these men intended to conserve, explicate, and expand Edwards' theology. Whether they preserved it or killed it has been a matter of debate. Most recent scholars, taking their cue from Sydney E. Ahlstrom's *A Religious History of the American People* (1972), have concluded along with him that Edwards "did not have a single disciple who was true to his essential genius" (*RHAP* 311) and that the New Divinity, in particular, "degraded Puritan theology by turning it into a lifeless system of apologetics" (*RHAP* 405).

Ahlstrom attributes the continuing degradation of Edwards' subtler thought to the simple fact that "no generation has been able to read and consider Edwards's complete works" (*RHAP* 312). Other scholars blame the decline on historical factors. Conrad Cherry, for instance, follows Joseph Haroutunian in his claim that, with the coming of the humanitarian movement, even for Calvinists moralism began to replace pietism (*PVM*). Cherry, claiming that the New Divinity took "the first step down the path to making theology legal in emphasis and nature didactic in import" (*NRI* 70), believes that "much of the theological preoccupation with law was a consequence of the self-confident democratic feelings spreading in the New Republic" (*NRI* 68).

Other scholars position their explanation of the New Divinity's decline from Edwards nearer to Ahlstrom's point about textual unavailability. James Hoopes, for example, suggests that because key Edwardsean texts remained unpublished, Edwards' disciples were "unaware of his idealist metaphysics" and consequently "unwittingly played into enemy [i.e., Arminian and Antinomian] hands by accepting the Lockean notion of the soul as a substance formed by experience" ("CCEB" 208 215). Ultimately, Hoopes contends, second-generation post-Edwards figures such as Lyman Beecher, who accepted the Lockean definition of substantive identity, would repudiate those fundamental Edwards doctrines—on free will, original sin, and infant damnation—that relied upon Edwards' repudiation of Locke's definition.

Unlike Ahlstrom, Haroutunian, Cherry, and Hoopes, some recent historians, most notably William Breitenbach, have decried the "myth" that Edwards' "most loyal disciples have been [his] betrayers" (B 177). Arguing against the "piety-versus-moralism" model of Puritan studies, Breitenbach discredits the "plot" typically imposed upon New England's religious history: "This interpretation, familiar to all students of American religion, describes a pure theocentric piety descending from the crags of Calvinism by way of covenant theology and worldly prosperity into the meadows of moralism, Arminianism, and Unitarianism, and finally losing itself—some would say, finding itself—in the swamps of Transcendentalism" (B 178).

Breitenbach strenuously objects to those who cast the New Divinity ministers either as fighting against or collaborating with encroaching moralists. No battle between Moralists and Pietists took place. To the contrary, the "*dominant* New England theological tradition," he asserts, "the clerical orthodoxy, was one of piety *and* moralism." Both Edwards and his New Divinity disciples followed in this tradition, occupying "the familiar middle ground, defending it against the extremes of Antinomianism and Arminianism" (B 179).

In many respects, Breitenbach's defense of the New Divinity is quite convincing. Nevertheless, it cannot be denied that even Edwards' most talented followers tended to overemphasize tenets that Edwards himself more carefully conditioned. For example, Bellamy insisted that God permits sin in order to perfect the universe, and Hopkins extended the concept of "disinterested benevolence" toward the "complete willingness to be damned if it be for the greater glory of God" (*RHAP* 408). This extension, as we have seen, is rhetorically implied, in some Edwardsean sermons, but it ignores the Edwardsean caveat that self-love is persistent, so that the self one is willing to damn is only one's "old" self.

After the New Divinity, the most important reform movement began with Timothy Dwight (1758–1817), Jonathan Edwards' grandson, president of Yale, and founder of the New Haven Theology. Dwight is known primarily for continuing his grandfather's tradition of promoting a mutually supportive relationship between Protestantism and empirical science while opposing Deistic claims of the sufficiency of natural religion.

Dwight's followers, including Lyman Beecher (1775–1863) and Nathaniel William Taylor (1786–1858), ushered in the Second Great Awakening, which occurred between 1797 and 1801. Taylor, Dwight's secretary and most promising student at Yale, provided the movement's intellectual foundation. Like Dwight, he was as strongly influenced by the Scottish Common Sense school as he was by Edwards. His greatest contribution was his clarification of Edwards' defence of original sin. As Ahlstrom puts it, "Taylor's fundamental insistence was that no man becomes depraved but by his own act" (*RHAP* 420). Sin, although inevitable, is not causally necessary. As we have seen, Edwards argued precisely this in his *Original Sin*. Oddly, Taylor, perhaps overly influenced by Arminian arguments against Edwards, presumed that he was correcting Edwards.

Taylor did go on to differ from Edwards, however, when he claims that man is never completely a determined part of nature but has always a "power to the contrary"—a capacity to negate the inclinations. Edwards, of course, would have replied that that is why men may act civilly out of self-love. Taylor's revision of Edwards provided a pseudo-Calvinistic justification for the humanitarian efforts, social benevolence, and moral reform movements—including temperance and abolition—that would characterize late eighteenth- and nineteenth-century American religion.

In Taylor's writing, the encyclopedic ideal and the notion of God as Moral Governor, both found in Edwards' continuation of the Richardsonian tradition, shifted emphasis. Edwards did indeed identify good actions with obedience, but for him devotion was the ultimate end of Christian practice. For Taylor, also, "the design of God's government" was "the happy harmony of the whole," but for him Christian practice resolved in the production of happiness for others (*NRI* 118–19). Edwards, no doubt, would have leveled the same argument at Taylor that he did at the Deists Taylor would abhor: like the watch found on the beach, the harmony of its parts is to no avail unless it serves the purpose intended by its maker. As Conrad Cherry has explained, in Taylor's view "the happiness which God is disposed to accomplish was not Edwardsean joyful appropriation and reflection of the power of God's presence; it was, instead, 'the love of doing good'" (*NRI* 125).

Taylor, Dwight, and other New Haven theologians were the last important American writers who depended significantly on Jonathan Edwards' work and reputation. Others, certainly, read and responded to his work, including Unitarians such as William Ellery Channing (1780–1842), who abandoned fundamental Calvinistic doctrines such as the trinitarian godhead, predestination, and original sin. Paradoxically, more so than the New Haven group, he saw human striving's end in communion with God and grace's end in disinterested benevolence. However, as his biographer Arthur W. Brown has pointed out, although in his early years Channing's "sense of piety was in kind and degree not very dissimilar from that of Jonathan Edwards," in later years "Edwardean piety would disappear; and he would love mankind for its dynamic potential of human goodness" (*WEC* 28). Like the Scottish philosophers Channing admired, he would come to believe in conscience as an inborn impulse toward benevolent feeling. Other Unitarians, such as Ralph Waldo Emerson, would move into Transcendentalism, in direct opposition to, if not disdain of, trinitarian Congregationalism and institutional religion in general.

Horace Bushnell (1802–76) was perhaps the only nineteenth-century American writer to display any real Edwardsean spirit. A student of Nathaniel Taylor's, Bushnell maintained the essential Calvinist doctrines of original sin and the need for grace. Drawing heavily upon European romantic thought and literature, Bushnell, according to Cherry, "recovered a symbolic view of religious truth very much like that of Jonathan Edwards" (*NRI* 159). Like Edwards, he focused sharply upon the problem of language as being central to the religious problem, although Coleridgean influence led him, of course, in quite different directions. Moreover, unlike most of his contemporaries who saw the proper end of human action in such principles as social harmony or duty to law, for Bushnell it was love, understood in a way not too distant from Edwards' consent to being. Finally, just as Edwards attempted to mediate between the New and Old Lights in his time by applying to the controversy his distinction between the sensible and the speculative, in works such as his *God in Christ* Bushnell expressed hope that his distinction between figurative and literal language would synthesize Calvinism and Unitarianism (*GIC* 85).

As social religion gained popularity in the nineteenth century, Edwards' importance declined, except perhaps as a ritual target for attacks. Mark A. Noll has noted that "during the nineteenth century at least forty-one substantial refutations of Edwards' major books appeared" ("JENT" 269). Of course, later significant influences can be traced, as Bruce Kuklick has shown with respect to John Dewey ("JEAP" 252–55) and as Sydney A. Ahlstrom has suggested of H. Richard Niebuhr (*RHAP* 940–41). For the most part, however, after 1850 Edwards' theology was less an active theological force and more a topic only of historical interest.

INFLUENCE INVISIBLE

Edwards' influence upon American literary rhetoric has been hardly touched upon by scholarship,[2] largely because that influence has been often indirect and sometimes indistinguishable from Puritanism's more general influence. Because of this lack of prior scholarship, we cannot offer an extensive survey of Edwards' unacknowledged influence upon American literary writing. Instead, we offer one example of the direction future scholarship might take.

Confused Conversions: Edwards and Harriet Beecher Stowe

From Stockbridge in the summer of 1751, Edwards wrote to the Reverend Thomas Gillespie of Carnock, Scotland, attempting to explain why he had been dismissed from his Northampton pulpit. The letter carefully, almost artfully, blames himself as much as his congregation for the strife and controversy, and it ends by weighing the success of the revivals he had engendered:

Many may be ready from things that are lately come to pass to determine that all Northampton religion is come to nothing, and that the famed awakenings and revivals of religion in that place prove to be nothing, but strange tides of a melancholy and whimsical humor. But they would draw no such conclusion if they exactly knew the true state of the case, and would judge it with full calmness and impartiality of mind. (*GA* 565–66)

Edwards' refusal to concede the failure of the awakenings is understandable. Their perceived success justified, in his and the world's eyes, his dogma's rightness and his methods' efficacy.

Yet Edwards did concede, many times, that considerable backsliding occured after the revivals, that most who appeared full of religion one month were obviously full of the world the next. He was, in addition, clearly distressed by the split between the New and Old Lights. His dismissal was only one of many signs that, although as a social movement the revivals were an obvious success, as instruments of spiritual change his sermons' effects were less than certain. Perhaps his sensing of that possibility made him all the more willing to be exiled from his typical audience and devote himself to writing treatises.

This much is certain: the results of Edwards' sermon rhetoric were largely unwanted. He regretted, and possibly feared, the mass hysteria, the submission to spiritual irrationality, the increased democratization and devaluation of religious authority, and the clerical community's subsequent polarization that accompanied, and can be rightly said to have resulted partially from, the sermon rhetoric he had developed.

Of course, many of these unwanted effects can be explained in terms of historical forces and conditions—economic, political, demographic, and intellectual—which would allow us to describe Edwards' audiences' responses as being well beyond his rhetorical control. At the same time, however, because later generations, including those proponents of social religion who disclaimed his Calvinist dogma, considered Edwards to be the revivalist preacher par excellence, his rhetorical techniques influenced religious conversion practices long after the historical conditions that might explain their effects had disappeared. When Edwards' conversion techniques were applied in a later age, by people of different faith, in a different genre, and yet produced analogous unwanted effects, we can conclude that the rhetorical strategies themselves were as much to blame for the effects as any extraneous factors.

One instance of such a later application ending in a similar rhetorical failure is Harriet Beecher Stowe's *Uncle Tom's Cabin*. Although Stowe's best-seller was "probably the most influential book ever written by an American" (*SD* 122), precisely because it made her into, as President Lincoln supposedly addressed her upon their meeting, "the little lady who made this big war" (JWW 480), it was a rhetorical failure in the sense that its effects did not match her intentions.

Today we may doubt that the book alone caused the war. In any case, as John William Ward has noted, "if *Uncle Tom's Cabin* played some small part in the coming of the war, one should remember that this is not the direction in which the book points." Stowe's "only hope" for her book, according to Ward, "was that men with changed hearts" would alter their own compliance with the horrible institution of slavery (JWW 492). Similarly, Jane Tompkins has argued that *Uncle Tom's Cabin* dramatized "the notion that historical change takes place only through religious conversion" (*SD* 133), and that although the book "was spectacularly persuasive in conventional political terms: it helped convince a nation to go to war," it was "a political failure" because "Stowe conceived her book as an instrument for bringing about the day when the world would be ruled not by force, but by Christian love" (*SD* 141).

If critics have noted Stowe's rhetorical failure, in the sense of her book's achieving unwanted effects, none have attempted to explain why it failed. Even Tompkins, who unlike her predecessors offers an explanation of why it achieved popularity, says only that "if history did not take the course [Stowe and other female sentimental writers] recommended, it is not because they were not political, but because they were insufficiently persuasive" (*SD* 141).

Tompkins' explanation of the book's popular success is that it depends upon a "storehouse of assumptions" held by its predominantly female, Protestant audience, to whom it offers an alternative, matriarchal system, one in which "the home is the center of all meaningful activity" and "women perform the most important tasks" (*SD* 127 141). Yet this still does not explain the martial response of the men who went to war or of the women who encouraged them. On this question, Tompkins' answer is no more helpful than that of the male critics she chastises for regarding the book's success "as some sort of mysterious eruption, inexplicable by natural causes" (*SD* 218n).

The Civil War was the last thing Stowe wanted her book to bring about, just as democratization and spiritual irrationality were the last things Edwards wanted his sermons to bring about. For both, changing their audiences' hearts would result in the desired social goal, not the other way around. The social goal did not have to precede the individual change of heart. Edwards did not seek the millennium because then the people would convert; Stowe did not seek just law because then the people would be just. Why, then, did their audiences tend to respond inappropriately?

For both authors the problem was the same; a confusion, on their audiences' part, of conversion with persuasion. Persuasion seeks to discover common ground and then works from that ground toward mutually sharable attitudes and ideas to induce mutually desirable actions. Kenneth Burke has located the central principle of persuasion in what he calls *identification*. "You persuade a man," says Burke, "only insofar as you can talk his language by speech, gesture, tonality, order, image, attitude, idea, *identifying* your ways with his" (*RM* 55). When considered as identification, persuasion must presume that beneath divisiveness and disagreement is an underlying cohesiveness, a sameness of substance, as Burke would put it, that, once assented to, allows transformations to be worked that more coherently unify postures, ideas, goals, concepts, and so forth, that initially seemed incommensurate. For this reason, although "the rhetorician may have to change the audience's opinion in one respect . . . he can succeed only insofar as he yields to that audience's opinions in other respects" (*RM* 56). Persuasion works to resolve superficial, although perhaps divisive, differences among people who are, or who can perceive themselves as being, fundamentally identical.

Conversion, however, works on a contrary principle. It assumes that although a community's members may share the same opinions, attitudes, ideas, language—everything—in common, they may in substance differ fundamentally. Moreover, the superficially shared surface may conceal that crucial difference. Accordingly, conversion systematically dis-covers the grounds upon which individuals historically established their values and purposes, revealing the inadequacy of those grounds and the individuals' incapacity to establish proper grounds, thus preparing them to surrender unconditionally to an exterior, transcendent authority.

As we have seen, Edwards' conversion sermons, both with imagery (as in "Sinners in the Hands of an Angry God") and with logic (as in "True Grace Distinguished from the Experience of Devils"), strive persistently to undercut the individual's confidence in his or her opinions, values, and especially attitudes. Such a dis-covering of the abyss over which the forms of personal and social identity hover is especially necessary to Calvinist conversion because the doctrine of God's sovereignty implies that finite beings are ultimately without free will. "Persuasion," as Burke reminds us, "involves choice, will; it is directed to a man only insofar as he is *free*" (*RM* 50). But conversion sermons are directed to their listeners' bound will. The sermons do not attempt to persuade listeners to choose rightly but to convince them that they cannot choose rightly and should submit to God's will.

In an eighteenth-century Puritan community like Northampton, of course, the ministerial and civic authorities represented God's will. Accordingly, the self-loathing accompanying the conversion experience could not be deflected toward the social structure that conditioned the self being loathed. At the same time, however, the self could not surrender to the social system either, even though the system stood for the transcendent authority being sought. Encyclopedic society was a complex of symbolic substitutions for an ideal subordination of self to God.

For this reason, although taken with seriousness, temporal relationships were not taken too seriously, for in the afterlife they would mean nothing. "The things and relations of this life," said Thomas Hooker, "are like prints left in Sand, there is not the least appearance or remembrance of them. The King remembers not his Crown, the Husband the Wife, Father the Child" (quoted in *PF* 20). As Edmund S. Morgan has explained:

For a child to make too much of its parents, a wife of her husband, a subject of his king was to place the creature before the creator, to reverse the order of creation, to repeat the sin of Adam. All social relations must be maintained with a respect to the order of things, in full recognition of the fact that man "ought to make God his immediate end." (*PF* 21)

When such an attitude toward social relationships, including authoritative ones, has been so long-standing, submission to a cult of personality or to a secular system is unlikely, although, one might argue, in George Whitefield's case it may have come close. Even so, Calvinist dogma militates against the individual's directing either loathing or adulation toward the social structure and its representatives.

Thus, in a Puritan community, conversion, when it goes wrong, can go one of two ways: it can become an extra-institutional revelling in emotion among individuals persuaded to share in presumably the same joyful experience; or, for those unpersuaded whose psychic defenses are nevertheless broken by the conversion process, it can become self-destructive, perhaps suicidal. In both cases, the energy released by the systematic breakdown of the individual's self-mastery is directed inward. Conflict with others can result only when the legitimacy of the individual's experience is denied, as it was by the Old Lights. However, although an us-them mentality did arise from the Old Lights' denial, their denial could not prevent the experience. Since revivalist experience did not depend upon the cooperation of others, Edwardsean converts had no motive to coerce others to submit along with them.

For a number of reasons, the conversion strategy at work in *Uncle Tom's Cabin* produced quite different, more violent responses. Like her brother Henry

Ward Beecher, Harriet Beecher Stowe may have rebelled against her grandfather Lyman Beecher's Taylorism, his inflammatory anti-Catholic agitation, and his paranoid fears of a foreign, Roman Catholic conspiracy to control the Mississippi Valley; nevertheless, she inherited from him the keen sense of conversionist strategy that had made him the most successful revivalist of the Second Great Awakening. What Stowe wished to convert her audience to, however, was poles apart from the Calvinist God of Jonathan Edwards.

In the "Concluding Remarks" of *Uncle Tom's Cabin* she addresses her readers directly, telling them exactly what they should do:

> But, what can any individual do? Of that, every individual can judge. There is one thing that every individual can do,—they can see to it that *they feel right*. An atmosphere of sympathetic influence encircles every human being; and the man or woman who *feels* strongly, healthily, and justly on the great interests of humanity, is a constant benefactor to the human race. See, then, to your sympathies in this matter! (*UTC* 472)

Stowe, like many in the humanitarian movement, discounted original sin. Though believing in a permanent principle of self-love, she and others also believed in a natural, God-created principle of "disinterested benevolence," a seat of sympathy and compassion, a divine principle informing the conscience which, because she also believed in free will, enabled the individual to contradict self-interest. A heart kept free of self-interest could feel the difference between virtue and vice.

This and similar views, developed during the eighteenth century by David Hume, Francis Hutcheson, William Wollaston, and others, came to Stowe primarily through her father and other New Divinity ministers, who were greatly influenced by them. Wollaston's description in *The Religion of Nature Delineated* is typical:

> There is something in *human* nature . . . which renders us obnoxious to the pains of others, causing us to sympathize with them. . . . It is grevous to see or hear (and almost to hear of) any man, or even any animal whatever, in *torment.* . . . It is therefore according to *nature* to be affected with the sufferings of other people and the contrary is *inhuman* and *unnatural.* (quoted in F 249)

In *The Nature of True Virtue,* Edwards attacked the association of conscience and sympathy with virtue.[3] The assumption that sympathy was God-given and therefore God-like led ultimately to the conclusion that a benevolent God would not condemn sinners to everlasting torment, especially for a sin they had inherited and not chosen to commit. Edwards' analysis sought to show that, as Norman Fiering puts it, "The highly touted moral sense is reducible to natural conscience, which is itself reducible to a primitive sense of desert and the natural desire for logical self-consistency, or rather, to the discomfort resulting from self-contradiction" (F 147). As a result, sympathy can be misplaced and self-serving.

Earlier, in *Some Thoughts Concerning the Revival*, Edwards had linked dependence upon conscience to spiritual pride:

But spiritual pride is the most secret of all sins. There is no sin so much like the Devil as this, for secrecy and subtlety, . . . undiscerned and unsuspected, and appearing as an angel of light. . . . It is a sin that has, as it were, many lives; if you kill it, it will live still; if you mortify it and suppress it in one shape, it rises in another; if you think it is all gone, yet it is there still. There are a great many kinds of it, that lie in different forms and shapes, one under another, and encompass the heart like the coats of an onion; if you pull one off there is another underneath. We had need therefore to have the greatest watch imaginable, over our hearts, with respect to this matter, and to cry most earnestly to the great Searcher of hearts, for his help. "He that trusts his own heart is a fool" [Prov. 28:26]. (*GA* 416–17)

Edwards would not have been surprised to hear that conversions to sympathy would contribute to the start of a bloody civil war.

Stowe's strategy of conversion to sympathy was simple: it sought to undermine the grounds for overriding the primitive, immediate, sympathetic response to others' distress that she assumed all individuals but the most corrupt felt. Thus from the beginning the strategy was more persuasive than convertive, for, being an humanitarian and not a Calvinist, she assumed that her readers, Southerners included, were fundamentally and originally good. She further assumed that two related forces had worked against her readers' natural sympathy. One was the force of habit and tradition that allowed Southerners, who witnessed slavery's horrors daily, simply not to feel in their hearts what they saw with their eyes. The other was the force of distance and abstraction that prevented Northerners from recognizing the slaves' basic humanity and allowed them to ignore their plight.

The latter case and Stowe's strategy against it is best illustrated by Chapter 9, "In Which it Appears that a Senator is But a Man." The chapter opens to a domestic scene involving Ohio state Senator Bird, who had recently returned from the legislature after arguing and winning the case for the Fugitive Slave Act of 1850, "a law," as his wife describes it, "forbidding people to give meat and drink to those poor colored people that come along" (*UTC* 91). On the senate floor, Bird, we learn later, had been

as bold as a lion about [the Act], and "mightily convinced" not only himself, but everybody that heard him;—but then his idea of a fugitive was only an idea of the letters that spell the word,—or at most, the image of a little newspaper picture of a man with a stick and bundle, with "Ran away from the subscriber" under it. The magic of the real presence of distress,—the imploring human eye, the frail, trembling hand, the despairing appeal of helpless agony,—these he had never tried. (*UTC* 102)

Stowe's employment of Edwards' distinction between speculative and sensible knowledge is obvious here. It implies that all the Senator's legal, rational argument is founded upon an empty concept of the fugitive, a mere sign, and that "the real presence" of one living slave would confound all his logic.

This, in fact, is exactly the tactic Mrs. Bird uses in her argument against her husband's position. Better stated, Mrs. Bird refuses to argue at all. When the Senator tells her, "I can state to you a very clear argument, to show—," she interrupts, "Oh, nonsense, John! you can talk all night, but you would n't do it. I put it to you, John,—would *you*, now, turn away a poor, shivering, hungry creature from your door, because he was a runaway?" (*UTC* 93). "Clear argument" is "nonsense." The Senator's contention that "we must put aside our private feelings" is overturned by Mrs. Bird's reply that "obeying God never brings on public evils" (*UTC* 93).

The issue becomes simply whether her husband is the kind of person who could act on mere law and reason in the face of human distress. Mrs. Bird refuses to believe that he could. She counters his every attempt to defer his personal feeling, whether to duty ("You know it is n't duty,—it can't be a duty!") or to reason ("I hate reasoning, John,—especially on such subjects"). The husband is silenced; his status as a good man is, in his wife's eyes, on the line.

Shortly after this conversation, Eliza and her child appear at the Bird's home seeking asylum. The Senator sheds tears—hiding them, of course—upon witnessing their misery. He has, as the novel has told us, "a particularly humane and accessible nature" (*UTC* 93), so we are not surprised that without being asked he arranges to convey Eliza to safety. "Your heart is better than your head, in this case, John" (*UTC* 100), his wife assures him, yet the reader is well aware that John's heart is in turmoil. As he sinks into "deep meditation" while "anxiously" putting on his boots before leaving with Eliza and her son, he mutters, "It 's a confounded awkward, ugly business . . . and that's a fact! It will have to be done, though, for aught I see,—hang it all!" (*UTC* 99). Because he "feels right," he has been thrown into the role of a hypocrite and criminal, and about that he cannot feel right. His conversion cannot be complete and satisfying because the system he serves is evil.

Senator Bird's predicament typifies that of Stowe's entire Northern audience. Since prior to the novel's publication the Fugitive Slave Act had been passed, what was once a Southern problem was now incontrovertibly an American problem: "Nothing of tragedy can be written, can be spoken, can be conceived, that equals the frightful reality of scenes daily and hourly acting on our shores, beneath the shadow of American law, and the shadow of the cross of Christ" (*UTC* 471). The North could no longer deny the slavery on our shores; it could no longer psychologically separate itself from the South. As John William Ward says, "No longer could it be maintained that it was 'they,' the Southerners, who supported slavery; it was 'we,' the people of the United States, who did" (JWW 488).

Stowe's novel, by making present the suffering of a people who for the North had been only abstract, distant figures—"only an idea of the letters that spell the word"—had made it possible for Northerners to feel for the slaves, but it was impossible for Northerners to "feel right" without first rectifying the system. Like Edwards, Stowe had sought to convert her readers, to undermine Southern justifications for slavery and Northern justifications for tolerating it. Like Edwards' call to repent, Stowe's call in the novel was meant for individuals. Nevertheless, she identified her audience as the "men and women of America" (*UTC* 471). Their social identity responded since it was their social identity that was condemned.

The psychology of sympathy explains why, although they came to see Southerners as part of "us" rather than as "them," Northerners were willing to exert violence toward them. In Stowe's book sympathy arises from imaginatively projecting oneself into another's situation, and the capacity for sympathy increases to the extent that the experience calling for compassion is shared. In Chapter 9, Mrs. Bird, who only a few pages before had told her husband that "folks do n't run away when they are happy" (*UTC* 93), asks Eliza why she had run away when by her own admission her master and mistress had been kind. Eliza responds by asking, "Ma'am, . . . have you ever lost a child." Mrs. Bird, bursting into tears, says, "Why do you ask that? I have lost a little one." And to this Eliza replies confidently, "Then you will feel for me" (*UTC* 97).

Consistently throughout the novel the slaves' misery demands sympathy, whereas the slave owners, such as Eliza's owners, the Shelbys, who might have been candidates for sympathy, find their demands for it undercut. Shelby, who sells Eliza's child out of the "cruel necessity" of impending foreclosure, shares his wife's self-condemnation for being "a fool to think I could make anything good out of such a deadly evil" as slavery "under laws like ours" (*UTC* 45). Their kindness is rendered cruel by the system with which they comply.

Far more unsympathetic than the Shelbys, however, is the disgusting slave trader who forced Shelby to sell the child, Haley, "a man of leather,—a man alive to nothing but trade and profit,—cool, and unhesitating, and unrelenting, as death and the grave" (*UTC* 46). Haley, more than any other single character, represents the slavery system, and he is, as Wollaston said of the unsympathetic, "*inhuman* and *unnatural*."

In *Uncle Tom's Cabin*, those capable of sympathy characteristically respond passionately and violently toward those who act unsympathetically. Mrs. Bird was ordinarily a quiet, restrained woman: "There was only one thing that was capable of arousing her, and that provocation came in on the side of her unusually gentle and sympathetic nature;—anything in the shape of cruelty would throw her into a passion" (*UTC* 92). The book goes on to tell how once, upon finding out her sons had been involved in "stoning a defenseless kitten,"

Mrs. Bird "whipped them" and "tumbled" them off to bed without any supper. The moral was that the "boys never stoned another kitten" (*UTC* 92).

Beyond implying that cruelty can be stopped only if violent punishment is enforced upon those who cause it, this little tale also suggests that the violence is even more understandable when the cruel party is part of oneself, part of the sympathetic one's family. Just as Edwards' conversions produced self-loathing toward the convert's sinful self, Stowe's, too, produced self-loathing, but toward that part of "us" that necessitated the Northern sympathetic response—the Southern slave owners. In effect, Stowe's novel implicitly demanded that its Northern readers obey the biblical injunction "If thine eye offend thee, pluck it out"—in short, that they wage war against the South.

Both Edwards and Stowe assumed that the horrors they presented as the products of a sinful perspective would induce individuals to change. They did, but not always as individuals. Edwards' and Stowe's rhetoric defined, or really created, their audiences, and simultaneously it asked them to separate themselves from the evil part of the identities the rhetoric had bestowed upon them. But when they heard as an audience, they were persuaded as an audience. Edwards' and Stowe's discourse did create a desire for change, but what their audiences saw fit to do as a group proved antithetical to what the authors would have had them do as individuals. The results, rhetorically speaking, were catastrophic.

For good or ill, Jonathan Edwards' influence on American life and letters extends far deeper and more extensively than we suppose. His legacy, like his life, is quietly persistent, a gift or a curse to those who encounter it. His vision of the abyss cannot with impunity be ignored; his alternative to the abyss cannot with serenity be contemplated. Still, his conviction, although perhaps only a fantasy for postmodernity, is as delightful to imagine as it is wistful to admire.

Notes

CHAPTER 1

1. According to Ola Winslow, "Trustee action [against Rector Cutler and Tutors Johnson and Browne] had defined these issues anew: orthodoxy consisted in the complete acceptance of the Saybrook Platform; heresy consisted in any variation therefrom, particularly in the direction of the Arminian doctrine and prelatical church government as opposed to Congregationalism" (W 84).

2. An enormous amount of scholarly confusion has resulted over the years because of Sereno Dwight's misdating of "The Mind" and other documents. Apparently, Edwards worked on "The Mind" well into his later years; if so, the idealistic philosophy of Edwards' youth must, in fact, inform his more mature writings, as this book assumes. See Wallace Anderson's report on Thomas Schaefer's dating of Edwards' miscellaneous works (A 326–29). See also James Hoopes' explanation of the significance of these dates to interpreting Edwards' later works ("CCEB" 297–315).

3. It is important to note, however, that Edwards was hardly alone in believing that preaching could not effect conversion. Although Edwards did not, most earlier Calvinists believed that original sin's chief consequence was the corruption of the faculties, and that this corruption rendered it impossible even for Jesus himself to convert all those who heard him. The important difference among Puritan divines centered about the preparatory processes. A few, like Thomas Hooker, perceived an infallible connection between the preparatory states and regeneration; others, like John Cotton, saw no connection and held that sinners "know only after the fact if fear has led to faith because preparation can go for nought" (GC 85; see also 83–85).

Hooker's belief could comfort those suffering humiliation, guilt, and a sense of helplessness while seeking salvation because they were to be saved "as surely as if [they] were invested [in the kingdom] already, and were now singing praises to the Lambe" (Hooker, *The Soules Humiliation* [London, 1637], quoted in *GC* 84). Cotton recognized no gracious operations prior to the actual conversion. Clearly, Hooker's view offered some relief from anxiety and the temptation to reject religion altogether in order to avoid the tension, while Cotton's offered no assurance whatsoever. Cotton, much as would Edwards' grandfather Solomon Stoddard, "identified conversion, illumination, and assurance" ("PMC" 276).

Like most Calvinists prior to Edwards, Stoddard and Cotton adhered to a faculty psychology wherein the intellect led and the heart followed (see *GC* 25–46). Thus Stoddard could preach, "he that has understood the gloriousness of God, is prepared and disposed to judge so from time to time. This discovery leaves such a sense and impression in the heart, as it inclines it forever to judge so concerning God" (*A Treatise Concerning Conversion* [Boston, 1719], quoted in "PMC" 276). Here as elsewhere in earlier Puritan theology, the understanding, properly prepared and set aright by grace, so inclines the will to accept God.

4. James Hoopes has noted that "as Norman Fiering has shown . . . , Edwards, like Locke, was not in rebellion against faculty psychology, but only against hypostatization of faculties, the assumption that faculties were distinct entities rather than different abilities or functions of a unitary mind" ("CCEB" 207; see also *JENT* 262–71). Hoopes argues that Edwards' psychological monism puts him further away from modern, Freudian psychology than his disciples who retained faculty division, because "the overarching psychological orthodoxy of the twentieth century" is "the view that the mind is capable of unconscious as well as conscious thought" ("CCEB" 207).

Hoopes' argument simply will not hold. Edwards had a thoroughgoing explanation of unconscious behavior, and his description of the sinful self as an image of God, its original, is amazingly similar to Freud's description of the neurotic ego's anxiety ridden relationship with the id. See Chapter 4 in this book, and Sigmund Freud, *Inhibitions, Symptoms, and Anxiety*, trans. Alix Strachey and Rev. James Strachey (New York and London: W. W. Norton, 1959), 22–23.

5. David Lyttle argues that "Edwards could not hold at the same time Locke's position on identity and the Calvinistic doctrine of Original Sin" ("JEPI" 163). Unfortunately, Lyttle takes the position that Edwards' use of Lockean terminology in *Original Sin*, "like his use of it in his definition of the Supernatural Light, is a mere facade in front of a medieval structure" ("JEPI" 163). Unable to see that for Edwards identity was determined by a position within a set of structural relationships, Lyttle assumed that, since Edwards obviously was not Lockean and did not believe that identity consisted in "same consciousness," he must therefore have taken the Cartesian view that Locke attacked—"that 'the indivisibility of the self or thinking substance is a self evident truth'" ("JEPI" 163).

CHAPTER 2

1. For the classic exposition of the Puritan social order, see Edmund S. Morgan, *The Puritan Family*. According to Morgan, "The essence of the social order lay in the superiority of husband over wife, parents over children, and master over servants in the family, ministers and elders over congregation in the church, rulers over subjects in the state" (*PF* 19).

2. David Laurence has suggested that Edwards' primary contribution to literary rhetoric is his representation of God's transformation during the conversion process from "impersonal force" to benevolent love:

Edwards's theology begins and, in the case of the damned, ends with the perception of naked impersonal power. His main effort as a writer is to represent force and worship of force as turning back on itself and overcoming itself, so that force and worship of force transform themselves into love and worship of love. Edwards's main literary task was to construct a figurative scheme in which a God whose natural form is naturalistic force is transformed into a God whose spiritual and human form is love, a system of metaphor in which a creature whose natural bent is to love power and who wants to be Fate comes to love love and learns to be human. ("JEF" 232–44)

CHAPTER 3

1. For a more complete analysis of *Original Sin* see Stephen R. Yarbrough, "The Beginning of Time: Jonathan Edwards' *Original Sin*," in *Early American Literature and Culture: Essays Honoring Harrison Meserole*, ed. Kathryn Zabelle Derounian (Newark: University of Delaware Press; London and Toronto: Associated University Press, 1992), 149–64.

2. Edwards' sense of the importance of vivacity or "liveliness" has been attributed to Lockean influences. Norman Fiering traces the influence of Locke and other thinkers (including Hutcheson and Shaftesbury) on Edwards' own thought. However, he explains that Edwards was deeply indebted to a number of earlier thinkers, including seventeenth-century Puritans. In addition, given Edwards' references to degrees of "liveliness" in his discussions of ideas, there is good reason to believe that Hume's *Enquiry Concerning Human Understanding* may have had a place in the background of his thought. However, it was not until the advent of George Campbell's *Philosophy of Rhetoric* (1776) that these features of experience were grounded in Lockean epistemology and given as a rationale for effective language. Perhaps Campbell was influenced by Edwards. Again, however, there is a tradition in Puritan rhetorical theory of connecting concrete imagery with appeals to the passions and, in turn, the will. In fact, Richardson's "Rhetorical Notes" are a primary source of this tradition, as

evidenced in Michael Wigglesworth's *Day of Doom* and other earlier Puritan literature. See John C. Adams, "Alexander Richardson and the Ramist Poetics of Michael Wigglesworth," *Early American Literature* 25 (1990): 271–88.

3. See John C. Adams, "Linguistic Values and Religious Experience: An Analysis of the Clothing Metaphors in Alexander Richardson's Ramist-Puritan Lectures on Speech," *Quarterly Journal of Speech* 75 (1990): 58–68.

4. See Lloyd Bitzer, "Aristotle's Enthymeme Revisited," *Quarterly Journal of Speech* 45 (1959): 399–408.

CHAPTER 4

1. For the most recent and sensitive account of Edwards' dismissal see Patricia Tracy, *Jonathan Edwards, Pastor*.

2. See John C. Adams, "Ramist Concepts of Testimony, Judicial Analogies, and the Puritan Conversion Narrative," *Rhetorica* 9 (1991): 251–68.

CHAPTER 5

1. For a more extensive analysis of Richardson's contribution to Puritan thought, see John C. Adams, "Alexander Richardson's Philosophy of Art and the Sources of the Puritan Social Ethic," *Journal of the History of Ideas* 50 (1989): 227–47.

2. Ramus' influence lasted at least until 1737 at Yale (see *SP* 206). However, according to Richard Warch, William Partridge gave Timothy Edwards a manuscript of George Downame's commentary on Ramus' *Dialectica*, and Edwards owned a copy of George Downame that includes a prolegomenon of art not unlike Richardson's (*SP* 205). See also Fiering on Richardson's possible influence on Edwards' concept of "consent," a key feature of his thinking on the subject of grace (F 114–15). Richardson actually uses the word "consentaniety" (as does Edwards) when he explains the harmony of the arts, as well as in his commentary on the Ramist dialectical *topos* of consentaniety argument. Richardson's commentary on Ramus' *Dialecticae libri duo* makes up the bulk of the first section of the 1657 edition of the *School-Master*. Fiering quotes Edwards' *Shadows or Images* (no. 8):

It is apparent . . . that there is a great and wonderful analogy in God's works. There is a wonderful resemblance in the effects which God produces, and consentaniety in His manner of working in one thing and another throughout all nature. . . . He makes the inferiour in imitation of the superior, the material the spiritual, on purpose to have a resemblance and shadow of them. (F 115 n. 26)

Moreover, Richardson employs the vocabulary of "types" in his discussion of primary and derived being. Finally, according to Warch there is evidence that a version of Richardson's "Notes of Physicks" was used at Yale possibly as late as 1729 (*SP* 208–9).

3. In addition to the image of a blow Richardson uses light passing through stained glass (*LSM* 23) and olfactory imagery of the scent of flowers (*LSM* 22) in his attempts to clarify how God's idea gets into peoples' heads.

CHAPTER 6

1. Harold Bloom's theory of influence, developed in such works as *The Anxiety of Influence* (1973), *A Map of Misreading* (1975), and *Poetry and Repression* (1976), although solely a theory of poetic influence, nevertheless provides the best guide available of the various subtle forms of influence relations among writers. His main point for the present study is that later writers always and necessarily revise earlier ones, inevitably seeking with their language to conceal either their departures from or reliance upon their precursors. In Bloom's work, such revision is revealed to have psychological origins; here, however, although for the most part content simply to identify instances of influence, we are more concerned with socio-historical origins.

2. George S. Lensing's "Robert Lowell and Jonathan Edwards: Poetry in the Hands of an Angry God" (*South Carolina Review* 6 [1974]: 7–17), Robert E. Morsberger's "'The Minister's Black Veil': 'Shrouded in a Blackness, Ten Times Black'" (*New England Quarterly* 46 [September 1973]: 454–63), Mason I. Lowance Jr.'s "From Edwards to Emerson to Thoreau: A Revaluation" (*American Transcendental Quarterly* 18 [Spring 1973]: 3–12), and Melinda Kaye Willard's "Jonathan Edwards and Nathaniel Hawthorne: Themes from the Common Consciousness" (*DAI* 39 [1979]: 6136A) are among the few scholarly works devoted to examining Edwards' influence on American literature.

3. Norman Fiering has extensively analyzed the intellectual context of Edwards' arguments in *The Nature of True Virtue* (see F 139–260). Fiering argues that "Edwards' reflections on the sympathetic emotions and their meaning were largely a reaction to Hutcheson, whom he had been reading extensively in the 1750s" (F 256).

Works Cited

Adams, John C. "Alexander Richardson and the Ramist Poetics of Michael Wigglesworth." *Early American Literature* 25 (1990): 271–88.

Adams, John C. "Alexander Richardson's Philosophy of Art and the Sources of the Puritan Social Ethic." *Journal of the History of Ideas* 50 (1989): 227–47.

Adams, John C. "Linguistic Values and Religious Experience: An Analysis of the Clothing Metaphors in Alexander Richardson's Ramist-Puritan Lectures on Speech." *Quarterly Journal of Speech* 75 (1990): 58–68.

Adams, John C. "Ramist Concepts of Testimony, Judicial Analogies, and the Puritan Conversion Narrative." *Rhetorica* 9 (1991): 251–68.

Ahlstrom, Sydney E. *A Religious History of the American People.* New Haven and London: Yale University Press, 1972.

Armstrong, Hilary. *St. Augustine and Christian Platonism.* Villanova: Villanova University Press, 1967.

Ames, William. *Technometry.* Ed. and trans. Lee W. Gibbs. College Park: State University of Pennsylvania Press, 1979.

Barlow, John. "The Good Mans Priviledge." London, 1618.

Breitenbach, William. "Piety and Moralism: Edwards and the New Divinity." In Jonathan Edwards and the American Experience, ed. Nathan O. Hatch and Harry S. Stout, 177–204. New York and Oxford: Oxford University Press, 1988.

Brown, Arthur W. *William Ellery Channing.* Twayne's United States Author's Series, no. 7. New Haven: College and University Press, 1961.

Burke, Kenneth. *A Rhetoric of Motives.* 1950. Reprint Berkeley, Los Angeles, and London: University of California Press, 1969.

Bushnell, Horace. *God in Christ.* Hartford, Conn.: Brown and Parsons, 1849.

Caldwell, Patricia. *The Puritan Conversion Narrative: The Beginnings of American Expression.* Cambridge: Harvard University Press, 1983.

Cherry, Conrad. *Nature and Religious Imagination: From Edwards to Bushnell.* Philadelphia: Fortress Press, 1980.

Cohen, Charles Lloyd. *God's Caress: The Psychology of Puritan Religious Experience.* New York: Oxford University Press, 1986.

Coolidge, John S. *The Pauline Renaissance in England.* New York: Oxford University Press, 1970.

Delattre, Roland. "Beauty and Theology: A Reappraisal of Jonathan Edwards." In *Critical Essays on Jonathan Edwards*, ed. William Scheik, 136–50. Boston: G. K. Hall, 1980.

Downame, George. *Commentarii in P. Rami Dialecticum.* 1605. Reprint. Frankfurt, 1610.

Edwards, Jonathan. *Images or Shadows of Divine Things* Ed. Perry Miller. New Haven: Yale University Press, 1948.

Elwood, Douglas J. *The Philosophical Theology of Jonathan Edwards.* New York: Columbia University Press, 1960.

Erdt, Terence. "The Calvinist Psychology of the Heart and the 'Sense' of Jonathan Edwards." *Early American Literature* 13 (1978): 165–80.

Faust, Clarence H., and Thomas H. Johnson, eds. *Jonathan Edwards: Representative Selections.* American Century Series. New York: Hill and Wang, 1962.

Ferm, Vergilius, ed. *Puritan Sage: Collected Writings of Jonathan Edwards.* New York: Library Publishers, 1953.

Fiering, Norman. *Jonathan Edwards's Moral Thought and Its British Context.* Chapel Hill: University. of North Carolina Press, 1981.

Flavel, John. *Husbandry Spiritualized or the Heavenly Use of Spiritual Things.* London, 1669.

Gay, Peter. *A Loss of Mastery: Puritan Historians in Colonial America.* Berkeley: University of California Press, 1966.

Goodwin, Thomas. *Works.* Vol. 4. London, 1649.

Haroutunian, Joseph. *Piety versus Moralism: The Passing of the New England Theology.* 1932. Reprinted. New York: Harper and Row, Harper Torchbooks, 1970.

Heidegger, Martin. *Nietzsche.* Trans. Frank A. Capuzzi. Vol. 4. San Francisco: Harper and Row, 1982.

Hickman, Edward, rev. and cor. *The Works of Jonathan Edwards.* 2 vols. London, 1835. Reprint. Edinburgh and Carlisle, Pa.: Banner of Truth Trust, 1979.

Hollingsworth, Richard. *Holy Ghost on the Bench.* London, 1656.

Hooker, Thomas. *A Survey of the Summe of Church-Discipline.* London, 1648.

Hoopes, James. "Calvinism and Consciousness from Edwards to Beecher." In *Jonathan Edwards and the American Experience*, ed. Nathan O. Hatch and

Harry S. Stout, 205–25. New York and Oxford: Oxford University Press, 1988.

Hoopes, James. *Consciousness in New England: From Puritanism and Ideas to Psychoanalysis and Semiotic.* Baltimore and London: John Hopkins University Press, 1989.

Johnson, Barbara. "The Frame of Reference: Poe, Lacan, Derrida." In *Contemporary Literary Criticism: Literary and Cultural Studies,* ed. Robert Con Davis and Ronald Schleifer, 322–50. 2d ed. New York and London: Longman, 1989.

Kimnach, Wilson H. "The Brazen Trumpet: Jonathan Edwards's Conception of the Sermon." In *Critical Essays on Jonathan Edwards,* ed. William J. Scheick, 277–86. Boston: G. K. Hall, 1980.

Kimnach, Wilson H. "The Literary Techniques of Jonathan Edwards." Ph. D. diss. University. of Pennsylvania, 1971.

Laurence, David. "Jonathan Edwards, Solomon Stoddard, and he Preparationist Model of Conversion." *Harvard Theological Review* 72 (1979): 267–83.

Locke, John. *An Essay Concerning Human Understanding.* Oxford: Oxford University Press, 1990.

Lyttle, David. "Jonathan Edwards on Personal Identity." *Early American Literature* 7 (1972): 163–71.

Marshall, David. *The Surprising Effects of Sympathy: Marivaux, Diderot, Rousseau, and Mary Shelley.* Chicago and London: University of Chicago Press, 1988.

Mather, Cotton. *Magnalia Christi Americana.* Trans. Lucius Robinson. 2 Vols. Hartford: Silus Andrus, 1855.

Mather, Samuel. *Figures and Types of the Old Testament.* London, 1648.

Miller, Perry. "Edwards, Locke, and the Rhetoric of Sensation." In *Critical Essays on Jonathan Edwards,* ed. William Scheick, 120–35. Boston, G.K. Hall, 1980.

Miller, Perry. *Errand Into the Wilderness.* Cambridge: Belknap Press, Harvard University Press, 1956.

Miller, Perry. *Jonathan Edwards.* American Men of Letters Series. New York: William Sloane Associates, 1949.

Miller, Perry. "Jonathan Edwards on the Sense of the Heart." *Harvard Theological Review* 41 (1948): 123–45.

Miller, Perry, and John E. Smith, gen. eds. *The Works of Jonathan Edwards.* New Haven and London: Yale University Press. Vol. 1, *Freedom of the Will,* ed. Paul Ramsey, 1957; vol. 2, *Religious Affections,* ed. John E. Smith, 1959; vol. 3, *Original Sin,* ed. Clyde A. Holbrook, 1970; vol. 4, *The Great Awakening,* ed. C. C. Goen, 1972; vol. 5, *Apocalyptic Writings,* ed. Stephen J. Stein, 1977; vol. 6, *Scientific and Philosophical Writings,* ed. Wallace E. Anderson, 1980; vol. 7, *The Life of David Brainard,* ed. Norman

Pettit, 1985; vol. 8, *Ethical Writings*, ed. Paul Ramsey, 1989; vol. 9, *A History of the Work of Redemption*, ed. John F. Wilson, 1989.

Morgan, Edmund S. *The Puritan Family: Religion and Domestic Relations in Seventeenth-Century New England.* 2nd. ed. New York: Harper and Row, Harper Torchbooks, 1966.

Morgan, Edmund S. *Visible Saints: The History of a Puritan Idea.* New York: New York University Press, 1963.

Owen, John. *Of the Divine Original.* London, 1659.

Pettit, Norman. *The Heart Prepared: Grace and Conversion in Puritan Spiritual Life.* New Haven and London: Yale University Press, 1966.

Richardson, Alexander. *The Logicians School-Master or a Comment Upon Ramus Logick. Whereunto are Added His Prelections.* London, 1657.

Richardson, Alexander. "Ethical Notes." *The Logicians School-Master*, sect. 2: 127–44. London, 1657.

Richardson, Alexander. "Rhetorical Notes." *The Logicians School-Master*, sect. 2: 29–85. London, 1657.

Scheick, William, ed. *Critical Essays on Jonathan Edwards.* Boston: G. K. Hall, 1980.

Smith, Adam. *The Theory of Moral Sentiments*, ed. D. D. Raphael and A. L. Macfie. 1979. Reprint. Indianapolis: Liberty Classics, 1982.

Stowe, Harriet Beecher. *Uncle Tom's Cabin.* Afterword by John William Ward. New York and Toronto: New American Library, 1966.

Stuart, Robert Lee. "Jonathan Edwards at Enfield: 'And Oh the Cheerfulness and Pleasantness . . .'" *American Literature* 48 (1976): 46–59.

Tompkins, Jane. *Sensational Designs: The Cultural Work of American Fiction, 1790–1860.* New York and Oxford: Oxford University Press, 1985.

Townsend, Harvey G., ed. *The Philosophy of Jonathan Edwards from His Private Notebooks.* Eugene: University of Oregon Press, 1955.

Tracy, Patricia J. *Jonathan Edwards, Pastor: Religion and Society in Eighteenth-Century Northampton.* American Century Series. New York: Hill and Wang, 1980.

Warch, Richard. *School of the Prophets: Yale College, 1701–1740.* New Haven and London: Yale University Press, 1973.

Westra, Helen. *The Minister's Task and Calling in the Sermons of Jonathan Edwards.* Studies in American Religion, vol. 17. Lewiston, N.Y.: Edwin Mellen, 1986.

Winslow, Ola Elizabeth. *Jonathan Edwards: 1703–1758.* New York: Macmillan Company, 1940.

Yarbrough, Stephen R. "The Beginning of Time: Jonathan Edwards' *Original Sin.*" In *Early American Literature and Culture: Essays Honoring Harrison Meserole*, ed. Kathryn Zabelle Derounian, 149–64. Newark: University of Delaware Press; London and Toronto: Associated University Press, 1992.

Yarbrough, Stephen R. "Jonathan Edwards on Rhetorical Authority." *Journal of the History of Ideas* 47 (1986): 395–408.

PART II
THREE SERMONS

"A Divine and Supernatural Light, Immediately Imparted to the Soul by the Spirit of God, Shown to be Both a Scriptural and Rational Doctrine"

MATT. xvi. 17.

And Jesus answered and said unto him, Blessed art thou, Simon Bar-jona: for flesh and blood hath not revealed it unto thee, but my Father which is in heaven.

CHRIST addresses these words to Peter upon occasion of his professing his faith in him as the Son of God. Our Lord was inquiring of his disciples, whom men said that he was; not that he needed to be informed, but only to introduce and give occasion to what follows. They answer, that some said he was John the Baptist, and some Elias, and others Jeremias, or one of the prophets. When they had thus given an account whom others said that he was, Christ asks them, whom they said that he was? Simon Peter, whom we find always zealous and forward, was the first to answer: he readily replied to the question, *Thou art Christ, the Son of the living God.*

Upon this occasion, Christ says as he does *to* him and *of* him in the text: in which we may observe,

1. That Peter is pronounced blessed on this account.—

Blessed art thou—"Thou art an happy man, that thou art not ignorant of this, that I *am Christ, the Son of the living God.* Thou art distinguishingly happy. Others are blinded, and have dark and deluded apprehensions, as you have now given an account, some thinking that I am Elias, and some that I am Jeremias, and some one thing, and some another; but none of them thinking right, all of them are misled. Happy art thou, that art so distinguished as to know the truth in this matter."

2. The evidence of this his happiness declared; *viz.* That God, and he *only*, had *revealed it* to him. This is an evidence of his being *blessed,*

First, As it shows how peculiarly favoured he was of God above others: *q.d.*
"How highly favoured art thou, that others, wise and great men, the scribes,
Pharisees, and rulers, and the nation in general are left in darkness, to follow
their own misguided apprehensions; and that thou shouldst be singled out, as it
were, by name, that my heavenly Father should thus set his love on *thee, Simon
Bar-jona.*—This argues thee *blessed,* that thou shouldst thus be the object of
God's distinguishing love."

Secondly, It evidences his blessedness also, as it intimates that this
knowledge is above any that *flesh* and *blood* can *reveal.* "This is such
knowledge as only my *Father which is in heaven* can give: it is too high and
excellent to be communicated by such means as other knowledge is. Thou art
blessed, that thou knowest what God alone can teach thee."

The original of this knowledge is here declared, both negatively and positively.
Positively, as God is here declared the author of it. *Negatively,* as it is declared,
that *flesh and blood* had *not revealed it.* God is the author of all knowledge and
understanding whatsoever. He is the author of all moral prudence, and all of the
skill that men have in their secular business. Thus it is said of all in Israel that
were *wise-hearted,* and skilled in embroidering, that God had *filled* them *with the
spirit of wisdom.* Exod. xxviii. 3.

God is the author of such knowledge; yet so that *flesh and blood reveals it.*
Mortal men are capable of imparting the knowledge of human arts and sciences,
and skill in temporal affairs. God is the author of such knowledge by those
means: *flesh and blood* is employed the *mediate* or *second* cause of it: he conveys
it by the power and influence of natural means. But this spiritual knowledge
spoken of in the text, is what God is the author of, none else: he *reveals it, and
flesh and blood reveals it not.* He imparts this knowledge immediately, not
making use of any intermediate natural causes, as he does in other knowledge.

What had passed in the preceding discourse naturally occasioned Christ to
observe this; because the disciples had been telling how others did not know
him, but were generally mistaken about him, divided and confounded in their
opinions of him: but Peter had declared his assured faith, that he was the *Son of
God.* Now it was natural to observe, how it was not *flesh and blood* that had
revealed it to him, but God; for if this knowledge were dependent on natural
causes or means, how came it to pass that they, a company of poor fishermen,
illiterate men, and persons of low education, attained to the knowledge of the
truth; while the Scribes and Pharisees, men of vastly higher advantages, and
greater knowledge and sagacity, in other matters, remained in ignorance? This
could be owing only to the gracious distinguishing influence and revelation of
the Spirit of God. Hence, what I would make the subject of my present
discourse, from these words, is this

DOCTRINE,

That there is such a thing as a spiritual and divine light, immediately imparted to the soul by God, of a different nature from any that is obtained by natural means—And on this subject I would,

I. Show what this divine light is.
II. How it is given immediately by God, and not obtained by natural means.
III. Show the truth of the doctrine.
And then conclude with a brief improvement.

I. I would show what this spiritual and divine light is. And in order to it would show,

First, In a few things what it is not. And here,

1. Those convictions that natural men may have of their sin and misery, is not this spiritual and divine light. Men in a natural condition may have convictions of the guilt that lies upon them, and of the anger of God, and their danger of divine vengeance. Such convictions are from the light of truth. That some sinners have a greater conviction of their guilt and misery than others, is because some have more light, or more of an apprehension of truth, than others. And this light and conviction may be from the Spirit of God; the Spirit convinces men of sin: but yet nature is much more concerned in it than in the communication of that spiritual and divine light that is spoken of in the doctrine; it is from the Spirit of God only as assisting natural principles, and not as infusing any new principles. Common grace differs from special, in that it influences only by assisting of nature; and not by imparting grace, or bestowing any thing above nature. The light that is obtained, is wholly natural, or of no superior kind to that mere nature attains to, though more of that kind be obtained than would be obtained if men were left wholly to themselves: or, in other words, common grace only assists the faculties of the soul to do that more fully which they do by nature, as natural conscience or reason will by mere nature make a man sensible of guilt, and will accuse and condemn him when he has done amiss. Conscience is a principle natural to men; and the work that it doth naturally, or of itself, is to give an apprehension of right and wrong, and to suggest to the mind the relation that there is between right and wrong and a retribution. The Spirit of God, in those convictions which unregenerate men sometimes have, assists conscience to do this work in a further degree than it would do if they were left to themselves. He helps it against those things that tend to stupify it, and obstruct its exercise. But in the renewing and sanctifying work of the Holy Ghost, those things are wrought in the soul that are above nature, and of which there is nothing of the like kind in the soul by nature; and they are caused to exist in the soul habitually, and according to such a stated constitution or law that lays such a foundation for exercises in a continued

course as is called a principle of nature. Not only are remaining principles assisted to do their work more freely and fully, but those principles are restored that were utterly destroyed by the fall; and the mind thenceforward habitually exerts those acts that the dominion of sin had made it as wholly destitute of as a dead body is of vital acts.

The Spirit of God acts in a very different manner in the one case, from what he doth in the other. He may indeed act upon the mind of a natural man, but he acts in the mind of a saint as an indwelling vital principle. He acts upon the mind of an unregenerate person as an extrinsic occasional agent; for in acting upon them, he doth not unite himself to them; for notwithstanding all his influences that they may possess, they are still sensual, having not the Spirit. Jude 19. But he unites himself with the mind of a saint, takes him for his temple, actuates and influences him as a new supernatural principle of life and action. There is this difference, that the Spirit of God, in acting in the soul of a godly man, exerts and communicates himself there in his own proper nature. Holiness is the proper nature of the Spirit of God. The Holy Spirit operates in the minds of the godly, by uniting himself to them, and living in them, and exerting his own nature in the exercise of their faculties. The Spirit of God may act upon a creature, and yet not in acting communicate himself. The Spirit of God may act upon inanimate creatures; as, *the Spirit moved upon the face of the waters,* in the beginning of the creation; so the Spirit of God may act upon the minds of men many ways, and communicate himself no more than when he acts upon an inanimate creature. For instance, he may excite thoughts in them, may assist their natural reason and understanding, or may assist other natural principles, and this without any union with the soul, but may act as it were, upon an external object. But as he acts in his holy influences and spiritual operations, he acts in a way of peculiar communication of himself; so that the subject is thence denominated spiritual.

2. This spiritual and divine light does not consist in any impression made upon the imagination. It is no impression upon the mind, as though one saw any thing with the bodily eyes. It is no imagination or idea of an outward light or glory, or any beauty of form or countenance, or a visible lustre or brightness of any object. The imagination may be strongly impressed with such things; but this is not spiritual light. Indeed when the mind has a lively discovery of spiritual things, and is greatly affected by the power of divine light, it may, and probably very commonly doth, much affect the imagination; so that impressions of an outward beauty or brightness may *accompany* those spiritual discoveries. But spiritual light is not that impression upon the imagination, but an exceedingly different thing. Natural men may have lively impressions on their imaginations; and we cannot determine but that the devil, who transforms himself into an angel of light, may cause imaginations of an outward beauty, or visible glory, and of sounds and speeches, and other such things; but these are things of a vastly inferior nature to spiritual light.

3. This spiritual light is not the suggesting of any new truths or propositions not contained in the word of God. This suggesting of new truths or doctrines to the mind, independent of any antecedent revelations of those propositions, either in word or writing, is inspiration; such as the prophets and apostles had, and such as some enthusiasts pretend to. But this spiritual light that I am speaking of, is quite a different thing from inspiration. It reveals no new doctrine, it suggests no new proposition to the mind, it teaches no new thing of God, or Christ, or another world, not taught in the Bible, but only gives a due apprehension of those things that are taught in the word of God.

4. It is not every affecting view that men have of religious things that is this spiritual and divine light. Men by mere principles of nature are capable of being affected with things that have a special relation to religion as well as other things. A person by mere nature, for instance, may be liable to be affected with the story of Jesus Christ, and the sufferings he underwent, as well as by any other tragical story. He may be the more affected with it from the interest he conceives mankind to have in it. Yea, he may be affected with it without believing it; as well as a man may be affected with what he reads in a romance, or sees acted in a stage-play. He may be affected with a lively and eloquent description of many pleasant things that attend the state of the blessed in heaven, as well as his imagination be entertained by a romantic description of the pleasantness of fairy land, or the like. And a common belief of the truth of such things, from education or otherwise, may help forward their affection. We read in Scripture of many that were greatly affected with things of a religious nature, who yet are there represented as wholly graceless, and many of them very ill men. A person therefore may have affecting views of the things of religion, and yet be very destitute of spiritual light. Flesh and blood may be the author of this: one man may give another an affecting view of divine things with but common assistance; but God alone can give a spiritual discovery of them.—But I proceed to show,

Secondly, Positively what this spiritual and divine light is.

And it may be thus described: A true sense of the divine excellency of the things revealed in the word of God, and a conviction of the truth and reality of them thence arising. This spiritual light primarily consists in the former of these, *viz.* A real sense and apprehension of the divine excellency of things revealed in the word of God. A spiritual and saving conviction of the truth and reality of these things, arises from such a sight of their divine excellency and glory; so that this conviction of their truth is an effect and natural consequence of this sight of their divine glory. There is therefore in this spiritual light,

1. A true sense of the divine and superlative excellency of the things of religion; a real sense of the excellency of God and Jesus Christ, and of the work of redemption, and the ways and works of God revealed in the gospel. There is a divine and superlative glory in these things; an excellency that is of a vastly higher kind, and more sublime nature, than in other things; a glory greatly

distinguishing them from all that is earthly and temporal. He that is spiritually enlightened truly apprehends and sees it, or has a sense of it. He does not merely rationally believe that God is glorious, but he has a sense of the gloriousness of God in his heart. There is not only a rational belief that God is holy, and that holiness is a good thing, but there is a sense of the loveliness of God's holiness. There is not only a speculatively judging that God is gracious, but a sense how amiable God is on account of the beauty of this divine attribute.

There is a twofold knowledge of good of which God has made the mind of man capable. The first, that which is merely notional; as when a person only speculatively judges that any thing is, which by the agreement of mankind, is called good or excellent, *viz*. that which is most to general advantage, and between which and a reward there is a suitableness,—and the like. And the other is, that which consists in the sense of the heart; as when the heart is sensible of pleasure and delight in the presence of the idea of it. In the former is exercised merely the speculative faculty, or the understanding, in distinction from the will or disposition of the soul. In the latter, the will, or inclination, or heart, are mainly concerned.

Thus there is a difference between having an *opinion*, that God is holy and gracious, and having a *sense* of the loveliness and beauty of that holiness and grace. There is a difference between having a rational judgment that honey is sweet, and having a sense of its sweetness. A man may have the former that knows not how honey tastes; but a man cannot have the latter unless he has an idea of the taste of honey in his mind. So there is a difference between believing a person is beautiful, and having a sense of his beauty. The former may be obtained by hearsay, but the latter only by seeing the countenance. When the heart is sensible of the beauty and amiableness of a thing, it necessarily feels pleasure in the apprehension. It is implied in a person's being heartily sensible of the loveliness of a thing, that the idea of it is pleasant to his soul; which is a far different thing from having a rational opinion that it is excellent.

2. There arises from this sense of the divine excellency of things contained in the word of God, a conviction of the truth and reality of them; and that, either indirectly or directly.

First, Indirectly, and that two ways.

1. As the prejudices of the heart, against the truth of divine things, are hereby removed; so that the mind becomes susceptive of the due force of rational arguments for their truth. The mind of man is naturally full of prejudices against divine truth. It is full of enmity against the doctrines of the gospel; which is a disadvantage to those arguments that prove their truth, and causes them to lose their force upon the mind. But when a person has discovered to him the divine excellency of Christian doctrines, this destroys the enmity, removes those prejudices, sanctifies the reason, and causes it to lie open to the force of arguments for their truth.

Hence was the different effect that Christ's miracles had to convince the disciples, from what they had to convince the scribes and Pharisees. Not that they had a stronger reason, or had their reason more improved; but their reason was sanctified, and those blinding prejudices, that the scribes and Pharisees were under, were removed by the sense they had of the excellency of Christ, and his doctrine.

2. It not only removes the hinderances of reason, but positively helps reason. It makes even the speculative notions more lively. It engages the attention of the mind, with more fixedness and intenseness to that kind of objects; which causes it to have a clearer view of them, and enables it more clearly to see their mutual relations, and occasions it to take more notice of them. The ideas themselves that otherwise are dim and obscure, are by this means impressed with the greater strength, and have a light cast upon them; so that the mind can better judge of them. As he that beholds objects on the face of the earth, when the light of the sun is cast upon them, is under greater advantage to discern them in their true forms and natural relations, than he that sees them in a dim twilight.

The mind, being sensible of the excellency of divine objects, dwells upon them with delight; and the powers of the soul are more awakened and enlivened to employ themselves in the contemplation of them, and exert themselves more fully and much more to the purpose. The beauty of the objects draws on the faculties, and draws forth their exercises; so that reason itself is under far greater advantages for its proper and free exercises, and to attain its proper end, free of darkness and delusion.—But,

Secondly, A true sense of the divine excellency of the things of God's word doth more directly and immediately convince us of their truth; and that because the excellency of these things is so superlative. There is a beauty in them so divine and God-like, that it greatly and evidently distinguishes them from things merely human, or that of which men are the inventors and authors; a glory so high and great, that when clearly seen, commands assent to their divine reality. When there is an actual and lively discovery of this beauty and excellency, it will not allow of any such thought as that it is the fruit of men's invention. This is a kind of intuitive and immediate evidence. They believe the doctrines of God's word to be divine, because they see a divine, and transcendent, and most evidently distinguishing glory in them; such a glory as, if clearly seen, does not leave room to doubt of their being of God, and not of men.

Such a conviction of the truths of religion as this, arising from a sense of their divine excellency, is included in saving faith. And this original of it, is that by which it is most essentially distinguished from that common assent, of which unregenerate men are capable.

II. I proceed now to the *second* thing proposed, *viz.* To shew how this light is immediately given by God, and not obtained by natural means. And here,

1. It is not intended that the natural faculties are not used in it. They are the subject of this light; and in such a manner, that they are not merely passive, but

active in it. God, in letting in this light into the soul, deals with man according to his nature, and makes use of his rational faculties. But yet this light is not the less immediately from God for that; the faculties are made use of as the subject, and not as the cause. As the use we make of our eyes in beholding various objects, when the sun arises, is not the cause of the light that discovers those objects to us.

2. It is not intended that outward means have no concern in this affair. It is not in this affair, as in inspiration, where new truths are suggested: for by this light is given only a due apprehension of the same truths that are revealed in the word of God; and therefore it is not given without the word. The gospel is employed in this affair. This light is the "light of the glorious gospel of Christ." 2 Cor. iv. 4. The gospel is as a glass, by which this light is conveyed to us. 1 Cor. iii. 12. "Now we see through a glass."—But,

3. When it is said that this light is given immediately by God, and not obtained by natural means, hereby is intended, that it is given by God without making use of any means that operate by their own power or natural force. God makes use of means; but it is not as mediate causes to produce this effect. There are not truly any second causes of it; but it is produced by God immediately. The word of God is no proper cause of this effect; but is made use of only to convey to the mind the subject-matter of this saving instruction: and this indeed it doth convey to us by natural force or influence. It conveys to our minds these doctrines; it is the cause of a notion of them in our heads, but not of the sense of their divine excellency in our hearts. Indeed a person cannot have spiritual light without the word. But that does not argue, that the word properly causes that light. The mind cannot see the excellency of any doctrine, unless that doctrine be first in the mind; but seeing the excellency of the doctrine may be immediately from the Spirit of God; though the conveying of the doctrine or proposition itself may be by the word. So that the notions which are the subject-matter of this light, are conveyed to the mind by the word of God; but that due sense of the heart, wherein this light formally consists, is immediately by the Spirit of God. As for instance, the notion that there is a Christ, and that Christ is holy and gracious, is conveyed to the mind by the word of God; but the sense of the excellency of Christ by reason of that holiness and grace, is nevertheless immediately the work of the Holy Spirit.—I come now,

III. To show the truth of the doctrine; that is, to show that there is such a thing as that spiritual light that has been described, thus immediately let into the mind by God. And here I would show briefly, that this doctrine is both *scriptural* and *rational*.

First, It is scriptural. My text is not only full to the purpose, but it is a doctrine with which the Scripture abounds. We are there abundantly taught, that the saints differ from the ungodly in this, that they have the knowledge of God, and a sight of God, and of Jesus Christ. I shall mention but few texts out of many: 1 John iii.6. "Whosoever sinneth, hath not seen him, nor known him."

3 John 11. "He that doth good, is of God: but he that doth evil, hath not seen God." John xiv. 19. "The world seeth me no more; but ye see me." John xvii. 3. "And this is eternal life, that they might know thee, the only true God, and Jesus Christ whom thou hast sent." This knowledge, or sight of God and Christ, cannot be a mere speculative knowledge; because it is spoken of as that wherein they differ from the ungodly. And by these scriptures, it must not only be a different knowledge in degree and circumstances, and different in its effects; but it must be entirely different in nature and kind.

And this light and knowledge is always spoken of as immediately given of God; Matt. xi. 25–27. "At that time Jesus answered and said, I thank thee, O Father, Lord of heaven and earth, because thou hast hid these things from the wise and prudent, and hast revealed them unto babes. Even so, Father, for so it seemed good in thy sight. All things are delivered unto me of my Father: and no man knoweth the Father, save the Son, and he to whomsoever the Son will reveal him." Here this effect is ascribed exclusively to the arbitrary operation and gift of God bestowing this knowledge on whom he will, and distinguishing those with it who have the least natural advantage or means for knowledge, even babes, when it is denied to the wise and prudent. And imparting this knowledge is here appropriated to the Son of God, as his sole prerogative. And again, 2 Cor. iv. 6. "For God who commanded the light to shine out of darkness, hath shined it in our hearts, to give the light of the knowledge of the glory of God, in the face of Jesus Christ." This plainly shows, that there is a discovery of the divine superlative glory and excellency of God and Christ, peculiar to the saints; and also, that it is as immediately from God, as light from the sun: and that it is the immediate effect of his power and will. For it is compared to God's creating the light by his powerful word in the beginning of the creation; and is said to be by the Spirit of the Lord, in the 18th verse of the preceding chapter. God is spoken of as giving the knowledge of Christ in conversion, as of what before was hidden and unseen, Gal. i. 15, 16. "But when it pleased God, who separated me from my mother's womb, and called me by his grace, to reveal his Son in me."—The scripture also speaks plainly of such a knowledge of the word of God, as has been described, as the immediate gift of God; Ps. cxix. 18. "Open thou mine eyes, that I may behold wondrous things out of thy law." What could the psalmist mean, when he begged of God to open his eyes? Was he ever blind? Might he not have resort to the law and see every word and sentence in it when he pleased? And what could he mean by those wondrous things? Were they the wonderful stories of the creation, and deluge, and Israel's passing through the Red sea, and the like? Were not his eyes open to read these strange things when he would? Doubtless by wondrous things in God's law, he had respect to those distinguishing and wonderful excellencies, and marvellous manifestations of the divine perfections and glory, contained in the commands and doctrines of the word, and those works and counsels of God that were there revealed. So the Scripture speaks of a knowledge of God's dispensation, and covenant of mercy and way of grace towards his people, as peculiar to the saints, and given only by God, Ps. xxv. 14. "The secret of the Lord is with them that fear him; and he will show them his covenant."

And that a true saving belief of the truth of religion is that which arises from such a discovery is also, what the Scripture teaches. As John vi. 40. "And this is the will of him that sent me, that every one who seeth the Son, and believeth on him, may have everlasting life;" where it is plain that a true faith is what arises from a spiritual sight of Christ. And John xvii. 6, 7, 8. "I have manifested thy name unto the men which thou gavest me out of the world.— Now they have known that all things whatsoever thou hast given me, are of thee. For I have given unto them the words which thou gavest me, and they have received them, and have known surely that I came out from thee, and they have believed that thou didst send me;" where Christ's manifesting God's name to the disciples, or giving them the knowledge of God, was that whereby they knew that Christ's doctrine was of God, and Christ himself proceeded from him, and was sent by him. Again, John xii. 44, 45, 46. "Jesus cried and said, He that believeth on me, believeth not on me, but on him that sent me. And he that seeth me, seeth him that sent me. I am come a light into the world, that whosoever believeth on me, should not abide in darkness." There believing in Christ, and spiritually seeing him, are parallel.

Christ condemns the Jews, that they did not know that he was the Messiah, and that his doctrine was true, from an inward distinguishing taste and relish of what was divine, in Luke xii. 56, 57. He having there blamed the Jews, that though they could discern the face of the sky and of the earth, and signs of the weather, that they could not discern those times—or as it is expressed in Matthew, the signs of those times—adds, "yea, and why even of your own selves, judge ye not what is right?" *i.e.* without extrinsic signs. Why have ye not that sense of true excellency, whereby ye may distinguish that which is holy and divine? Why have ye not that savour of the things of God, by which you may see the distinguishing glory, and evident divinity, of me and my doctrine?

The apostle Peter mentions it as what gave him and his companions good and well-grounded assurance of the truth of the gospel, that they had seen the divine glory of Christ.—2 Pet. i. 16. "For we have not followed cunningly devised fables, when we made known unto you the power and coming of our Lord Jesus Christ, but we were eye-witnesses of his majesty." The apostle has respect to that visible glory of Christ which they saw in his transfiguration: that glory was so divine, having such an ineffable appearance and semblance of divine holiness, majesty, and grace, that it evidently denoted him to be a divine person. But if a sight of Christ's outward glory might give a rational assurance of his divinity, why may not an apprehension of his spiritual glory do so too? Doubtless Christ's spiritual glory is itself as distinguishing, and as plainly shows his divinity, as his outward glory,—nay, a great deal more: for his spiritual glory is that wherein his divinity consists: and the outward glory of his transfiguration showed him to be divine, only as it was a remarkable image or representation of that spiritual glory. Doubtless, therefore, he that has had a clear sight of the spiritual glory of Christ, may say, I have not followed cunningly devised fables, but have been an eye-witness of his majesty, upon as good grounds as the apostle, when he had respect to the outward glory of Christ that he had seen. But this brings me to what was proposed next, *viz.* to show that,

Secondly, This doctrine is rational.

1. It is rational to suppose, that there is really such an excellency in divine things—so transcendent and exceedingly different from what is in other things—that, if it were seen, would most evidently distinguish them. We cannot rationally doubt but that things divine, which appertain to the Supreme Being, are vastly different from things that are human; that there is a high, glorious, and God-like excellency in them, that does most remarkably difference them from the things that are of men; insomuch that if the difference were but seen, it would have a convincing, satisfying influence upon any one, that they are divine. What reason can be offered against it? unless we would argue, that God is not remarkably distinguished in glory from men.

If Christ should now appear to any one as he did on the mount at his transfiguration; or if he should appear to the world in his heavenly glory, as he will do at the day of judgment; without doubt, his glory and majesty would be such as would satisfy every one, that he was a divine person, and that his religion was true: and it would be a most reasonable and well-grounded conviction too. And why may there not be that stamp of divinity, or divine glory, on the word of God, on the scheme and doctrine of the gospel, that may be in like manner distinguishing and as rationally convincing, provided it be but seen? It is rational to suppose, that when God speaks to the world, there should be something in his word vastly different from men's word. Supposing that God never had spoken to the world, but we had notice that he was about to reveal himself from heaven, and speak to us immediately himself, or that he should give us a book of his own inditing; after what manner should we expect that he would speak? Would it be rational to suppose, that his speech would be exceeding different from men's speech, that there should be such an excellency and sublimity in his word, such a stamp of wisdom, holiness, majesty, and other divine perfections, that the word of men, yea of the wisest of men, should appear mean and base in comparison of it? Doubtless it would be thought rational to expect this, and unreasonable to think otherwise. When a wise man speaks in the exercise of his wisdom, there is something in every thing he says, that is very distinguishable from the talk of a little child. So, without doubt, and much more, is the speech of God to be distinguished from that of the wisest of men; agreeable to Jer. xxiii. 28, 29. God having there been reproving the false prophets that prophesied in his name, and pretended that what they spake was his word, when indeed it was their own word, says, "The prophet that hath a dream, let him tell a dream; and he that hath my word, let him speak my word faithfully: what is the chaff to the wheat? saith the Lord. Is not my word like as a fire? saith the Lord: and like a hammer that breaketh the rock in pieces?"

2. If there be such a distinguishing excellency in divine things; it is rational to suppose that there may be such a thing as seeing it. What should hinder but that it may be seen? It is no argument, that there is no such distinguishing excellency, or that it cannot be seen, because some do not see it, though they may be discerning men in temporal matters. It is not rational to suppose, if there be any such excellency in divine things, that wicked men should see it. Is it rational to suppose, that those whose minds are full of spiritual pollution, and under the power of filthy lusts, should have any relish or sense of divine beauty or excellency; or that their minds should be susceptive of that light that is in its own nature so pure and heavenly? It need not seem at all strange, that sin should so blind the mind, seeing that men's particular natural tempers and dispositions will so much blind them in secular matters; as when men's natural temper is melancholy, jealous, fearful, proud, or the like.

3. It is rational to suppose, that this knowledge should be given immediately by God, and not be obtained by natural means. Upon what account should it seem unreasonable, that there should be any immediate communication between God and the creature? It is strange that men should make any matter of difficulty of it. Why should not he that made all things, still have something immediately to do with things that he has made? Where lies the great difficulty, if we own the being of a God, and that he created all things out of nothing, of allowing some immediate influence of God on the creation still? And if it be reasonable to suppose it with respect to any part of the creation, it is especially so with respect to reasonable intelligent creatures; who are next to God in the gradation of the different orders of beings, and whose business is most immediately with God; and reason teaches that man was made to serve and glorify his Creator. And if it be rational to suppose that God immediately communicates himself to man in any affair, it is in this. It is rational to suppose that God would reserve that knowledge and wisdom, which is of such a divine and excellent nature, to be bestowed immediately by himself; and that it should not be left in the power of second causes. Spiritual wisdom and grace is the highest and most excellent gift that ever God bestows on any creature: in this the highest excellency and perfection of a rational creature consists. It is also immensely the most important of all divine gifts: it is that wherein man's happiness consists, and on which his everlasting welfare depends. How rational is it to suppose that God, however he has left lower gifts to second causes, and in some sort in their power, yet should reserve this most excellent, divine, and important of all divine communications, in his own hands, to be bestowed immediately by himself, as a thing too great for second causes to be concerned in. It is rational to suppose, that this blessing should be immediately from God, for there is no gift or benefit that is in itself so nearly related to the divine nature. Nothing which the creature receives is so much a participation of the Deity: it is a kind of emanation of

God's beauty, and is related to God as the light is to the sun. It is therefore congruous and fit, that when it is given of God, it should be immediately from himself, and by himself, according to his own sovereign will.

It is rational to suppose, that it should be beyond man's power to obtain this light by the mere strength of natural reason; for it is not a thing that belongs to reason, to see the beauty and loveliness of spiritual things; it is not a speculative thing, but depends on the sense of the heart. Reason indeed is necessary in order to it, as it is by reason only that we are become the subjects of the means of it; which means I have already shown to be necessary in order to it, though they have no proper causal influence in the affair. It is by reason that we become possessed of a notion of those doctrines that are the subject-matter of this divine light, or knowledge; and reason may many ways be indirectly and remotely an advantage to it. Reason has also to do in the acts that are immediately consequent on this discovery: for seeing the truth of religion from hence, is by reason; though it be but by one step, and the inference be immediate. So reason has to do in that accepting of and trusting in Christ, *that* is consequent on it. But if we take *reason* strictly—,not for the faculty of mental perception in general, but for ratiocination, or a power of inferring by arguments—the perceiving of spiritual beauty and excellency no more belongs to reason, than it belongs to the sense of feeling to perceive colours, or to the power of seeing to perceive the sweetness of food. It is out of reason's province to perceive the beauty or loveliness of anything: such a perception does not belong to that faculty. Reason's work is to perceive truth and not excellency. It is not ratiocination that gives men the perception of the beauty and amiableness of a countenance, though it may be many ways indirectly an advantage to it; yet it is no more reason that immediately perceives it, than it is reason that perceives the sweetness of honey: it depends on the sense of the heart.—Reason may determine that a countenance is beautiful to others, it may determine that honey is sweet to others; but it will never give me a perception of its sweetness.

I will conclude with a very brief improvement of what has been said.

First, This doctrine may lead us to reflect on the goodness of God, that has so ordered it, that a saving evidence of the truth of the gospel is such, as is attainable by persons of mean capacities and advantages, as well as those that are of the greatest parts and learning. If the evidence of the gospel depended only on history, and such reasonings as learned men only are capable of, it would be above the reach of far the greatest part of mankind. But persons with an ordinary degree of knowledge are capable, without a long and subtile train of reasoning, to see the divine excellency of the things of religion: they are capable of being taught by the Spirit of God, as well as learned men. The evidence that is this way obtained, is vastly better and more satisfying, than all that can be obtained by the arguing of those that are most learned, and greatest masters of reason. And babes are as capable of knowing these things, as the wise and prudent; and they are often hid from these when they are revealed to those. 1 Cor. i. 26, 27.

For ye see your calling, brethren, how that not many wise men after the flesh, not many mighty, not many noble, are called. But God hath chosen the foolish things of the world—."

Secondly, This doctrine may well put us upon examining ourselves, whether we have ever had this divine light let into our souls. If there be such a thing, doubtless it is of great importance whether we have thus been taught by the Spirit of God; whether the light of the glorious gospel of Christ, who is the image of God, hath shined unto us, giving us the light of the knowledge of the glory of God in the face of Jesus Christ; whether we have seen the Son, and believed on him, or have that faith of gospel-doctrines which arises from a spiritual sight of Christ.

Thirdly, All may hence be exhorted, earnestly to seek this spiritual light. To influence and move to it, the following things may be considered.

1. This is the most excellent and divine wisdom that any creature is capable of. It is more excellent than any human learning; it is far more excellent than all the knowledge of the greatest philosophers or statesmen. Yea, the least glimpse of the glory of God in the face of Christ doth more exalt and ennoble the soul, than all the knowledge of those that have the greatest speculative understanding in divinity without grace. This knowledge has the most noble object that can be, *viz.* the divine glory and excellency of God and Christ. The knowledge of these objects is that wherein consists the most excellent knowledge of the angels, yea, of God himself.

2. This knowledge is that which is above all others sweet and joyful. Men have a great deal of pleasure in human knowledge, in studies of natural things; but this is nothing to that joy which arises from this divine light shining into the soul. This light gives a view of those things that are immensely the most exquisitely beautiful, and capable of delighting the eye of the understanding. This spiritual light is the dawning of the light of glory in the heart. There is nothing so powerful as this to support persons in affliction, and to give the mind peace and brightness in this stormy and dark world.

3. This light is such as effectually influences the inclination, and changes the nature of the soul. It assimilates our nature to the divine nature, and changes the soul into an image of the same glory that is beheld. 2 Cor. iii. 18. "But we all with open face, beholding as in a glass the glory of the Lord, are changed into the same image, from glory to glory, even as by the Spirit of the Lord." This knowledge will wean from the world, and raise the inclination to heavenly things. It will turn the heart to God as the fountain of good, and to choose him for the only portion. This light, and this only, will bring the soul to a saving close with Christ. It conforms the heart to the gospel, mortifies its enmity and opposition against the scheme of salvation therein revealed: it causes the heart to embrace the joyful tidings, and entirely to adhere to, and acquiesce in the revelation of Christ as our Saviour: it causes the whole soul to accord and symphonize with it, admitting it with entire credit and respect, cleaving to it

with full inclination and affection; and it effectually disposes the soul to give up itself entirely to Christ.

4. This light, and this only, has its fruit in an universal holiness of life. No merely notional or speculative understanding of the doctrines of religion will ever bring to this. But this light, as it reaches the bottom of the heart, and changes the nature, so it will effectually dispose to an universal obedience. It shows God as worthy to be obeyed and served. It draws forth the heart in a sincere love to God, which is the only principle of a true, gracious, and universal obedience; and it convinces of the reality of those glorious rewards that God has promised to them that obey him.*

---

*Preached at Northampton, and published at the desire of some of the hearers, in the year 1734.

"Sinners in the Hands of an Angry God"

DEUT. XXXII. 35.

—Their foot shall slide in due time.—

In this verse is threatened the vengeance of God on the wicked unbelieving Israelites, who were God's visible people, and who lived under the means of grace; but who, notwithstanding, all God's wonderful works toward them, remained (as ver. 28.) void of counsel, having no understanding in them. Under all the cultivations of Heaven, they brought forth bitter and poisonous fruit; as in the two verses next preceding the text.—The expression I have chosen for my text, *Their foot shall slide in due time*, seems to imply the following things, relating to the punishment and destruction to which these wicked Israelites were exposed.

1. That they were always exposed to *destruction*; as one that stands or walks in slippery places is always exposed to fall. This is implied in the manner of their destruction coming upon them, being represented by their foot sliding. The same is expressed, Psalm lxxiii. 18. "Surely thou didst set them in slippery places; thou castedst them down into destruction."

2. It implies, that they were always exposed to sudden unexpected destruction. As he that walks in slippery places is every moment liable to fall, he cannot forsee one moment whether he shall stand or fall the next; and when he does fall, he falls at once without warning: which is also expressed in Psalm lxxiii. 18, 19. "Surely thou didst set them in slippery places; thou castedst them down into destruction: how are they brought into desolation as in a moment?"

3. Another thing implied is, that they are liable to fall *of themselves*, without being thrown down by the hand of another; as he that stands or walks on slippery ground needs nothing but his own weight to throw him down.

4. That the reason why they are not fallen already, and do not fall now, is only that God's appointed time is not come. For it is said that when that due time, or appointed time, comes, *their foot shall slide*. Then they shall be left to fall, as they are inclined by their own weight. God will not hold them up in these slippery places any longer, but will let them go; and then, at that very instant, they shall fall into destruction; as he that stands on such slippery declining ground, on the edge of a pit, he cannot stand alone, when he is let go he immediately falls and is lost.

The observation from the words that I would now insist upon is this.—"There is nothing that keeps wicked men at any one moment out of hell, but the mere pleasure of God"—By the *mere* pleasure of God, I mean his *sovereign* pleasure, his arbitrary will, restrained by no obligation, hindered by no manner of difficulty, any more than if nothing else but God's mere will had in the least degree, or in any respect whatsoever, any hand in the preservation of wicked men one moment.—The truth of this observation may appear by the following considerations.

1. There is no want of *power* in God to cast wicked men into hell at any moment. Men's hands cannot be strong when God rises up: the strongest have no power to resist him, nor can any deliver out of his hands.—He is not only able to cast wicked men into hell, but he can most easily do it. Sometimes an earthly prince meets with a great deal of difficulty to subdue a rebel, who has found means to fortify himself, and has made himself strong by the numbers of his followers. But it is not so with God. There is no fortress that is any defence from the power of God. Though hand join in hand, and vast multitudes of God's enemies combine and associate themselves, they are easily broken in pieces. They are as great heaps of light chaff before the whirlwind; or large quantities of dry stubble before devouring flames. We find it easy to tread on and crush a worm that we see crawling on the earth; so it is easy for us to cut or singe a slender thread that any thing hangs by: thus easy is it for God, when he pleases, to cast his enemies down to hell. What are we, that we should think to stand before him, at whose rebuke the earth trembles, and before whom the rocks are thrown down?

2. They *deserve* to be cast into hell; so that divine justice never stands in the way, it makes no objection against God's using his power at any moment to destroy them. Yea, on the contrary, justice calls aloud for an infinite punishment of their sins. Divine justice says of the tree that brings forth such grapes of Sodom, "Cut it down, why cumbereth it the ground?" Luke xiii. 7. The sword of divine justice is every moment brandished over their heads, and it is nothing but the hand of arbitrary mercy, and God's mere will, that holds it back.

3. They are already under a sentence of *condemnation* to hell. They do not only justly deserve to be cast down thither, but the sentence of the law of God, that eternal and immutable rule of righteousness that God has fixed between him

and mankind, is gone out against them, and stands against them; so that they are bound over already to hell. John iii. 18. "He that believeth not is condemned already." So that every unconverted man properly belongs to hell: that is his place; from thence he is, John viii. 23. "Ye are from beneath," and thither he is bound; it is the place that justice, and God's word, and the sentence of his unchangeable law assign to him.

4. They are now the objects of that very same *anger* and wrath of God, that is expressed in the torments of hell. And the reason why they do not go down to hell at each moment, is not because God, in whose power they are, is not then very angry with them; as he is with many miserable creatures now tormented in hell, who there feel and bear the fierceness of his wrath. Yea, God is a great deal more angry with great numbers that are now on earth; yea, doubtless with many that are now in this congregation, who it may be are at ease, than he is with many of those who are now in the flames of hell.—So that it is not because God is unmindful of their wickedness, and does not resent it, that he does not let loose his hand and cut them off. God is not altogether such a one as themselves, though they imagine him to be so. The wrath of God burns against them, their damnation does not slumber; the pit is prepared, the fire is made ready, the furnace is now hot, ready to receive them; the flames do now rage and glow. The glittering sword is whet, and held over them, and the pit hath opened its mouth under them.

5. The *devil* stands ready to fall upon them, and seize them as his own, at what moment God shall permit him. They belong to him; he has their souls in his possession, and under his dominion. The Scripture represents them as his goods, Luke xi. 12. The devils watch them; they are ever by them, at their right hand; they stand waiting for them, like greedy hungry lions that see their prey, and expect to have it, but are for the present kept back. If God should withdraw his hand, by which they are restrained, they would in one moment fly upon their poor souls. The old serpent is gaping for them; hell opens its mouth wide to receive them; and if God should permit it, they would be hastily swallowed up and lost.

6. There are in the souls of wicked men those hellish *principles* reigning, that would presently kindle and flame out into hell-fire, if it were not for God's restraints. There is laid in the very nature of carnal men, a foundation for the torments of hell. There are those corrupt principles, in reigning power in them, and in full possession of them, that are seeds of hell-fire. These principles are active and powerful, exceeding violent in their nature, and if it were not for the restraining hand of God upon them, they would soon break out, they would flame out after the same manner as the same corruptions, the same enmity, does in the hearts of damned souls, and would beget the same torments as they do in them. The souls of the wicked are in Scripture compared to the troubled sea, Isaiah. lvii. 20. For the present, God restrains their wickedness by his mighty power, as he does the raging waves of the troubled sea, saying, "Hitherto shalt

thou come, but no further;" but if God should withdraw that restraining power, it would soon carry all before it. Sin is the ruin and misery of the soul; it is destructive in its nature; and if God should leave it without restraint, there would need nothing else to make the soul perfectly miserable. The corruption of the heart of man is immoderate and boundless in its fury; and while wicked men live here, it is like fire pent up by God's restraints, whereas if it were let loose, it would set on fire the course of nature; and as the heart is now a sink of sin, so, if sin was not restrained, it would immediately turn the soul into a fiery oven, or a furnace of fire and brimstone.

7. It is no security to wicked men for one moment, that there are no visible means of death at hand. It is no security to a natural man, that he is now in health, and that he does not see which way he should now immediately go out of the world by any accident, and that there is no visible danger in any respect in his circumstances. The manifold and continual experience of the world in all ages, shows this is no evidence, that a man is not on the very brink of eternity, and that the next step will not be into another world. The unseen, unthought of ways and means of persons going suddenly out of the world are innumerable and unconceivable. Unconverted men walk over the pit of hell on a rotten covering, and there are innumerable places in this covering so weak that they will not bear their weight, and these places are not seen. The arrows of death fly unseen at noon-day; the sharpest sight cannot discern them. God has so many different unsearchable ways of taking wicked men out of the world and sending them to hell, that there is nothing to make it appear, that God had need to be at the expense of a miracle, or go out of the ordinary course of his providence, to destroy any wicked man, at any moment. All the means that there are of sinners going out of the world, are so in God's hands, and so universally and absolutely subject to his power and determination, that it does not depend at all the less on the mere will of God, whether sinners shall at any moment go to hell, than if means were never made use of, or at all concerned in the case.

8. Natural men's prudence and care to preserve their own lives, or the care of others to preserve them, do not secure them a moment. To this, divine providence and universal experience does also bear testimony. There is this clear evidence that mens' own wisdom is no security to them from death; that if it were otherwise we should see some difference between the wise and politic men of the world, and others, with regard to their liableness to early and unexpected death: but how is it in fact? Eccles. ii. 16. "How dieth the wise man? even as the fool."

9. All wicked men's pains and *contrivance* which they use to escape hell, while they continue to reject Christ, and so remain wicked men, do not secure them from hell one moment. Almost every natural man that hears of hell, flatters himself that he shall escape it; he depends upon himself for his own security; he flatters himself in what he has done, in what he is now doing, or what he intends to do. Every one lays out matters in his own mind how he shall

avoid damnation, and flatters himself that he contrives well for himself, and that his schemes will not fail. They hear indeed that there are but few saved, and that the greater part of men that have died heretofore are gone to hell; but each one imagines that he lays out matters better for his own escape than others have done. He does not intend to come to that place of torment; he says within himself, that he intends to take effectual care, and to order matters so for himself as not to fail.

But the foolish children of men miserably delude themselves in their own schemes, and in confidence in their own strength and wisdom; they trust to nothing but a shadow. The greater part of those who heretofore have lived under the same means of grace, and are now dead, are undoubtedly gone to hell; and it was not because they were not as wise as those who are now alive: it was not because they did not lay out matters as well for themselves to secure their own escape. If we could speak with them, and inquire of them, one by one, whether they expected, when alive, and when they used to hear about hell, ever to be the subjects of that misery, we, doubtless, should hear one and another reply, "No, I never intended to come here: I had laid out matters otherwise in my mind; I thought I should contrive well for myself: I thought my scheme good. I intended to take effectual care; but it came upon me unexpected: I did not look for it at that time, and in that manner; it came as a thief: Death outwitted me: God's wrath was too quick for me. Oh, my cursed foolishness! I was flattering myself, and pleasing myself with vain dreams of what I would do hereafter; and when I was saying, Peace and safety, then sudden destruction came upon me."

10. God has laid himself under *no obligation*, by any promise, to keep any natural man out of hell one moment. God certainly has made no promises either of eternal life, or of any deliverance or preservation from eternal death, but what are contained in the covenant of grace, the promises that are given in Christ, in whom all the promises are yea and amen. But surely they have no interest in the promises of the covenant of grace who are not the children of that covenant, who do not believe in any of the promises, and have no interest in the Mediator of the covenant.

So that, whatever some have imagined and pretended about promises made to natural men's earnest seeking and knocking, it is plain and manifest, that whatever pains a natural man takes in religion, whatever prayers he makes, till he believes in Christ, God is under no manner of obligation to keep him a moment from eternal destruction.

So that thus it is that natural men are held in the hand of God over the pit of hell; they have deserved the fiery pit, and are already sentenced to it; and God is dreadfully provoked, his anger is as great towards them as to those that are actually suffering the executions of the fierceness of his wrath in hell, and they have done nothing in the least to appease or abate that anger, neither is God in the least bound by any promise to hold them up one moment: the devil is waiting for them, hell is gaping for them, the flames gather and flash about them, and would fain lay hold on them, and swallow them up; the fire pent up in their own hearts is struggling to break out; and they have no interest in any Mediator, there are no means within reach that can be any security to them. In short, they have no refuge, nothing to take hold of; all that preserves them every moment is the mere arbitrary will, and uncovenanted, unobliged forbearance, of an incensed God.

APPLICATION

The use of this awful subject may be for awakening unconverted persons in this congregation. This that you have heard is the case of every one of you that are out of Christ.—That world of misery, that lake of burning brimstone, is extended abroad under you. There is the dreadful pit of the glowing flames of the wrath of God; there is hell's wide gaping mouth open; and you have nothing to stand upon, nor any thing to take hold of; there is nothing between you and hell but the air; it is only the power and mere pleasure of God that holds you up.

You probably are not sensible of this; you find you are kept out of hell, but do not see the hand of God in it; but look at other things, as the good state of your bodily constitution, your care of your own life, and the means you use for your own preservation. But indeed these things are nothing; if God should withdraw his hand, they would avail no more to keep you from falling, than the thin air to hold up a person that is suspended in it.

Your wickedness makes you as it were heavy as lead, and to tend downwards with great weight and pressure towards hell; and if God should let you go, you would immediately sink and swiftly descend and plunge into the bottomless gulf; and your healthy constitution, and your own care and prudence, and best contrivance, and all your righteousness, would have no more influence to uphold you and keep you out of hell, than a spider's web would have to stop a fallen rock. Were it not for the sovereign pleasure of God, the earth would not bear you one moment; for you are a burden to it: the creation groans with you; the creature is made subject to the bondage of your corruption, not willingly; the sun does not willingly shine upon you to give you light to serve sin and Satan; the earth does not willingly yield her increase to satisfy your lusts; nor is it willingly a stage for your wickedness to be acted upon; the air does not willingly serve you for breath to maintain the flame of life in your vitals, while you spend your life in the service of God's enemies. God's creatures are good, and were made for men to serve God with, and do not willingly subserve to any other purpose, and groan when they are abused to purposes so directly contrary to their nature and end. And the world would spew you out, were it not for the sovereign hand of him who hath subjected it in hope. There are black clouds of God's wrath now hanging directly over your heads, full of the dreadful storm, and big with thunder; and were it not for the restraining hand of God, it would immediately burst forth upon you. The sovereign pleasure of God, for the present, stays his rough wind; otherwise it would come with fury, and your destruction would come like a whirlwind, and you would be like the chaff of the summer threshing-floor.

The wrath of God is like great waters that are dammed for the present; they increase more and more, and rise higher and higher, till an outlet is given; and the longer the stream is stopped, the more rapid and mighty is its course, when once it is let loose. It is true, that judgment against your evil works has not been executed hitherto; the floods of God's vengeance have been withheld; but your guilt in the mean time is constantly increasing, and you are every day treasuring up more wrath; the waters are constantly rising, and waxing more and more mighty; and there is nothing but the mere pleasure of God, that holds the waters back, that are unwilling to be stopped, and press hard to go forward. If God should only withdraw his hand from the flood-gate, it would immediately fly open, and the fiery floods of the fierceness and wrath of God, would rush forth with inconceivable fury, and would come upon you with omnipotent power; and if your strength were ten thousand times greater than it is, yea, ten thousand times greater than the strength of the stoutest, sturdiest devil in hell, it would be nothing to withstand or endure it.

The bow of God's wrath is bent, and the arrow made ready on the string, and justice bends the arrow at your heart, and strains the bow, and it is nothing but the mere pleasure of God, and that of an angry God, without any promise or obligation at all, that keeps the arrow one moment from being made drunk with your blood. Thus all you that never passed under a great change of heart, by the mighty power of the Spirit of God upon your souls; all you that were never born again, and made new creatures, and raised from being dead in sin, to a state of new, and before altogether unexperienced, light and life, are in the hands of an angry God. However you may have reformed your life in many things, and may have had religious affections, and may keep up a form of religion in your families and closets, and in the house of God, it is nothing but his mere pleasure that keeps you from being this moment swallowed up in everlasting destruction. However unconvinced you may now be of the truth of what you hear, by and by you will be fully convinced of it. Those that are gone from being in the like circumstances with you, see that it was so with them; for destruction came suddenly upon most of them; when they expected nothing of it, and while they were saying, Peace and safety: now they see, that those things on which they depended for peace and safety, were nothing but thin air and empty shadows.

The God that holds you over the pit of hell, much as one holds a spider, or some loathsome insect, over the fire, abhors you, and is dreadfully provoked: his wrath towards you burns like fire; he looks upon you as worthy of nothing else, but to be cast into the fire; he is of purer eyes than to bear to have you in his sight; you are ten thousand times more abominable in his eyes, than the most hateful venomous serpent is in ours. You have offended him infinitely more than ever a stubborn rebel did his prince: and yet, it is nothing but his hand that holds you from falling into the fire every moment. It is to be ascribed to nothing else, that you did not go to hell the last night; that you was suffered to awake again in this world, after you closed your eyes to sleep. And there is no other reason to be given, why you have not dropped into hell since you arose in the morning, but that God's hand has held you up. There is no other reason to be given why you have not gone to hell, since you have sat here in the house of God, provoking his pure eyes by your sinful wicked manner of attending his solemn worship. Yea, there is nothing else that is to be given as a reason why you do not this very moment drop down into hell.

O sinner! Consider the fearful danger you are in: it is a great furnace of wrath, a wide and bottomless pit, full of the fire of wrath, that you are held over in the hand of that God, whose wrath is provoked and incensed as much against you, as against many of the damned in hell. You hang by a slender thread, with the flames of divine wrath flashing about it, and ready every moment to singe it, and burn it assunder; and you have no interest in any Mediator, and nothing to lay hold of to save yourself, nothing to keep off the flames of wrath, nothing of your own, nothing that you ever have done, nothing that you can do, to induce God to spare you one moment.—And consider here more particularly,

1. *Whose* wrath it is: it is the wrath of the infinite God. If it were only the wrath of man, though it were of the most potent prince, it would be comparatively little to be regarded. The wrath of kings is very much dreaded, especially of absolute monarchs, who have the possessions and lives of their subjects wholly in their power, to be disposed of at their mere will. Prov. xx 2. "The fear of a king is as the roaring of a lion: whoso provoketh him to anger, sinneth against his own soul." The subject that very much enrages the arbitrary prince, is liable to suffer the most extreme torments that human art can invent, or human power can inflict. But the greatest earthly potentates, in their greatest majesty and strength, and when clothed in their greatest terrors, are but feeble, despicable worms of the dust, in comparison of the great and almighty Creator and King of heaven and earth. It is but little that they can do, when most enraged, and when they have exerted the utmost of their fury. All the kings of the earth, before God, are as grasshoppers; they are nothing, and less than nothing: both their love and their hatred is to be despised. The wrath of the great King of kings, is as much more terrible than theirs, as his majesty is greater. Luke xii. 4, 5. "And I say unto you, my friends, Be not afraid of them that kill the body, and after that, have no more that they can do. But I will forewarn ye whom you shall fear: Fear him, which after he hath killed, hath power to cast into hell; yea, I say unto you, Fear him."

2. It is the *fierceness* of his wrath that you are exposed to. We often read of the fury of God; as in Is. lix. 18. "According to their deeds, accordingly he will repay fury to his adversaries." So Isaiah lxvi. 15. "For behold, the Lord will come with fire, and with his chariots like a whirlwind, to render his anger with

fury, and his rebuke with flames of fire." And in many other places. So, Rev. xix. 15. we read of "the wine-press of the fierceness and wrath of Almighty God." The words are exceeding terrible. If it had only been said, "the wrath of God," the words would have implied that which is infinitely dreadful: but it is "the fierceness and wrath of God." The fury of God! the fierceness of Jehovah! O how dreadful must that be! Who can utter or conceive what such expressions carry in them? But it is also "the fierceness and wrath of *Almighty* God." As though there would be a very great manifestation of his almighty power in what the fierceness of his wrath should inflict; as though omnipotence should be as it were enraged, and exerted, as men are wont to exert their strength in the fierceness of their wrath. Oh! then, what will be the consequence! What will become of the poor worm that shall suffer it! Whose hands can be strong? and whose heart can endure? To what a dreadful, inexpressible, inconceivable depth of misery must the poor creature be sunk who shall be the subject of this!

Consider this, you that are here present, that yet remain in an unregenerate state. That God will execute the fierceness of his anger, implies, that he will inflict wrath without any pity. When God beholds the ineffable extremity of your case, and sees your torment to be so vastly disproportioned to your strength, and sees how your poor soul is crushed, and sinks down, as it were, in an infinite gloom; he will have no compassion upon you, he will not forebear the executions of his wrath, or in the least lighten his hand; there shall be no moderation or mercy, nor will God then at all stay his rough wind; he will have no regard to your welfare, nor be at all careful lest you should suffer too much in any other sense, than only that you shall *not suffer beyond what strict justice requires*. Nothing shall be withheld, because it is hard for you to bear. Ezek. viii. 18. "Therefore will I also deal in fury; mine eye shall not spare, neither will I have pity; and though they cry in mine ears with a loud voice, yet I will not hear them." Now God stands ready to pity you; this is a day of mercy; you may cry now with some encouragement of obtaining mercy. But when once the day of mercy is past, your most lamentable and dolorous cries and shrieks will be in vain; you will be wholly lost and thrown away of God, as to any regard to your welfare. God will have no other use to put you to, but to suffer misery; you shall be continued in being to no other end; for you will be a vessel of wrath fitted to destruction; and there will be no other use of this vessel, but to be filled full of wrath. God will be far from pitying you when you cry to him, that it is said he will only "laugh and mock," Prov. i. 25, 26, &c.

How awful are those words, Isa. lxiii. 3, which are the words of the great God, "I will tread them in mine anger, and will trample them in my fury, and their blood shall be sprinkled upon my garments, and I will stain all my raiment." It is perhaps impossible to conceive of words that carry in them greater manifestations of these three things, *viz.* contempt, and hatred, and fierceness of indignation. If you cry to God to pity you, he will be so far from pitying you in your doleful case, or showing you the least regard or favour, that, instead of

that, he will only tread you under foot. And though he will know that you
cannot bear the weight of omnipotence treading upon you, yet he will not regard
that, but he will crush you under his feet without mercy; he will crush out your
blood, and make it fly, and it shall be sprinkled on his garments, so as to stain
all his raiment. He will not only hate you, but he will have you in the utmost
contempt; no place shall be thought fit for you, but under his feet to be trodden
down as the mire of the streets.

3. The misery you are exposed to is that which God will inflict to that end,
that he might show what that wrath of Jehovah is. God hath had it on his heart
to show to angels and men, both how excellent his love is, and also how terrible
his wrath is. Sometimes earthly kings have a mind to show how terrible their
wrath is, by the extreme punishments they would execute on those that provoke
them. Nebuchadnezzar, that mighty and haughty monarch of the Chaldean
empire, was willing to show his wrath when enraged with Shadrach, Mesech,
and Abednego; and accordingly gave order that the burning fiery furnace should
be heated seven times hotter than it was before: doubtless, it was raised to the
utmost degree of fierceness that human art could raise it. But the great God is
also willing to show his wrath, and magnify his awful majesty and mighty
power, in the extreme sufferings of his enemies. Rom. ix. 22. "What if God,
willing to show his wrath, and to make his power known, endured with much
long-suffering the vessels of wrath fitted to destruction?" And seeing this is his
design, and what he has determined, even to show how terrible the unrestrained
wrath, the fury and fierceness, of Jehovah is, he will do it to effect. There will
be something accomplished and brought to pass that will be dreadful with a
witness. When the great and angry God hath risen up and executed his awful
vengeance on the poor sinner, and the wretch is actually suffering the infinite
weight and power of his indignation, then will God call upon the whole universe
to behold that awful majesty and mighty power that is to be seen in it. Isaiah.
xxxiii. 12—14. "And the people shall be as the burnings of lime, as thorns cut
up shall they be burnt in the fire. Hear, ye that are far off, what I have done; and
ye that are near, acknowledge my might. The sinners in Zion are afraid;
fearfulness hath surprised the hypocrites," &c.

Thus it will be with you that are in an unconverted state, if you continue in it;
the infinite might, and majesty, and terribleness of the omnipotent God shall be
magnified upon you, in the ineffable strength of your torments. You shall be
tormented in the presence of the holy angels, and in the presence of the Lamb;
and when you shall be in this state of suffering, the glorious inhabitants of
heaven shall go forth and look on the awful spectacle, that they may see what
the wrath and fierceness of the Almighty is; and when they have seen it, they
will fall down and adore the great power and majesty. Isaiah lxvi. 23, 24. "And
it shall come to pass, that from one new moon to another, and from one sabbath
to another, shall all flesh come to worship before me, saith the Lord. And they
shall go forth and look upon the carcasses of the men that have transgressed

against me; for their worm shall not die, neither shall their fire be quenched, and they shall be an abhorring unto all flesh."

4. It is *everlasting* wrath. It would be dreadful to suffer this fierceness and wrath of Almighty God one moment; but you must suffer it to all eternity. There will be no end to this exquisite horrible misery. When you look forward, you shall see a long forever, a boundless duration before you, which will swallow up your thoughts, and amaze your soul; and you will absolutely despair of ever having any deliverance, any end, any mitigation, any rest at all. You will know certainly that you must wear out long ages, millions and millions of ages, in wrestling and conflicting with this almighty merciless vengeance; and then when you have so done, when so many ages have actually been spent by you in this manner, you will know that all is but a point to what remains. So that your punishment will indeed be infinite. Oh who can express what the state of a soul in such circumstances is! All that we can possibly say about it, gives but a very feeble, faint representation of it; it is inexpressible and inconceivable: for "who knows the power of God's anger?"

How dreadful is the state of those that are daily and hourly in the danger of this great wrath and infinite misery! But this is the dismal case of every soul in this congregation that has not been born again, however moral and strict, sober and religious, they may otherwise be. Oh that you would consider it, whether you be young or old! There is reason to think, that there are many in this congregation now hearing this discourse, that will actually be the subjects of this very misery to all eternity. We know not who they are, or in what seats they sit, or what thoughts they now have. It may be they are now at ease, and hear all these things without much disturbance, and are now flattering themselves that they are not the persons, promising themselves that they shall escape. If we knew that there was one person, and but one, in the whole congregation, that was to be the subject of this misery, what an awful thing would it be to think of! If we knew who it was, what an awful sight would be to see such a person! How might all the rest of the congregation lift up a lamentable and bitter cry over him! But, alas! instead of one, how many is it likely will remember this discourse in hell! And it would be a wonder, if some that are now present should not be in hell in a very short time, even before this year is out. And it would be no wonder if some persons, that now sit here, in some seats of this meeting-house, in health, quiet and secure, should be there before to-morrow morning. Those of you that finally continue in a natural condition, that shall keep out of hell longest, will be there in a little time! your damnation does not slumber; it will come swiftly, and, in all probability, very suddenly, upon many of you. You have reason to wonder that you are not already in hell. It is doubtless the case of some whom you have seen and known, that never deserved hell more than you, and that heretofore appeared as likely to have been now alive as you. Their case is past all hope; they are crying in extreme misery and perfect despair; but here you are in the land of the living, and in the house of God, and have an opportunity to obtain salvation. What would not those poor damned, hopeless souls give for one day's opportunity such as you now enjoy!

And now you have an extraordinary opportunity, a day wherein Christ has thrown the door of mercy wide open, and stands in calling, and crying with a loud voice to poor sinners; a day wherein many are flocking to him, and pressing into the kingdom of God. Many are daily coming from the east, west, north, and south; many that were very lately in the same miserable condition that you are in, are now in a happy state, with their hearts filled with love to him who has loved them, and washed them from their sins in his own blood, and rejoicing in hope of the glory of God. How awful it is to be left behind at such a day! To see so many others feasting, while you are pining and perishing! To see so many rejoicing and singing for joy of heart, while you have cause to mourn for sorrow of heart, and howl for vexation of spirit! How can you rest one moment in such a condition? Are not your souls as precious as the souls of the people at Suffield, where they are flocking from day to day to Christ?

Are there not many here who have lived long in the world, and are not to this day born again? and so are aliens from the commonwealth of Israel, and have done nothing ever since they have lived, but treasure up wrath against the day of wrath? Oh, Sirs, your case, in an especial manner, is extremely dangerous. Your guilt and hardness of heart is extremely great. Do you not see how generally persons of your years are passed over and left, in the present remarkable and wonderful dispensation of God's mercy? You had need to consider yourselves, and awake thoroughly out of sleep. You cannot bear the fierceness and wrath of the infinite God.—And you, young men and young women, will you neglect this precious season which you now enjoy, when so many others of your age are renouncing all youthful vanities, and flocking to Christ? You especially have now an extraordinary opportunity; but if you neglect it, it will soon be with you as with those persons who spent all the precious days of youth in sin, and are now come to such a dreadful pass in blindness and hardness.—And you, children, who are unconverted, do not you know that you are going down to hell, to bear the dreadful wrath of that God, who is now angry with you every day and every night? Will you be content to be the children of the devil, when so many other children in the land are converted, and are become the holy and happy children of the King of Kings?

And let every one that is yet out of Christ, and hanging over the pit of hell, whether they be old men and women, or middle aged, or young people, or little children, now hearken to the loud calls of God's word and providence. This acceptable year of the Lord, a day of such great favour to some, will doubtless be a day of as remarkable vengeance to others. Men's hearts harden, and their guilt increases apace, at such a day as this, if they neglect their souls; and never was there so great danger of such persons being given up to hardness of heart and blindness of mind. God seems now to be hastily gathering in his elect in all parts of the land; and probably the greater part of adult persons that ever shall be saved, will be brought in now in a little time, and that it will be as it was on the great out-pouring of the Spirit upon the Jews in the apostles' days, the election will obtain, and the rest will be blinded. If this should be the case with you, you will eternally curse this day, and will curse the day that ever you was born, to see such a season of the pouring out of God's Spirit, and will wish that you had died and gone to hell before you had seen it. Now undoubtedly it is, as it was in the days of John the Baptist, the axe is in an extraordinary manner laid at the root of the trees, that every tree which brings not forth good fruit, may be hewn down and cast into the fire.

Therefore, let every one that is out of Christ, now awake and fly from the wrath to come. The wrath of Almighty God is now undoubtedly hanging over a great part of this congregation: Let every one fly out of Sodom: "Haste and escape for your lives, look not behind you, escape to the mountain, lest you be consumed."*

---

*Preached at Enfield, July 8, 1741, at a time of great awakenings; and attended with remarkable impressions on many of the hearers.

"True Grace Distinguished From the Experience of Devils"

JAMES ii. 19.

Thou believest that there is one God; thou dost well: the devils also believe, and tremble.

OBSERVE in these words,—1. Something that some depended on, as an evidence of their good estate and acceptance, as the objects of God's favour, *viz.* a speculative faith, or belief of the doctrines of religion. The great doctrine of the existence of one only God is particularly mentioned; probably, because this was a doctrine wherein, especially, there was a visible and noted distinction between professing Christians and the heathens, amongst whom the Christians in those days were dispersed. And therefore, this was what many trusted in, as what recommended them to, or at least was an evidence of their interest in, the great spiritual and eternal privileges, in which real Christians were distinguished from the rest of the world.

2. How much is allowed concerning this faith, *viz.* That it is a good attainment; "Thou dost well." It was good, as it was necessary. This doctrine was one of the fundamental doctrines of Christianity; and, in some respects, above all others fundamental. It was necessary to be believed, in order to salvation. To be without the belief of this doctrine, especially in those that had such advantage to know as they had to whom the apostle wrote, would be a great sin, and what would vastly aggravate their damnation. This belief was also good, as it had a good tendency in many respects.

3. What is implicitly denied concerning it, *viz.* That it is any evidence of a person's being in a state of salvation. The whole context shows this to be the design of the apostle in the words. And it is particularly manifest, by the conclusion of the verse; which is,

4. The thing observable in the words, *viz.* The argument by which the apostle proves, that this is no sign of a state of grace, *viz.* that it is found in the devils. They believe that there is one God, and that he is a holy, sin-hating God; and that he is a God of truth, and will fulfil his threatenings, by which he has denounced future judgments, and a great increase of misery on them; and that he is an almighty God, and able to execute his threatened vengeance upon them.

Therefore, the doctrine I infer from the words to make the subject of my present discourse, is this, *viz.* Nothing in the mind of man, that is of the same nature with what the devils experience, or are the subjects of, is any sure sign of saving grace.

If there be any thing that the devils have, or find in themselves, which is an evidence of the saving grace of the Spirit of God, then the apostle's argument is not good; which is plainly this: "That which is in the devils, or which they do, is no certain evidence of grace. But the devils believe that there is one God. Therefore, thy believing that there is one God, is no sure evidence that thou art gracious." So that the whole foundation of the apostle's argument lies in that proposition:—"That which is in the devils, is no certain sign of grace."— Nevertheless, I shall mention two or three further reasons, or arguments of the truth of this doctrine.

I. The devils have no degree of holiness: and therefore those things which are nothing beyond what they are the subjects of, cannot be holy experiences.

The devil once was holy; but when he fell, he lost all his holiness, and became perfectly wicked. He is the greatest sinner, and in some sense the father of all sin. John viii. 44. "Ye are of your father the devil, and the lusts of your father ye will do: he was a murderer from the beginning, and abode not in the truth, because there was no truth in him. When he speaketh a lie, he speaketh of his own: for he is a liar, and the father of it." 1 John iii. 8. . . .

Therefore, surely, those things which the minds of devils are the subjects of, can have nothing of the nature of true holiness in them. The knowledge and understanding which they have of the things of God and religion, cannot be of the nature of divine and holy light, nor any knowledge that is merely of the same kind. No impressions made on their hearts, can be of a spiritual nature. That kind of sense which they have of divine things, however great, cannot be a holy sense. Such affections as move their hearts, however powerful, cannot be holy affections. If there be no holiness in them as they are in the devil, there can be no holiness in them as they are in man; unless something be added to them beyond what is in the devil. And if any thing be added to them, then they are not the same things; but are something beyond what devils are the subjects of; which is contrary to the supposition; for the proposition which I am upon is, that those things which are of the same nature, and nothing beyond what devils are the subjects of, cannot be holy experiences. It is not the subject that makes the affection, or experience, or quality holy; but it is the quality that makes the subject holy.

And if those qualities and experiences which the devils are the subjects of, have nothing of the nature of holiness in them, then they can be no certain signs, that persons which have them are holy or gracious. There is no certain sign of true grace, but those things which are spiritual and gracious. It is God's image that is his seal and mark, the stamp by which those that are his are known. But that which has nothing of the nature of holiness, has nothing of this image. That which is a sure sign of grace, must either be something which has the nature and essence of grace, or flows from, or some way belongs to, its essence: for that which distinguishes things one from another is the essence, or something appertaining to their essence. And therefore, that which is sometimes found wholly without the essence of holiness or grace, can be no essential, sure, or distinguishing mark of grace.

II. The devils are not only absolutely without all true holiness, but they are not so much as the subjects of any common grace.

If any should imagine, that some things may be signs of grace which are not grace itself, or which have nothing of the nature and essence of grace and holiness in them; yet, certainly they will allow, that the qualifications which are sure evidences of grace, must be things that are near akin to grace, or having some remarkable affinity with it. But the devils are not only wholly destitute of any true holiness, but they are at the greatest distance from it, and have nothing in them in any wise akin to it.

There are many in this world who are wholly destitute of saving grace, who yet have common grace. They have no true holiness, but nevertheless have something of that which is called moral virtue; and are the subjects of some degree of the common influences of the Spirit of God. It is so with those in general that live under the light of the gospel, and are not given up to judicial blindness and hardness. Yea, those that are thus given up, yet have some degree of restraining grace while they live in this world; without which the earth could not bear them, and they would in no measure be tolerable members of human society. But when any are damned, or cast into hell, as the devils are, God wholly withdraws his restraining grace, and all merciful influences of his Spirit whatsoever. They have neither saving grace nor common grace; neither the *grace* of the Spirit, nor any of the common *gifts* of the Spirit; neither true holiness, nor moral virtue of any kind. Hence arises the vast increase of the exercise of wickedness in the hearts of men when they are damned. And herein is the chief difference between the damned in hell, and unregenerate and graceless men in this world. Not that wicked men in this world have any more holiness or true virtue than the damned, or have wicked men, when they leave this world, any principles of wickedness infused into them: but when men are cast into hell, God perfectly takes away his Spirit from them, as to all its merciful common influences, and entirely withdraws from them all restraints of his Spirit and good providence.

III. It is unreasonable to suppose, that a person's being in any respect as the devil is, should be a certain sign that he is very unlike and opposite to him, and hereafter shall not have his part with him. True saints are extremely unlike and contrary to the devil, both relatively and really. They are so *relatively*. The devil is the grand rebel; the chief enemy of God and Christ; the object of God's greatest wrath; a condemned malefactor, utterly rejected and cast off by him; for ever shut out of his presence; the prisoner of his justice; an everlasting inhabitant of the infernal world. The saints, on the contrary, are the citizens of the heavenly Jerusalem; members of the family of the glorious King of heaven; the children of God; the brethren and spouse of his dear Son; heirs of God; joint-heirs with Christ; kings and priests unto God. And they are extremely different *really*. The devil, on account of this hateful nature, and those accursed dispositions which reign in him, is called Satan, the adversary, Abaddon and Apollyon, the great destroyer, the wolf, the roaring lion, the great dragon, the old serpent. The saints are represented as God's holy ones, his anointed ones, the excellent of the earth; the meek of the earth; lambs and doves; Christ's little children; having the image of God, pure in heart; God's jewels; lilies in Christ's garden; plants of paradise; stars of heaven; temples of the living God. The saints, so far as they are saints, are as diverse from the devil, as heaven is from hell; and much more contrary than light is to darkness: and the eternal state that they are appointed to, is answerably diverse and contrary.

Now, it is not reasonable to suppose, that being in any respect as Satan is, or being the subject of any of the same properties, qualifications, affections, or actions, that are in him, is any certain evidence that persons are thus exceeding different from him, and in circumstances so diverse, and appointed to an eternal state so extremely contrary in all respects. Wicked men are in Scripture called the children of the devil. Now is it reasonable to suppose, that men's being in any respect as the devil is, can be a certain sign, that they are not his children, but the children of the infinitely holy and blessed God? We are informed, that wicked men shall hereafter have their part with devils; shall be sentenced to the same everlasting fire which is prepared for the devil and his angels. Now, can a man's being like the devil in any respect be a sure token that he shall not have his part with him, but with glorious angels, and with Jesus Christ, dwelling with him, where he is, that he may behold and partake of his glory?

IMPROVEMENT

The *first* use may lie in several inferences, for our *instruction*.

I. From what has been said, it may be inferred, by parity of reason, that nothing that damned men *do*, or ever will *experience*, can be any sure sign of grace.

Damned men are like the devils, are conformed to them in nature and state. They have nothing better in them than the devils, have no higher principles in their hearts; experience nothing, and do nothing, of a more excellent kind; as they are the children and servants of the devil, and as such, shall dwell with him, and be partakers with him of the same misery. . . .

Each of the forementioned reasons, given to show the truth of the doctrine with respect to devils, holds good with respect to damned men. Damned men have no degree of holiness; and therefore those things which are nothing beyond what they have, cannot be holy experiences. Damned men are not only absolutely destitute of all true holiness, but they have not so much as any common grace. And lastly, it is unreasonable to suppose, that a person's being in any respect as the damned in hell are, should be a certain sign that they are very unlike and opposite to them, and hereafter shall not have their portion with them.

II. We may hence infer, that no degree of *speculative knowledge* of things of religion is any certain sign of saving grace. The devil, before his fall, was among those bright and glorious angels of heaven, which are represented as morning-stars, and flames of fire, that excel in strength and wisdom. And though he be now become sinful, yet his sin has not abolished the faculties of the angelic nature; as when man fell, he did not lose the faculties of the human nature.—Sin destroys spiritual principles, but not the natural faculties. It is true, sin, when in full dominion, entirely prevents the exercise of the natural faculties in holy and spiritual understanding; and lays many impediments in the way of their proper exercise in other respects. It lays the natural faculty of reason under great disadvantages, by many and strong prejudices; and in fallen men the faculties of the soul are, doubtless, greatly impeded in their exercise, through that great weakness and disorder of the corporeal organ to which it is strictly united, and which is the consequence of sin.—But there seems to be nothing in the nature of sin, or moral corruption, that has any tendency to destroy the natural capacity, or even to diminish it, properly speaking. If sin were of such a nature as necessarily to have that tendency and effect; then it might be expected, that wicked men, in a future state, where they are given up entirely to the unrestrained exercise of their corruptions and lusts, and sin is in all respects brought to its greatest perfection in them, would have the capacity of their souls greatly diminished. This we have no reason to suppose; but rather, on the contrary, that their capacities are greatly enlarged, and that their actual knowledge is vastly increased; and that even with respect to the Divine Being, and the things of religion, and the great concerns of the immortal souls of men, the eyes of wicked men are opened, when they go into another world.

The greatness of the abilities of devils may be argued, from the representation in Eph. vi. 12. "We wrestle not against flesh and blood, but against principalities, against powers," &c. The same may also be argued from what the Scripture says of Satan's subtlety. Gen. iii. 1. 2 Cor. xi. 3. Acts xiii. 10. And as the devil has a faculty of understanding of large capacity, so he is capable of a great speculative knowledge of the things of God, and the invisible and eternal world, as well as other things; and must needs actually have a great understanding of these things; as these have always been chiefly in his view; and as his circumstances, from his first existence, have been such as have tended chiefly to engage him to attend to these things. Before his fall, he was one of those angels who continually beheld the face of the Father in heaven: and sin has no tendency to destroy the memory, and therefore has no tendency to blot out of it any speculative knowledge that was formerly there.

As the devil's subtlety shows his great capacity; so the way in which his subtlety is exercised and manifested—which is principally in his artful management with respect to things of religion, his exceeding subtle representations, insinuations, reasonings, and temptations, concerning these things—demonstrates his great actual understanding of them; as, in order to be a very artful disputant in any science, though it be only to confound and deceive such as are conversant in it, a person had need to have a great and extensive acquaintance with the things which pertain to that science.

Thus the devil has undoubtedly a great degree of speculative knowledge in divinity; having been, as it were, educated in the best divinity school in the universe, viz. the heaven of heavens. He must needs have such an extensive and accurate knowledge concerning the nature and attributes of God, as we, worms of the dust, in our present state, are not capable of. And he must have a far more extensive knowledge of the works of God, as of the work of creation in particular; for he was a spectator of the creation of this visible world; he was one of those morning-stars (Job xxxviii. 4–7.) "who sang together, and of those sons of God, that shouted for joy, when God laid the foundations of the earth, and laid the measures thereof, and stretched the line upon it." And so he must have a very great knowledge of God's works of providence. He has been a spectator of the series of these works from the beginning; he has seen how God has governed the world in all ages; and he has seen the whole train of God's wonderful successive dispensations of providence towards his church, from generation to generation. And he has not been an indifferent spectator; but the great opposition between God and him, in the whole course of those dispensations, has necessarily engaged his attention in the strictest observation of them. He must have a great degree of knowledge concerning Jesus Christ as the Saviour of men, and the nature and method of the work of redemption, and the wonderful wisdom of God in this contrivance. It is that work of God wherein, above all others, God has acted in opposition to him, and in which he has chiefly set himself in opposition to God. It is with relation to this affair, that the mighty warfare has been maintained, which has been carried on between Michael and his angels, and the devil and his angels, through all ages from the beginning of the world, and especially since Christ appeared. The devil has had enough to engage his attention to the steps of divine wisdom in this work: for it is to that wisdom he has opposed his subtlety; and he has seen and found, to his great disappointment and unspeakable torment, how divine wisdom, as exercised in that work, has baffled and confounded his devices. He has a great knowledge of the things of another world; for the things of that world are in his immediate view. He has a great knowledge of heaven, for he has been an inhabitant of that world of glory: and he has a great knowledge of hell, and the nature of its misery; for he is the first inhabitant of hell; and above all the other inhabitants, has experience of its torments, and has felt them constantly, for more than fifty-seven hundred years. He must have a great knowledge of the Holy Scriptures; for it is evident, he is not hindered from knowing what is written there, by the use he made of the words of scriptures; for it is evident he is not hindered from knowing what is written there, by the use he made of the words of Scripture in his temptation of our Saviour. And if he can know, he has much opportunity to know, and must needs have a disposition to know, with the greatest exactness; that he may, to greater effect, pervert and wrest the Scripture, and prevent such an effect of the word of God on the hearts of men, as shall tend to overthrow his kingdom. He must have a great knowledge of the nature of mankind, their capacity, their dispositions, and the corruptions of their hearts; for he has had long and great observation and experience. The heart of man is what he had chiefly to do with, in his subtle devices, mighty efforts, restless and indefatigable operations and exertions of himself, from the beginning of the world. And it is evident that he has a great speculative knowledge of the nature of experimental religion, by his being able to imitate it so artfully, and in such a manner as to transform himself into an angel of light.

Therefore, it is manifest, from my text and doctrine, that no degree of speculative knowledge of religion is any certain sign of true piety. Whatever clear notions a man may have of the attributes of God, the doctrine of the Trinity, the nature of the two covenants, the economy of the persons of the Trinity, and the part which each person has in the affair of man's redemption; if he can discourse never so excellently of the offices of Christ, and the way of salvation by him, and the admirable methods of divine wisdom, and the harmony of the various attributes of God in that way; if he can talk never so clearly and exactly of the method of the justification of a sinner, and of the nature of conversion, and the operations of the Spirit of God, in applying the redemption of Christ; giving good distinctions, happily solving difficulties, and answering objections, in a manner tending greatly to enlighten the ignorant, to the edification of the church of God, and the conviction of gainsayers, and the great increase of light in the world: if he has more knowledge of this sort than hundreds of true saints of an ordinary education, and most divines; yet all is no certain evidence of any degree of saving grace in the heart. . . .

III. It may also be inferred from what has been observed, that for persons merely to yield a *speculative assent* to the doctrines of religion as true, is no certain evidence of a state of grace. My text tells us, that the devils believe; and as they believe that there is one God, so they believe the truth of the doctrines of religion in general. The devil is orthodox in his faith; he believes the true scheme of doctrine; he is no Deist, Socinian, Arian, Pelagian, or antinomian; the articles of his faith are all sound, and in them he is thoroughly established.

Therefore, for a person to believe the doctrines of Christianity merely from the force of arguments, as discerned only by speculation, is no evidence of grace.

It is probably a very rare thing for unregenerate men to have a strong persuasion of the truth of the doctrines of religion, especially such of them as are very mysterious, and much above the comprehension of reason. Yet if he be very confident of the truth of Christianity and its doctrines, and is able to argue most strongly for the proof of them, in this he goes nothing beyond the devil; who doubtless has a great knowledge of the rational arguments by which the truth of the christian religion and its several principles are evinced.

And therefore when the scripture speaks of *believing that Jesus is the Son of God,* as a sure evidence of grace, as in 1 John v. 1. and other places, it must be understood, not of a mere speculative assent, but of *another kind and manner* of believing, which is called faith of God's elect, Titus i. 1. There is a *spiritual* conviction of the truth, which is a believing with the whole heart, peculiar to true saints; of which I shall speak more particularly.

IV. It may be inferred from the doctrine which has been insisted on, that it is no certain sign of persons being savingly converted, that they have been subjects of very great *distress and terrors* of mind, through apprehensions of God's wrath, and fears of damnation.

That the devils are the subjects of great terrors, through apprehensions of God's wrath, and fears of its future effects, is implied in my text; which speaks not only of their believing, but *trembling.* It must be no small degree of terror which should make those principalities and powers, those mighty, proud, and sturdy beings, to tremble.

There are many terrors that some persons who are concerned for their salvation, are the subjects of, which are not from any proper awakenings of conscience, or apprehensions of truth, but from melancholy or frightful impressions on their imagination; or some groundless apprehensions, and the delusions and false suggestions of Satan. But if they have had never so great and long-continued terrors from real awakenings, and convictions of truth, and views of things as they are, this is no more than what is in the devils, and will be in all wicked men in another world. . . . —Therefore, if persons have been first awakened, and afterwards have had comfort and joy, it is no certain sign that their comforts are of the right hand, because they were preceded by very great terrors.

V. It may be further inferred from the doctrine, That no *work of the law* on men's hearts, in conviction of guilt, and just desert of punishment, is a sure argument that a person has been savingly converted.

Not only are no awakenings and terrors any certain evidence of this, but no mere legal work whatsoever, though carried to the utmost extent. Nothing wherein there is no grace or spiritual light, but only the mere conviction of natural conscience, and those acts and operations of the mind which are the result of this—and so are, as it were, merely forced by the clear light of conscience, without the concurrence of the heart and inclination with that light—is any certain sign of the saving grace of God, or that a person was ever savingly converted.

The evidence of this, from my text and doctrine, is demonstrative; because the devils are the subjects of these things; and all wicked men that shall finally perish, will be the subjects of the same. Natural conscience is not extinguished in the damned in hell; but, on the contrary, remains there in its greatest strength, and is brought to its most perfect exercise; most fully to do its proper office as God's vicegerent in the soul, to condemn those rebels against the King of heaven and earth, and manifest God's just wrath and vengeance, and by that means to torment them, and be as a never-dying worm within them. Wretched men find means in this world to blind the eyes and stop the mouth of this vicegerent of a sin-revenging God; but they shall not be able to do it always. In another world, the eyes and mouth of conscience will be fully opened. . . . When the King of heaven and earth comes to judgment, their consciences will be so perfectly enlightened and convinced by the all-searching Light they shall then stand in, that their mouths will be effectually stopped, as to all excuses for themselves, all pleading of their own righteousness to excuse or justify them, and all objections against the justice of their Judge, that their conscience will condemn them only, and not God.

Therefore it follows from the doctrine, That it can be no certain sign of grace, that persons have had great convictions of sin. Suppose they have had their sins of life, with their aggravations, remarkably set before them, so as greatly to affect and terrify them; and withal, have had a great sight of the wickedness of their hearts, the greatness of the sin of unbelief, and of the unexcusableness and heinousness of their most secret spiritual iniquities. Perhaps they have been convinced of the utter insufficiency of their own righteousness, and they despair of being recommended to God by it; have been convinced that they are wholly without excuse before God, and deserve damnation; and that God would be just in executing the threatened punishment upon them, though it be so dreadful. All these things will be in the ungodly at the day of judgment, when they shall stand with devils, at the left hand, and shall be doomed as accursed to everlasting fire with them. . . .

Indeed the want of a thorough sense of guilt, and desert of punishment, and conviction of the justice of God in threatening damnation, is a sign that a person never was converted, and truly brought with the whole soul to embrace Christ as a Saviour from this punishment: for it is easily demonstrable, that there is no such thing as entirely and cordially accepting an offer of a Saviour from a punishment which we think we do not deserve. But having such a conviction is no certain sign that persons have true faith, or have ever truly received Christ as their Saviour. And if persons have great comfort, joy, and confidence suddenly let into their minds, after great convictions, it is no infallible evidence that their comforts are built on a good foundation.

It is manifest, therefore, that too much stress has been laid by many persons, on a great work of the law preceding their comforts, who seem not only to have looked on such a work of the law as necessary to precede faith, but also to have esteemed it as the chief evidence of the truth and genuineness of succeeding faith and comforts. By this means it is to be feared very many have been deceived, and established in a false hope. And what is to be seen in the event of things, in multitudes of instances, confirms this. It may be safely allowed that it is not so usual for great convictions of conscience to prove abortive, and fail of a good issue, as for lesser convictions; and that more generally when the Spirit of God proceeds so far with sinners, in the work of the law, as to give them a great sight of their hearts, and of the heinousness of their spiritual iniquities; and to convince them that they are without excuse;—and that all their righteousness can do nothing to merit God's favour; but they lie justly exposed to God's eternal vengeance without mercy—a work of saving conversion follows. But we can have no warrant to say it is universally so, or to lay it down as an infallible rule, that when convictions of conscience have gone thus far, saving faith and repentance will surely follow. . . .

If he may give some degree that may finally be in vain, who shall set the bounds, and say how great the degree shall be? Who can, on sure grounds, determine, that when a sinner has so much of that conviction which the devils and damned in hell have, true faith and eternal salvation will be the certain consequence? This we may certainly determine, that, if the apostle's argument in the text be good, not any thing whatsoever that the devils have is certainly connected with such a consequence. Seeing sinners, while such, are capable of the most perfect convictions, and will have them at the day of judgment, and in hell; who shall say that God never shall cause reprobates to anticipate the future judgment and damnation in that respect? And if he does so, who shall say to him, what doest thou? or call him to account concerning his ends in so doing? . . .

And let it be considered, where is our warrant in Scripture, to make use of any legal convictions, or any method or order of successive events in a work of the law, and consequent comforts, as a sure sign of regeneration. The Scripture is abundant, in expressly mentioning evidences of grace, and of a state of favour with God, as characteristics of true saints. . . .

These were the characteristics of those that are truly happy given by our Saviour in the beginning of his sermon on the mount. These are the things that Christ mentions, as the true evidences of being his real disciples, in his last and dying discourse to his disciples, in the 14th, 15th, and 16th chapters of John, and in his intercessary prayer, chap. xvii. These are the things which the apostle Paul often speaks of as evidences of his sincerity, and sure title to a crown of glory. And these are the things he often mentions to others, in his epistles, as the proper evidences of real Christianity, a justified state, and a title to glory.

He insists on the fruits of the Spirit; love, joy, peace, long-suffering, gentleness, goodness, faith, meekness, temperance; as the proper evidences of being Christ's, and living in the Spirit: Gal. v. 22–25. It is that charity, or divine love, which is pure, peaceable, gentle, easy to be entreated, full of mercy, &c. that he insists on, as the most essential evidence of true godliness; without which, all other things are nothing. . . . If persons have such things as these apparently in them, it ought to be determined that they are truly converted, without its being first known what method the Spirit of God took to introduce these things into the soul, which oftentimes is altogether untraceable. All the works of God are in some respects unsearchable: but the Scripture often represents the works of the Spirit of God as peculiarly so: Isaiah xl. 13. "Who hath directed the Spirit of the Lord, or being his counsellor, hath taught him?" Eccles. xi. 5. "As thou knowest not what is the way of the Spirit, nor how the bones do grow in the womb of her that is with child: so thou knowest not the works of God, who maketh all." John iii. 8. "The wind bloweth where it listeth, and thou hearest the sound thereof, but canst not tell whence it cometh, and whither it goeth: so is every one that is born of the Spirit."

VI. It follows from my text and doctrine, That it is no certain sign of grace, that persons have earnest desires and longings after salvation.

The devils, doubtless, long for deliverance from the misery they suffer, and from that greater misery which they expect. If they tremble through fear of it, they must, necessarily, earnestly desire to be delivered from it. Wicked men are, in Scripture, represented as longing for the privileges of the righteous, when the door is shut, and they are shut out from among them: they come to the door, and cry, Lord, Lord, open to us. Therefore, we are not to look on all desires that are very earnest and vehement, as certain evidences of a pious heart. There are earnest desires of a religious nature, which the saints have, that are the proper breathings of a new nature, and distinguishing qualities of true saints: but there are also longings, which unregenerate men may have, which are often mistaken for marks of godliness. They think they hunger and thirst after righteousness, and have earnest desires after God and Christ, and long for heaven; when, indeed, all is to be resolved into self-love; and so is a longing which arises from no higher principles than the earnest desires of devils.

VII. It may be inferred from what has been observed, That persons who have no grace may have a great apprehension of an external glory in things heavenly and divine, and of whatsoever is external pertaining to religion.

If persons have impressed strongly on their minds ideas obtained by the external senses, whether by the ear, as any kind of sound, pleasant music, or words spoken of excellent signification; words of Scripture, suitable to their case, or adapted to the subject of their meditations: or ideas obtained by the eye, as of a visible beauty and glory, a shining light, golden streets, gates of precious stone, a most magnificent throne surrounded by angels and saints in shining ranks: or any thing external belonging to Jesus Christ, either in his humbled state, as hanging on the cross, with his crown of thorns, his wounds open, and blood trickling down; or in his glorified state, with awful majesty, or ravishing beauty and sweetness in his countenance; his face shining above the brightness of the sun, and the like: these things are no certain signs of grace. . . .

VIII. It may be inferred from the doctrine, That persons who have no grace may have a very great and affecting sense of many divine things on their hearts.

The devil has not only great speculative knowledge, but he has a sense of many divine things, which deeply affects him, and is most strongly impressed on his heart. As,

1. The devils and damned souls have a great sense of the vast importance of the things of another world. They are in the invisible world, and they see and know how great the things of that world are: their experience teaches them in the most affecting manner. They have a great sense of the worth of salvation, and the worth of immortal souls, and the vast importance of those things that concern men's eternal welfare. The parable in the latter end of the 16th chapter of Luke teaches this, in representing the rich man in hell, as entreating that Lazarus might be sent to his five brothers, to testify unto them, lest they should come to that place of torment. They who endure the torments of hell have doubtless a most lively and affecting sense of the vastness of an endless eternity, and of the comparative momentariness of this life, and the vanity of the concerns and enjoyments of time.—They are convinced effectually, that all the things of this world, even those that appear greatest and most important to the inhabitants of the earth, are despicable trifles, in comparison of the things of the eternal world. They have a great sense of the preciousness of time, and of the means of grace, and the inestimable value of the privileges which they enjoy which live under the gospel. They are fully sensible of the folly of those that go on in sin; neglect their opportunities; make light of the counsels and warnings of God; and bitterly lament their exceeding folly in their own sins, by which they have brought on themselves so great and remediless misery. When sinners, by woeful experience, know the dreadful issue of their evil way, they will mourn at the last, saying, How have I hated instruction, and my heart despised reproof, and have not obeyed the voice of my teachers, nor inclined mine ear to them that instructed me! Prov. iv. 11, 12, 13.

Therefore, however true godliness is now attended with a great sense of the importance of divine things—and it is rare that men who have no grace maintain such a sense in any steady and persevering manner—yet it is manifest those things are no certain evidences of grace. Unregenerate men may have a sense of the importance of eternity, and the vanity of time; the worth of immortal souls; the preciousness of time and the means of grace, and the folly of the way of allowed sin. They may have such a sense of those things, as may deeply affect them, and cause them to mourn for their own sins, and be much concerned for others; though it be true, they have not these things in the same manner, and in all respects from the same principles and views, as godly men have them.

2. Devils and damned men have a strong and most affecting sense of the awful greatness and majesty of God. This is greatly made manifest in the execution of divine vengeance on his enemies. . . .

It is evident, therefore, that a sense of God's terrible majesty is no certain evidence of saving grace: for we see that wicked men and devils are capable of it; yea, many wicked men in this world have actually had it. This is a manifestation which God made of himself in the sight of that wicked congregation at mount Sinai, which they saw, and with which they were deeply affected, so that all people in the camp trembled.

3. Devils and damned men have some kind of conviction and sense of all attributes of God, both natural and moral, that is strong and very affecting.

The devils know God's almighty *power*: they saw a great manifestation of it, when they saw God lay the foundation of the earth, &c. and were much affected with it. . . . So the devils have a great knowledge of the *wisdom* of God: they have had unspeakably more opportunity and occasion to observe it in the work of creation, and also in the works of providence, than any mortal man has ever had; and have been themselves the subjects of innumerable affecting manifestations of it, in God's disappointing and confounding them in their most subtle devices, in so wonderful and amazing a manner. So they see and find the infinite purity and *holiness* of the divine nature, in the most affecting manner, as this appears in his infinite hatred of sin, in what they feel of the dreadful effects of that hatred. They know already by what they suffer, and will know hereafter to a greater degree, and far more affecting manner, that such is the opposition of God's nature to sin, that it is like a consuming fire, which burns with infinite vehemence against it. They, also, will see the holiness of God, as exercised in his love to righteousness and holiness, in the glory of Christ and his church; which also will be very affecting to devils and wicked men. And the exact *justice* of God will be manifested to them in the clearest and strongest, most convincing and most affecting light, at the day of judgment; when they will also see great and affecting demonstrations of the riches of his *grace*, in the marvellous fruits of his love to the vessels of *mercy*; when they shall see them at the right hand of Christ, shining as the sun in the kingdom of their Father, and shall hear the blessed sentence pronounced upon them; and will be deeply affected with it, as seems naturally implied in Luke xiii. 28, 29. The devils know God's *truth*, and therefore they believe his threatenings, and tremble in expectation of their accomplishment. And wicked men that now doubt his truth, and dare not trust his word, will hereafter, in the most convincing, affecting manner, find his word to be true in all that he has threatened, and will see that he is faithful to his promises in the rewards of his saints. Devils and damned men know that God is eternal and unchangeable; and therefore, they despair of there ever being an end to their misery. Therefore it is manifest, that merely persons having an affecting sense of some, or even of all God's attributes, is no certain sign that they have the true grace of God in their hearts. . . . My text has reference, not only to the act of the understandings of the devils in believing, but to that affection of their hearts which accompanies the views they have; as trembling is an effect of the affection of the heart. Which shows, that if men have both the same views of understanding, and also the same affections of heart, that the devils have, it is no sign of grace.

And as to the particular degree to which these things may be carried in men in this world without grace, it appears not safe to make use of it as an infallible rule to determine men's state. I know not where we have any rule to go by, to fix the precise degree in which God by his providence, or his common influences on the mind, will excite in wicked men in this world, the same views and affections which the wicked have in another world; which, it is manifest, the former are capable of as well as the latter, having the same faculties and principles of soul; and which views and affections, it is evident, they often are actually the subjects of in some degree, some in a greater and some in a less degree. The infallible evidences of grace which are laid down in Scripture are of another kind: they are all of a holy and spiritual nature; and therefore things of that kind which a heart that is wholly carnal and corrupt cannot receive or experience, 1 Cor. ii. 14. I might also here add, that observation and experience, in very many instances, seem to confirm what Scripture and reason teaches in these things.

The *second* use may be of *self-examination*.

Let the things which have been observed put all on examining themselves, and inquiring, whether they have any better evidences of saving grace, than such as have been mentioned.

We see how the infallible Spirit of God, in the text, plainly represents the things of which the devils are the subjects, as no sure sign of grace. And we have now, in some instances, observed how far the devils and damned men go, and will go, in their experience, their knowledge of divine things, their belief of truth, their awakenings and terrors of conscience, their conviction of guilt, and of the justice of God in their eternal dreadful damnation, their longings after salvation, their sight of the external glory of Christ and heavenly things, their sense of the vast importance of the things of religion, and another world; their sense of the awful greatness and terrible majesty of God, yea, of all God's attributes. These things may well put us on serious self-examination, whether we have any thing to evidence our good estate, beyond what the devils have. . . .

Here, it may be, some will be ready to say, I have something besides all these things; what the devils have not, even love and joy.

I answer, You may have something besides the experiences of devils, and yet nothing beyond them. Though the experience be different, yet it may not be owing to any different principle, but only the different circumstances under which these principles are exercised. The principles from whence the fore-mentioned things in devils and damned men arise, are these two, natural understanding and self-love. It is from these principles of natural understanding and self-love, as exercised about their own dispositions and actions, and God as their judge, that they have natural conscience, and have such convictions of conscience as have been spoken of. . . . And that you have a kind of love, or gratitude and joy, which devils and damned men have not, may possibly not arise from any other principles in your heart different from these two, but only from these principles as exercised in different circumstances. As for instance, your being a subject of the restraining grace of God, and under circumstances of hope. The natural understanding and self-love of devils possibly might affect them in the same manner if they were in the same circumstances. If your love to God has its first source from nothing else than a supposed immediate divine witness, or any other supposed evidence, that Christ died for you in particular, and that God loves you; it springs from no higher principles than self-love; which is a principle that reigns in the hearts of devils. Self-love is sufficient, without grace, to cause men to love those that love them, or that they imagine love them, and make much of them; Luke vi. 32. "For if ye love them which love you, what thank have you? For sinners also love those that love them." And would not the hearts of devils be filled with great joy, if they, by any means, should take up a confident persuasion that God pardoned them, and was become their friend, and that they should be delivered from that wrath of which they now are in trembling expectation. If the devils go so far as you have heard, even in their circumstances, being totally cast off, and given up to unrestrained wickedness, being without hope, knowing that God is and ever will be their enemy, they suffering his wrath without mercy: how far may we reasonably suppose they might go, in imitation of grace and pious experience, if they had the same degree of knowledge, as clear views, and as strong conviction, under circumstances of hope, and offers of mercy; and being the subjects of common grace, restraining their corruptions, and assisting and exciting the natural principles of reason, conscience, &c.! Such things, or any thing like them, in the heart of a sinner in this world; at the same time that he, from some strong impression on his imagination, has suddenly, after great terrors, imbibed a confidence, that now this great God is his Friend and Father, has released him from all the misery he feared, and has promised him eternal happiness: I say, such things would, doubtless, vastly heighten his ecstasy of joy, and raise the exercise of natural gratitude, (that principle from whence sinners love those that love them,) and would occasion a great imitation of many graces in strong exercises. Is it any wonder then that multitudes under such a sort of affection are deceived? Especially when they have devils to help forward the delusion, whose great subtlety has chiefly been exercised in deceiving mankind through all past generations.

INQ. Here possibly some may be ready to inquire, If there be so many things which men may experience from no higher principles than are in the minds and hearts of devils; what are those exercises and affections that are of a higher nature, which I must find in my heart, and which I may justly look upon as sure signs of the saving grace of God's Spirit?

Ans. I answer, Those exercises and affections which are good evidences of grace, differ from all that the devils have, and all that can arise from such principles as are in their hearts, in two things, *viz.* their *foundation* and their *tendency*.

1. They differ in their *foundation,* or in that belonging to them which is the foundation of all the rest that pertains to them, *viz.* an apprehension or sense of the *supreme holy beauty* and comeliness of divine things, as they are in themselves, or in their own nature.

Of this the devils and damned in hell are, and for ever will be, entirely destitute. This the devils once had, while they stood in their integrity; but they wholly lost it when they fell. And this is the *only* thing that can be mentioned pertaining to the devil's apprehension and sense of the Divine Being, that he did lose. Nothing else belonging to the knowledge of God, can be devised, of which he is destitute. . . .

The wicked, at the day of judgment, will see every thing else in Christ, but his beauty and amiableness. There is no one quality or property of his person that can be thought of, but what will be set before them in the strongest light at that day, but only such as consist in this. . . .

Therefore in a sight or sense of this fundamentally consists the difference between the saving grace of God's Spirit, and the experiences of devils and damned souls. This is the foundation of every thing else that is distinguishing in true christian experience. This is the foundation of the faith of God's elect. This gives the mind a saving belief of the truth of divine things. It is a view of the excellency of the gospel, or sense of the divine beauty and amiableness of the scheme of doctrine there exhibited, that savingly convinces the mind that it is indeed divine or of God. This account of the matter is plainly implied; 2 Cor. iv. 3, 4. "But if our gospel be hid, it is hid to them that are lost, in whom the God of this world hath blinded the minds of them that believe not, lest the light of the glorious gospel of Christ, who is the image of God, should shine into them." And, verse 6, "For God, who commanded the light to shine out of darkness, hath shined in our hearts, to give the light of the knowledge of the glory of God in the face of Jesus Christ." It is very evident that a saving belief of the gospel, is here spoken of by the apostle as arising from a view of the divine glory or beauty of the things it exhibits. It is by this view that the soul of a true convert is enabled savingly to see the sufficiency of Christ for his salvation. He that has his eyes opened to behold the divine superlative beauty and loveliness of Jesus Christ, is convinced of his sufficiency to stand as a Mediator between him, a guilty hell-deserving wretch, and an infinitely holy God, in an exceeding different manner than ever he can be convinced by the arguments of authors or preachers, however excellent.

When he once comes to see Christ's divine loveliness, he wonders no more that he is thought worthy by God the Father to be accepted for the vilest sinner.

Now it is not difficult for him to conceive how the blood of Christ should be esteemed by God so precious as to be worthy to be accepted as a compensation for the greatest sins. The soul now properly sees the preciousness of Christ, and so does properly see and understand the very ground and reason of his acceptableness to God, and the value God sets on his blood, obedience, and intercession. This satisfies the poor guilty soul, and gives it rest, when the finest and most elaborate discourses about the sufficiency of Christ and suitableness of the way of salvation, would not do it. . . . A sight of the greatness of God in his attributes may overwhelm men, and be more than they can endure; but the enmity and opposition of the heart may remain in its full strength, and the will remain inflexible. Whereas one glimpse of the moral and spiritual glory of God, and the supreme amiableness of Jesus Christ shining into the heart, overcomes and abolishes this opposition, and inclines the soul to Christ, as it were, by an omnipotent power. So that now, not only the understanding, but the will and the whole soul, receives and embraces the Saviour. This is most certainly the discovery, which is the first internal foundation of a saving faith in Christ in the soul of the true convert, and not any immediate outward or inward witness, that Christ loves him, or that he died for him in particular, and is his Saviour; so begetting confidence and joy, and a seeming love to Christ, because he loves him. By such faith and conversion, (demonstrably vain and counterfeit,) multitudes have been deluded. The sight of the glory of God, in the face of Jesus Christ, works true supreme love to God. This is a sight of the proper foundation of supreme love to God, *viz. the supreme loveliness of his nature*; and a love to him on this ground is truly above any thing that can come from a mere principle of self-love, which is in the hearts of devils as well as men. And this begets true spiritual and holy joy in the soul, which is indeed joy in God, and glorying in him, and not rejoicing in ourselves. . . .

This *sense of divine beauty* is the first thing in the actual change made in the soul in true conversion, and is the foundation of every thing else belonging to that change; as is evident by those words of the apostle, 2 Cor. iii. 18. "But we all with open face, beholding, as in a glass, the glory of the Lord, are changed into the same image, from glory to glory, even as by the Spirit of the Lord."

2. Truly gracious affections and exercises of mind differ from such as are counterfeit, which arise from no higher principles than are in the hearts of devils, in their *tendency*; and that in these two respects.

(1.) They are of a tendency and influence very contrary to that which was especially the devil's sin, even pride. . . . False and delusive experiences evermore tend to this, though oftentimes under the disguise of great and extraordinary humility. Spiritual pride is the prevailing temper and general character of hypocrites, deluded with false discoveries and affections. . . . False experience is conceited of itself, and affected with itself. Thus he that has false humility is much affected to think how he is abased before God. He that has false love is affected, when he thinks of the greatness of his love. The very food and nourishment of false experience is to view itself, and take much notice of itself; and its very breath and life is to be some way showing itself. Whereas truly gracious views and affections are of a quite contrary tendency. They nourish no self-conceit; no exalting notion of the man's own righteousness, experience, or privileges; no high conceit of his humiliations. They incline to no ostentation, nor self-exaltation, under any disguise whatsoever. . . . The light of God's beauty, and that alone, truly shows the soul its own deformity, and effectually inclines it to exalt God and abase itself.

(2.) These gracious exercises and affections differ from the other in their tendency to destroy Satan's interest; and that in two respects:

First, in the *person himself*. They cause the soul to hate every evil and false way, and to produce universal holiness of heart and life, disposing him to make the service of God, the promotion of his glory and the good of mankind, the very business of his life: whereas those false discoveries and affections have not this effect. . . .

2. Truly gracious experiences have a tendency to destroy Satan's interest in *the world*.

When false religion, consisting in the counterfeits of the operations of the Spirit of God, and in high pretences and great appearances of inward experimental religion, prevails among a people—though for the present it may surprise many, and may be the occasion of alarming and awakening some sinners—it tends greatly to wound and weaken the cause of vital religion, and to strengthen the interest of Satan, desperately to harden the hearts of sinners, exceedingly to fill the world with prejudice against the power of godliness, to promote infidelity and licentious principles and practices, to build up and make strong the devil's kingdom in the world, more than open vice and profaneness, or professed atheism, or public persecution, and, perhaps, more than any thing else whatsoever.

But it is not so with true religion in its genuine beauty.—That, if it prevails in great power, will doubtless excite the rage of the devil, and many other enemies of religion. However, it gives great advantage to its friends, and exceedingly strengthens their cause, and tends to convince or confound enemies. True religion is a divine light in the souls of the saints; and as it shines out in the conversation before men, it tends to induce others to glorify God. There is nothing like it (as to means) to awaken the consciences of men, to convince infidels, and to stop the mouths of gainsayers. . . .

The *third* use may be of *exhortation*, to seek those distinguishing qualifications and affections of soul which neither the devil, nor any unholy being, has or can have.

How excellent is that inward virtue and religion which consists in those! Herein consists the most excellent experiences of saints and angels in heaven. Herein consists the best experience of the man Christ Jesus, whether in his humbled or glorified state. Herein consists the image of God.—Yea, this is spoken of in Scripture as a communication of something of God's own beauty and excellency. . . . Yea, by means of this divine virtue, there is a mutual indwelling of God and the saints; 1 John iv. 16. "God is love; and he that dwelleth in love, dwelleth in God, and God in him."

This qualification must render the person that has it excellent and happy indeed, and doubtless is the highest dignity and blessedness of any creature. This is the peculiar gift of God, which he bestows only on his special favourites. As to silver, gold, and diamonds, earthly crowns and kingdoms, he often throws them out to those whom he esteems as dogs and swine; but this is the peculiar blessing of his dear children.—This is what flesh and blood cannot impart. God alone can bestow it. This was the special benefit which Christ died to procure for his elect, the most excellent token of his everlasting love; the chief fruit of his great labours, and the most precious purchase of his blood.

By this, above all things, do men glorify God. By this, above all other things, do the saints shine as lights in the world, and are blessings to mankind. And this, above all things, tends to their own comfort; from hence arises that "peace which passeth all understanding," and that "joy which is unspeakable and full of glory." And this is that which will most certainly issue in the eternal salvation of those who have it. It is impossible that the soul possessing it should sink and perish. It is an immortal seed; it is eternal life begun; and therefore they that have it can never die. It is the dawning of the light of glory. It is the day-star risen in the heart, that is a sure forerunner of that sun's rising which will bring on an everlasting day. This is that water which Christ gives, which is in him that drinks it "a well of water springing up into everlasting life;" John iv. 14. It is something from heaven, of a heavenly nature, and tends to heaven. And those that have it, however they may now wander in a wilderness, or be tossed to and fro on a tempestuous ocean, shall certainly arrive in heaven at last, where this heavenly spark shall be increased and perfected, and the souls of the saints all be transformed into a bright and pure flame, and they shall shine forth as the sun in the kingdom of their Father. Amen.*

---

*Preached before the Synod of New York, convened at Newark, in New Jersey, on September 28, N.S. 1752.

Chronology

LIFE

1703	October 5, Jonathan Edwards born, at East Winsdor, Connecticut.
1715	*Of Insects.*
1716	Entered Yale College.
1720	Graduated from Yale College.
1720–22	Studied theology in New Haven.
1721	Beginning of his conversion.
1722	Went as minister to a Presbyterian church in New York City.
1723	Left the New York church.
1724	Elected to the office of tutor at Yale.
1725	Teaching career interrupted by illness.
1726	Resigned tutorship; became colleague of his grandfather, Rev. Solomon Stoddard, in Northampton, Massachusetts.
1727	Married Sarah Pierrepont.
1731	*God Glorified in the Work of Redemption.*
1734	Preached "A Divine and Supernatural Light" at Northampton.
1737	*A Faithful Narrative.*
1739	*Narrative of His Conversion.*
1738	*Charity and Its Fruits*
1741	Preached "Sinners in the Hands of an Angry God" at Enfield.
1742	*Some Thoughts Concerning the Present Revival.*
1746	*A Treatise Concerning Religious Affections.*
1747	*A Humble Attempt.*
1748	Beginning of dissension at Northampton.
1749	*An Account of the Life of . . . David Brainerd.*

1750   Preached "A Farewell Sermon" at Northampton.
1751   Settled at Stockbridge.
1752   *Misrepresentations Corrected, and Truth Vindicated.*
1752   Preached "True Grace Distinguished from the Experience of
            Devils" at the Synod of New York.
1754   *Freedom of the Will.*
1755   *Two Dissertations.*
1757   Chosen president of the College of New Jersey.
1758   January, assumed office of president.   March 22, died of
            smallpox.

WORKS PUBLISHED DURING EDWARDS' LIFETIME

1731   *God Glorified in the Work of Redemption, by the Greatness of
            Man's Dependence upon him in the Whole of it.* Boston.
1734   *A Divine and Supernatural Light, Immediately imparted to the
            Soul by the Spirit of God, Shown to be both a Scriptural and
            Rational Doctrine.* Boston.
1736   *Part of a Large Letter from the Rev. Mr. Edwards of
            Northampton giving an account of the Late Wonderful Work
            of God in those Parts.* Boston.
1737   *A Faithful Narrative of the Surprizing Work of God in the
            Conversion of Many Hundred Souls in Northampton and the
            Neighboring Towns and Villages.* Boston.
1738   *Discourses on Various Important Subjects. Nearly concerning
            the great Affair of the Soul's Eternal Salvation.* Boston.
1741   *The Distinguishing Marks of a Work of the Spirit of God.*
            Boston.
1741   *The Resort and Remedy of those that are bereaved by the Death
            of an Eminent Minister; A Sermon preached at Hatfield, Sept.
            2, 1741. Being the Day of the Interment of the Reverend Mr.
            William Williams, the aged and venerable Pastor of that
            church.* Boston.
1741   *Sinners in the Hands of an Angry God: A Sermon preached at
            Enfield, July 8th, 1741, at a Time of great Awakening.*
            Boston.
1742   *Some Thoughts Concerning the Present Revival of Religion in
            New-England.* Boston.
1743   *The Great Concern of a Watchman for Souls, In a Sermon
            Preach's at the Ordination of the Reverend Mr. Jonathan Judd,
            June 8, 1743.* Boston.

1744	*The True Excellency of a Minister of the Gospel: A Sermon preached at Pelham, Aug. 30, 1744 at the ordination of the Rev. Mr. Robert Abercrombie.* Boston.
1745	*An Expostulatory Letter from the Rev. Mr. Edwards of Northampton to the Rev. Mr. Clap, Rector of Yale-College in New-Haven.* Boston.
1745	*Copies of the Two Letters cited by Rev. Mr. Clap in his late printed Letter to a Friend in Boston.* Boston.
1746	*A Treatise Concerning Religious Affections; in Three Parts.* Boston.
1746	*The Church's Marriage to her Sons, and to her God: A Sermon Preached at the Instalment of the Rev. Mr. Samuel Buel as Pastor . . . at East-Hampton on Long-Island, September 19, 1746.* Boston.
1747	*True Saints when Absent from the Body are Present with the Lord: A Sermon Preached at the Funeral of Mr. David Brainerd.* Boston.
1748	*A Strong Rod broken and withered: A Sermon Preached at Northampton, . . . June 26, 1748, On the Death of the Honourable John Stoddard, Esq.* Boston.
1749	*An Account of the Life of the Late Reverend Mr. David Brainerd—chiefly taken from his own diary and other Private Writings, written for his own Use and now Published.* Boston.
1749	*Christ the great Example of Gospel Ministers: A Sermon Preach'd at Portsmouth, at the Ordination of the Reverend Mr. Job Strong. . . . June 29, 1749.* Boston.
1749	*An Humble Inquiry into the Rules of the Word of God, Concerning the Qualifications Requisite to a Compleat Standing and full Communion in the Visible Christian Church.* Boston.
1750	Preface to Joseph Bellamy's *True Religion Delineated.* Boston.
1751	*A Farewell-Sermon Preached at the first Precinct in Northampton After the People's publick Rejection of their Minister. . . . on June 22, 1750.* Boston.
1752	*Misrepresentations Corrected, and Truth Vindicated, In a Reply to the Rev. Mr. Solomon Williams' Book.* Boston.
1753	*True Grace Distinguished from the Experience of Devils: in a Sermon, Preached before the Synod of New-York, . . . Sept. 28, 1752.* Boston.

1754   *A Careful and Strict Enquiry into the Modern prevailing Notions
            of that Freedom of Will, which is supposed to be essential to
            Moral Agency, Vertue and Vice, Reward and Punishment,
            Praise and Blame.* Boston.

Selected Bibliography

WORKS BY JONATHAN EDWARDS

Collected Works

The Works of President Edwards. Ed. Samuel Austin. 8 vols. Worcester, Mass.: Isaiah Thomas, 1808–09.

The Works of President Edwards. Ed. Sereno Dwight. 10 vols. New York: Converse, 1829–30.

The Works of President Edwards. Ed. Samuel Austin. A reprint of the Worcester edition of 1808–09 with some additions. 4 vols. New York: Leavitt & Allen, 1843.

The Works of Jonathan Edwards. Vols. 1–2 gen. ed. Perry Miller, vol. 3– gen. ed. John E. Smith. New Haven and London: Yale University Press, 1957–.

The Works of Jonathan Edwards. Rev. and corr. Edward Hickman. 2 vols. London, 1835. Reprint. Edinburgh and Carlisle, Pa.: Banner of Truth Trust, 1979.

Additional Works

The Great Christian Doctrine of Original Sin Defended. Boston, 1758.

The Life and Character of the late Reverend and Pious Mr. Jonathan Edwards . . . together with a Number of his Sermons on Various Important Subjects. Ed. Samuel Hopkins. Boston, 1765.

Two Dissertations: I, Concerning the End for which God created the World; II, The Nature of True Virtue. Boston, 1765.

A History of the Work of Redemption, Containing the Outlines of a Body of Divinity. Edinburgh, 1774.

Sermons. Ed. Jonathan Edwards the younger. Hartford, 1780.

Christian Cautions, or, The Necessity of Self-Examination. Edinburgh, 1788.

Practical Sermons on Various Subjects. Edinburgh, 1789.

Miscellaneous Observations on Important Theological Subjects. Ed. John Erskine. Edinburgh, 1793.

Remarks on Important Theological Controversies. Edinburgh, 1796.

Practical Sermons never before published. Edinburgh, 1797.

An Unpublished Essay of Edwards on the Trinity. Ed. G. P. Fisher. New York, 1903.

Images or Shadows of Divine Things. Ed. Perry Miller. New Haven: Yale University Press, 1948.

"Notes on the Mind." In *The Philosophy of Jonathan Edwards From His Private Notebooks*, ed. Harry G. Townsend. Eugene: University of Oregon Press, 1955.

Reprinted Selections

Faust, Clarence H. and Thomas H. Johnson, eds. *Jonathan Edwards: Representative Selections.* American Century Series. New York: Hill and Wang, 1962.

Ferm, Vergilius, ed. *Puritan Sage: Collected Writings of Jonathan Edwards.* New York: Library Publishers, 1953.

Goen, C. C. *The Great Awakening.* New Haven: Yale University Press, 1972.

Simonson, Harold P., ed. *Selected Writings of Jonathan Edwards.* New York: F. Ungar, 1970.

Manuscripts

Yale Collection, Yale University Library: "Interleaved Bible"; "Miscellanies" (notebooks, 1,360 entries); Sermons. (1,150 manuscripts).

Andover Collection, Andover-Harvard Theological Seminary Library: Letters; "Miscellanies" (notebooks, a continuation of the Yale notebooks); Sermons (five sermons and about fifty sermon outlines, mostly from Stockbridge years).

Scattered Manuscript Items: Princeton University Library; Massachusetts Historical Society; American Antiquarian Society; Library of Congress; New York Public Library; Boston Athenaeum; Congregational Libraries of Boston and London.

Bibliographies

Johnson, Thomas H. *The Printed Writings of Jonathan Edwards, 1703–1758, A Bibliography.* Princeton: Princeton University Press, 1940.

Lesser, M. X. *Jonathan Edwards: A Reference Guide.* Boston: G. K. Hall, 1981.

Manspeaker, Nancy. *Jonathan Edwards: Bibliographical Synopses.* New York and Toronto: E. Mellen Press, 1981.

WORKS ON JONATHAN EDWARDS

Books

Aldridge, Alfred Owen. *Jonathan Edwards.* New York: Washington Square Press, 1964.

Allen, A.V.G. *Life and Writings of Jonathan Edwards.* Edinburgh: T. & T. Clark, 1889.

Carmody, Denise Lardner. *The Republic of Many Mansions: Foundations of American Religious Thought.* New York: Paragon House, 1990.

Cherry, Conrad. *Nature and Religious Imagination: From Edwards to Bushnell.* Philadelphia: Fortress Press, 1980.

Cherry, Conrad. *The Theology of Jonathan Edwards: A Reappraisal.* Garden City, N.Y.: Doubleday, Anchor Books, 1966.

Cohen, Charles Lloyd. *God's Caress: The Psychology of Puritan Religious Experience.* New York: Oxford University Press, 1986.

Delattre, Roland A. *Beauty and Sensibility in the Thought of Jonathan Edwards: An Essay in Aesthetics and Theological Ethics.* New Haven: Yale University Press, 1968.

De Prospo, R. C. *Theism in the Discourse of Jonathan Edwards.* Newark: University of Delaware Press; London: Associated University Presses, 1985.

Elwood, Douglas J. *The Philosophical Theology of Jonathan Edwards.* New York: Columbia University Press, 1960.

Erdt, Terence. *Jonathan Edwards, Art and the Sense of the Heart.* Amherst: University of Massachusetts Press, 1980.

Feidelson, Charles. *Symbolism and American Literature.* Chicago: University of Chicago Press, 1953.

Fiering, Norman. *Jonathan Edwards's Moral Thought and its British Context.* Chapel Hill: University of North Carolina Press, 1981.

Foster, Stephen. *The Long Argument: English Puritanism and the Shaping of New England Culture, 1570–1700.* Chapel Hill and London: University of North Carolina Press, 1991.

Gaustad, Edwin Scott. *The Great Awakening in New England*. New York: Harper, 1957.

Gay, Peter. *A Loss of Mastery: Puritan Historians in Colonial America*. Berkeley: University of California Press, 1966.

Geissler, Suzanne. *Jonathan Edwards to Aaron Burr, Jr.: From the Great Awakening to Democratic Politics*. Lewiston, N.Y.: E. Mellen Press, 1981.

Griffin, Edward M. *Jonathan Edwards*. Minneapolis: University of Minnesota Press, 1971.

Guelzo, Allen C. *Edwards on the Will: A Century of Theological Debate*. Middletown, Conn.: Wesleyan University Press, 1989.

Hall, Richard A. S. *The Neglected Northampton Texts of Jonathan Edwards: Edwards on Society and Politics*. Lewiston, N.Y.: E. Mellen Press, 1990.

Haroutunian, Joseph. *Piety versus Moralism: The Passing of the New England Theology*. 1932. Reprinted. New York: Harper and Row, Harper Torchbooks, 1970.

Hatch Nathan O., and Harry S. Stout, eds. *Jonathan Edwards and the American Experience*. New York and Oxford: Oxford University Press, 1988.

Heimert, Alan. *Religion and the American Mind: From the Great Awakening to the Revolution*. Cambridge: Harvard University Press, 1966.

Heimert, Alan, and Perry Miller, eds. *The Great Awakening: Documents Illustrating the Crisis and Its Consequences*. Indianapolis and New York: Bobbs-Merrill, 1967.

Hoopes, James. *Consciousness in New England: From Puritanism to Ideas of Psychoanalysis and Semiotic*. Baltimore and London: Johns Hopkins University Press, 1989.

Howard, Leon. *"The Mind" of Jonathan Edwards: A Reconstructed Text*. Berkeley: University of California Press, 1963.

Jensen, Robert W. *America's Theologian: A Recommendation of Jonathan Edwards*. New York: Oxford University Press, 1988.

Kuklick, Bruce. *Churchmen and Philosophers: From Jonathan Edwards to John Dewey*. New Haven: Yale University Press, 1985.

Lee, Sang Hyun. *The Philosophical Theology of Jonathan Edwards*. Princeton: Princeton University Press, 1988.

Lesser, M. X. *Jonathan Edwards*. Boston: Twayne, 1988.

Levin, David, ed. *Jonathan Edwards: A Profile*. New York: Hill & Wang, 1969.

Lewis, R. W. B. *The American Adams*. Chicago: U of Chicago Press, 1955.

McGiffert, Arthur C., Jr. *Jonathan Edwards*, New York: Harper, 1932.

Miller, Perry. *Errand Into the Wilderness*. Cambridge: Harvard University Press, Belknap Press, 1956.

Miller, Perry. *Jonathan Edwards*. New York: Meridian Books, 1959.

Miller, Perry. *Nature's Nation*. Cambridge: Harvard University Press, 1967.

Miller, Perry. *Orthodoxy in Massachusetts.* Cambridge: Harvard University Press, 1933.

Morgan, Edmund S. *The Puritan Family: Religion and Domestic Relations in Seventeenth-Century New England.* 2nd. ed. New York: Harper and Row, Harper Torchbooks, 1966.

Morgan, Edmund S. *Visible Saints: The History of a Puritan Idea.* New York: New York University Press, 1963.

Opie, John, ed. *Edwards and the Enlightenment.* Lexington, Mass.: Heath, 1969.

Pettit, Norman. *The Heart Prepared: Grace and Conversion in Puritan Spiritual Life.* New Haven and London: Yale University Press, 1966.

Pfisterer, Karl Dietrich. *The Prism of Scripture: Studies on History and Historicity in the Work of Jonathan Edwards.* Frankfurt: Herbert Lang, 1975.

Scheick, William J., ed. *Critical Essays on Jonathan Edwards.* Boston: G. K. Hall, 1980.

Scheick, William J. *The Writings of Jonathan Edwards: Theme, Motif, and Style.* College Station: Texas A & M University Press, 1975.

Schneider, Herbert W. *A History of American Philosophy.* New York: Columbia University Press, 1947.

Schneider, Herbert W. *The Puritan Mind.* Ann Arbor: University of Michigan Press, Ann Arbor Paperback, 1958.

Simonson, Harold Peter. *Jonathan Edwards, Theologian of the Heart.* 1974. Reprint. Macon, Ga.: Mercer University Press/Rose, 1982.

Stearns, Monroe. *The Great Awakening, 1720–1760.* New York: Watts, 1970.

Tracy, Patricia J. *Jonathan Edwards, Pastor: Religion and Society in Eighteenth-Century Northampton.* New York: Hill and Wang, 1980.

Warch, Richard. *School of the Prophets: Yale College, 1701–1740.* New Haven and London: Yale University Press, 1973.

White, Morton. *Document in the History of American Philosophy: From Jonathan Edwards to John Dewey.* New York: Oxford University Press, 1972.

Wilson-Kastner, Patricia. *Coherence in a Fragmented World: Jonathan Edwards' Theology of the Holy Spirit.* Washington, D.C.: University Press of America, 1978.

Winslow, Ola Elizabeth. *Jonathan Edwards: 1703–1758.* New York: Macmillan Company, 1940.

Articles

Aijian, Paul M. "The Relation of the Concepts of Being and Value in Calvinism to Jonathan Edwards." Ph.D. diss. University of Southern California, 1950.

Bushman, Richard L. "Jonathan Edwards as Great Man: Identity, Conversion and Leadership in the Great Awakening." *Soundings* 52 (1969): 15–46.

Carpenter, Frederick L. "The Radicalism of Jonathan Edwards." *New England Quarterly* 4 (1931): 629–44.

Holmes, Oliver Wendell. "Jonathan Edwards." *International Review* 9 (1880): 1–28.

Hornberger, Theodore. "The Effect of the New Science Upon the Thought of Jonathan Edwards." *American Literature* 9 (1937): 196–207.

Johnson, Thomas H. "Jonathan Edwards' Background Reading." *Colonial Society of Massachusetts Publications* 28 (1931): 193–222.

Laurence, David. "Jonathan Edwards, Solomon Stoddard, and the Preparationist Model of Conversion." *Harvard Theological Review* 72 (1979): 267–83.

Lowance, Mason I. "Images or Shadows of Divine Things: The Typology of Jonathan Edwards." *Early American Literature* 5 (1984–85): 141–81.

Lyttle, David James. "The Sixth Sense of Jonathan Edwards." *Church Quarterly Review* 167 (1966): 50–59.

MacCracken, John Henry. "The Sources of Jonathan Edwards's Idealism." *Philosophical Review* 11 (1902): 26–42.

Munk, Linda. "His Dazzling Absence: The Shekinah in Jonathan Edwards." *Early American Literature* 27 (1992): 1–30.

Nagy, Paul J. "Jonathan Edwards and the Metaphysics of Consent." *The Personalist* 51 (1970): 434–46.

Reaske, Christopher R. "The Devil and Jonathan Edwards." *Journal of the History of Ideas* 33 (1972): 123–38.

Rupp, George. "The 'Idealism' of Jonathan Edwards." *Harvard Theological Review* 62 (1969): 209–26.

Rusch, Frederick L. "Reality and the Puritan Mind: Jonathan Edwards and Ethan Frome." *Journal of Evolutionary Psychology.* 4 (1983): 238–47.

Simonson, Harold P. "Jonathan Edwards and His Scottish Connections." *Journal of American Studies* 21 (1987): 353–76.

Slater, John F. "The Sleepwalker and the Great Awakening: Brown's Edgar Huntly and Jonathan Edwards." *Papers on Language and Literature* 19 (1983): 199–217.

Sliwoski, Richard S. "Doctoral Dissertations on Jonathan Edwards." *Early American Literature* 14 (1979–80): 318–27.

Smith, Claude A. "Jonathan Edwards and 'The Way of Ideas.'" *Harvard Theological Review* 59 (1966): 153–73.

Stein, Stephen J. "Providence and the Apocalypse in the Early Writings of Jonathan Edwards." *Early American Literature* 13 (1978–79): 250–67.

Stein, Stephen J. "The Quest for the Spiritual Sense: The Biblical Hermeneutics of Jonathan Edwards." *Harvard Theological Review* 70 (1977): 99–113.

Weber, Donald. "The Figure of Jonathan Edwards." *American Quarterly* 35 (1983): 556– 64.

Westbrook, Robert B. "Social Criticism in the Heavenly City of Jonathan Edwards." *Soundings* 59(1976): 396–412.

Books and Articles on Edwardsean and Puritan Rhetoric

Adams, John C. "Alexander Richardson and the Ramist Poetics of Michael Wigglesworth." *Early American Literature* 25 (1990): 271–88.

Adams, John C. "Linguistic Values and Religious Experience: An Analysis of the Clothing Metaphors in Alexander Richardson's Ramist-Puritan Lectures on Speech." *Quarterly Journal of Speech* 75 (1990): 58–68.

Adams, John C. "Ramist Concepts of Testimony, Judicial Analogies, and the Puritan Conversion Narrative." *Rhetorica* 9 (1991): 251–68.

Anderson, Wilbert. "The Preaching Power of Jonathan Edwards." *Congregationalist and Christian World* 88 (1903): 463–66.

Baumgartner, Paul. "Jonathan Edwards: The Theory Behind His Uses of Figurative Language." *PMLA* 78 (1963): 321–25.

Bercovitch, Sacan. *The American Jeremiad.* Madison: University of Wisconsin Press, 1978.

Bercovitch, Sacan. "Colonial Puritan Rhetoric and the Discovery of American Identity." *Canadian Review of American Studies* 6 (1975): 131–50.

Bercovitch, Sacan. "Puritan New England Rhetoric and the Jewish Problem." *Early American Literature* 5 (1970): 63–73.

Bercovitch, Sacan. *Typology and Early American Literature* Amherst: University of Massachusetts Press, 1972.

Bercovitch, Sacan, and Gerald J. Kennedy, eds. *The Modernity of American Puritan Rhetoric.* Baton Rouge: Louisiana State University Press, 1987.

Blanke, Gustav. *Puritan Contributions to the Rhetoric of America's World Mission.* Frankfort: Lang, 1983.

Bormann, Ernest G. "Fetching Good Out of Evil: A Rhetorical Use of Calamity." *Quarterly Journal of Speech* 63 (1977): 130–39.

Bosco, Ronald, ed. *The Puritan Sermon in America 1630–1750.* Delmar, N.Y.: Scholars' Facsimiles and Reprints, 1978.

Buckingham, Willis J. "Stylistic Artistry in the Sermons of Jonathan Edwards." *Papers on Language and Literature* 6 (1970): 136–51.

Cady, E. H. "The Artistry of Jonathan Edwards." *New England Quarterly* 22 (1949): 61–72.

Caldwell, Patricia. *The Puritan Conversion Narrative: The Beginnings of American Expression.* Cambridge: Harvard University Press, 1983.

Cherry, Conrad. "Word and Spirit." In *The Theology of Jonathan Edwards: A Reappraisal.* Garden City, N.Y.: Doubleday, Anchor Books, 1966.

Clift, Arlene Louise. "Rhetoric and Reason-Revelation Relationship in the Writings of Jonathan Edwards. Ph.D. diss. Harvard University, 1969.

Collins, Edward M., Jr. "The Rhetoric of Sensation Challenges the Rhetoric of the Intellect: An Eighteenth-Century Controversy." In *Preaching in American History: Selected Issues in the American Pulpit, 1630–1967*, ed. De Witte Holland, 98–117. Nashville, Tenn.: Abingdon Press, 1969.

Cowan, James C. "Jonathan Edwards' Sermon Style: 'The Future Punishment of the Wicked Unavoidable and Intolerable." *South Central Bulletin* 29 (1969): 119–22.

Cowing, Cedric B. "Sex and Preaching in the Great Awakening." *American Quarterly* 20 (1968): 624–44.

Davidson, Edward H. "God's Well-Trodden Foot-Path: Puritan Preaching and Sermon Form." *Texas Studies in Literature and Language: A Journal of the Humanities* 25 (1983): 503–27.

De Prospo, R. C. "The 'New Simple Idea' of Edwards' Personal Narrative." *Early American Literature* 14 (1979–80): 193–204.

Erdt, Terence. "The Calvinist Psychology of the Heart and the 'Sense' of Jonathan Edwards." *Early American Literature* 13 (1978): 165–80.

Garrison, Joseph M. Jr. "Teaching Early American Literature: Some Suggestions." *College English* 31 (1970): 487–97.

Grazier, James Lewis. "The Preaching of Jonathan Edwards: A Study of His Published Sermons with Special Reference to the Great Awakening." Ph.D. diss. Temple University, 1957.

Gura, Philip F. "Sowing for the Harvest: William Williams and the Great Awakening." *Journal of Presbyterian History* 56 (1978): 326–41.

Haims, Lynn. "The Face of God: Puritan Iconography in Early American Poetry, Sermons, and Tombstone Carving." *Early American Literature* 14 (1979): 15–47.

Hubbard, Dolan. "David Walker's Appeal and the American Puritan Jeremiadic Tradition." *Centennial Review* 30 (1986): 331–46.

Hulme, Peter, Francis Barker, Margaret Iverson, and Diana Loxley, eds. *Polytropic Man: Tropes of Sexuality and Mobility in Early Colonial Discourse*. Colchester: University of Essex Press, 1985.

Jacobson, David. "Jonathan Edwards and the 'American Difference': Pragmatic Reflections on the 'Sense of the Heart.'" *Journal of American Studies* 21 (1987): 377–85.

Johnson, Paul David. "Jonathan Edwards's 'Sweet Conjunction.'" *Early American Literature* 16 (1981–82): 270–82.

Jones, Phyllis. "Biblical Rhetoric and the Pulpit Literature of New England." *Early American Literature* 11 (1976–77): 245–58.

Kibbey, Ann. *The Interpretation of Material Shapes in Puritanism: A Study of Rhetoric, Prejudice and Violence*. Cambridge and New York: Cambridge University Press, 1986.

Kimnach, Wilson H. "The Brazen Trumpet: Jonathan Edwards's Conception of the Sermon." In *Critical Essays on Jonathan Edwards*, ed. William J. Scheick, 277–86. Boston: G. K. Hall, 1980.

Kimnach, Wilson H. "Jonathan Edwards' Early Sermons: New York, 1722–1723." *Journal of Presbyterian History* 55 (1977): 255–56.

Kimnach, Wilson H. "Jonathan Edwards' Sermon Mill." *Early American Literature* 10 (1975): 167–77.

Kimnach, Wilson H. "The Literary Techniques of Jonathan Edwards." Ph.D. diss., University of Pennsylvania, 1971.

Kolodny, Annette. "Imagery in the Sermons of Jonathan Edwards." *Early American Literature* 7 (1972): 172–82.

Laurence, David. "Jonathan Edwards, John Locke and the Canon of Experience." *Early American Literature* 15 (1980): 217–21.

Lensing, George S. "Robert Lowell and Jonathan Edwards: Poetry in the Hands of an Angry God." *South Carolina Review* 6 (1974): 7–17.

Lyttle, David. "Jonathan Edwards on Personal Identity." *Early American Literature* 7 (1972): 163–71.

McGraw, James. "The Preaching of Jonathan Edwards." *Preacher's Magazine* 32 (1957): 9–12.

Martin, Howard H. "Puritan Preaching: Notes on American Colonial Rhetoric." *Quarterly Journal of Speech* 50 (1964): 285–92.

Medlicott, Alexander. "In the Wake of Mr. Edwards's 'Most Awakening' Sermon at Enfield." *Early American Literature* 15 (1980–81): 217–21.

Miller, Perry. "Edwards, Locke, and the Rhetoric of Sensation." In *Critical Essays on Jonathan Edwards*, ed. William J. Scheick, 120–35. Boston: G. K. Hall, 1980.

Miller, Perry. "Jonathan Edwards on the Sense of the Heart." *Harvard Theological Review* 41 (1948): 123–45.

Morris, William S. "The Genius of Jonathan Edwards." In *Reinterpretation in American Church History*, ed. Jerald C. Bauer, 29–65. Chicago and London: University of Chicago Press, 1968.

Murphy, Murray G. "The Psychodynamics of Puritan Conversion." *American Quarterly* 31 (1979): 135–47.

Potter, David, and Gordon L. Thomas, eds. *The Colonial Idiom*. Carbondale: Southern Illinois University Press, 1970.

Powell, Lyman P. *Heavenly Heretics*. New York: G. P. Putnam's Sons, 1909.

Shea, Daniel B. "Deconstruction Comes to Early 'America': The Case of Edwards." *Early American Literature* 21 (1986–87): 268–74.

Slotkin, Richard. *Regeneration Through Violence: The Mythology of the American Frontier, 1600–1860*. Middletown, Conn.: Wesleyan University Press, 1973.

Steele, Thomas J., and Eugene R. Delay. "Vertigo in History: The Threatening Tactility of 'Sinners in the Hands of an Angry God.'" *Early American Literature* 18 (1983–84): 242–56.

Stein, Stephen J. "The Spirit and the Word: Jonathan Edwards and Scriptural Exegesis." In *Jonathan Edwards and the American Experience*, ed. Nathan O. Hatch and Harry S. Stout. Eds. Oxford: Oxford University Press, 1988.

Stuart, Robert Lee. "Jonathan Edwards at Enfield: 'And Oh the Cheerfulness and Pleasantness . . .'" *American Literature* 48 (1976): 46–59.

Wainwright, William J. "Jonathan Edwards and the Language of God." *Journal of the Academy of Religion* 48 (1980): 519–30.

Weber, Donald. *Rhetoric and History in Revolutionary New England.* New York and Oxford: Oxford University Press, 1988.

Westra, Helen. *The Minister's Task and Calling in the Sermons of Jonathan Edwards.* Lewiston, N.Y.: E. Mellen Press, 1986.

White, Eugene. "Cotton Mather's 'A Companion for Communicants' and Rhetorical Genre." *Southern Speech Communication Journal* 51 (1986): 326–43.

White, Eugene. *Puritan Rhetoric: The Issue of Emotion in Religion.* Carbondale: Southern Illinois University Press, 1972.

Wolf, Carl J. C., ed. *Jonathan Edwards on Evangelism.* Westport, Conn.: Greenwood Press, 1981.

Yarbrough, Stephen R. "Jonathan Edwards on Rhetorical Authority." *Journal of the History of Ideas* 47 (1986): 395–408.

Ziff, Larzer. "Revolutionary Rhetoric and Puritanism." *Early American Literature* 13 (1978): 45–49.

Index

About the Authors

STEPHEN R. YARBROUGH, Associate Professor of English, Skidmore College, has written at length on critical theory and American literature.

JOHN C. ADAMS, Assistant Professor of the Department of Speech Communication, Syracuse University, has written many articles for professional journals on American rhetoric and the history of public addresses.

Great American Orators

Henry Ward Beecher: Peripatetic Preacher
Halford R. Ryan

Edward Everett: Unionist Orator
Ronald F. Reid

Theodore Roosevelt and the Rhetoric of Militant Decency
Robert V. Friedenberg

Patrick Henry, The Orator
David A. McCants

Anna Howard Shaw: Suffrage Orator and Social Reformer
Wil A. Linkugel and Martha Solomon

William Jennings Bryan: Orator of Small-Town America
Donald K. Springen

Robert M. La Follette, Sr.: The Voice of Conscience
Carl R. Burgchardt

Ronald Reagan: The Great Communicator
Kurt Ritter and David Henry

Clarence Darrow: The Creation of an American Myth
Richard J. Jensen

"Do Everything" Reform: The Oratory of Frances E. Willard
Richard W. Leeman

Abraham Lincoln the Orator: Penetrating the Lincoln Legend
Lois J. Einhorn

Mark Twain: Protagonist for the Popular Culture
Marlene Boyd Vallin